LEGENDARY PIONEERS OF BLACK RADIO

GILBERT A. WILLIAMS

PRAEGER   Westport, Connecticut
London

Library of Congress Cataloging-in-Publication Data

Williams, Gilbert Anthony, 1951–
    Legendary pioneers of Black radio / Gilbert A. Williams.
      p. cm.
    Includes bibliographical references and index.
    ISBN 0–275–95888–4 (alk. paper)
    1. Disc jockeys—United States—Interviews. 2. Afro-American disc
jockeys—United States—Interviews. 3. Afro-Americans in radio
broadcasting. I. Title.
ML406.W56 1998
791.44′089′96073—dc21   97–38995

British Library Cataloguing in Publication Data is available.

Library of Congress Catalog Card Number: 97–38995
ISBN: 0–275–95888–4

First published in 1998

Praeger Publishers, 88 Post Road West, Westport, CT 06881
An imprint of Greenwood Publishing Group, Inc.

Printed in the United States of America

♾™

The paper used in this book complies with the
Permanent Paper Standard issued by the National
Information Standards Organization (Z39.48–1984).

10 9 8 7 6 5 4 3 2

This book is dedicated to Ann I. Alchin, at one time a co-worker in the Department of Telecommunication at Michigan State University, and now a very true friend. Ann has generously offered her time and assistance in the preparation of this book, for which I will always be grateful.

Contents

Photo section follows chapter 7.

Preface

Sociologist Lawrence Levine argues that culture is not "fixed, static and unchanging;" instead it is "dynamic, always changing, and adapting."[1] African-American culture has adapted to changes in American society over time. Moreover, it has been "a cushion between" African Americans and "their environment," and enabled them to survive slavery, Jim Crow laws and racial discrimination.[2]

African Americans used the reservoir of Central and West African cultures that was their collective consciousness and created an improvisational culture. For example, scholars have written about improvisational features in African-American language, black dialect and "communication style." Also, linguists have shown that black dialect uses grammatical structure, idioms and speech patterns commonly found in West and Central African languages.[3]

In dance, several "elements or motifs characteristic of African dancing" are "integral parts of American Black dancing."[4] Moreover, African-American religious practices have the imprint of African culture. Scholars have generally considered these elements in isolation or as African survivals or retentions in African-American culture. Taken as a whole, however, the features of improvisational culture exist as "conceptual approaches—as unique ways of doing things and making things happen." Improvisational culture is not fixed, but is a process and a unique way of doing things.[5]

Black DJs epitomize improvisational culture. They are the masters of improvisation. They can combine music, timing, tempo and other elements to keep audiences entertained.

As purveyors of African-American popular culture, black DJs promote ideas and values their communities need to hear. As griots or storytellers, they help shape the moral character of their listeners. As pioneers in radio broadcasting, they have helped other African Americans find work in this field. Finally, as ministers, teachers and jesters, they have become cultural heroes.

Before anyone can comprehend the many roles these individuals have played, one must understand the perspectives that they brought to their work. Some black DJs had worked in vaudeville and had learned about show business in that arena. Others were college educated and spoke middle-American English. On the other hand, some black DJs had only a basic education but knew "people." A few had been ministers, while others had worked in advertising, using sound trucks to sell merchandise.

In other words, the African-American men and women who became DJs came from all walks of life and were not a part of any elite group. Moreover, as purveyors of popular culture, they had to deal with issues and concerns that affected most African Americans. In this way and others, they were truly *of* the people.

Like culture heroes of earlier times, who brought fire and other new "technology" back to villages, black DJs brought electronic communication, the lifeblood of modern society, back to their village people. Black DJs became cultural heroes because they were the vanguard of African-American culture. As thousands of African Americans left farms and plantations, they needed someone to tell them how to survive in the concrete jungles of urban America. Black DJs performed this vital role.

Black DJs helped boost the spirits of migrants by playing the blues, jazz, gospel, rhythm and blues and soul music. To make listeners laugh they told jokes and made outlandish boasts and toasts. To help their people remember the past, they told stories about achievement and struggle.

While black DJs played music that African Americans wanted to hear, they also helped maintain African traditions and oral culture. As the griots in African villages memorized the collective history of their people, black DJs kept alive the traditions of improvisational culture. Moreover, through their work, they influenced American culture.

African-American creativity behind the microphone influenced listeners of all races. Many whites emulated black DJs. For instance, during the 1960s, Bill Drake, a radio consultant for the RKO Corporation, "indoctrinated stations in such basics as . . . deejays talking over intros and endings" of records, a practice black DJs had created two decades earlier.[6]

Significantly, black DJs helped corporations market their products to black consumers as they were able to communicate effectively with and sell products to African Americans. Therefore, corporations recognized the importance of having black DJs ad-lib commercials and endorse products.

As illustrated briefly, black DJs are the embodiments of improvisational culture and have been for the past seventy years through their unique style of communicating and their participaton in improvisational culture. This culture fulfills psychological and sociological needs of African Americans. By creating this process and unique way of doing things, African Americans have survived in American society. Black DJs promote and help perpetuate improvisational culture by using it and teaching others how to use improvisation in their work, social activities and American society in general.

NOTES

1. Levine, Lawrence W. (1977), *Black Culture and Black Consciousness*. New York: Oxford University Press, p. 5.

2. Brown, Ina Corrine (1963), *Understanding Other Cultures*. Englewood Cliffs, NJ: Prentice Hall, pp. 5–24.

3. Assante, Molefe Kete, "African Elements in African-American English," in Joseph E. Holloway (ed.) (1990), *Africanisms in American Culture*. Bloomington and Indianapolis: Indiana University Press, pp. 19–33.

4. Brooks, Tilford (1984), *America's Black Musical Heritage*. Englewood Cliffs, NJ: Prentice Hall, p. 29.

5. Maultsby, Portia K., "Africanisms in African-American Music," in Joseph E. Holloway (ed.) (1990), *Africanisms in American Culture*. Bloomington and Indianapolis: Indiana University Press, pp. 185–210.

6. Spaulding, Norman W. (1981), "History of Black Oriented Radio in Chicago, 1929–1963," Ph.D. dissertation, University of Illinois, Urbana-Champaign, p. 124. See also, Heimenz, Jack, "DeeJay Blues: The Story of Rock Radio," *Sound*, September 1975, pp. 28–30.

Acknowledgments

I wish to acknowledge my parents, L. V. and Johnyne Williams (in memory), and my sisters and brothers—Donald, Sandra, Janice, Diane (in memory), Victor, Terry, Michael, Elmer, Kathy, Greg and Jennifer—for their strong and continuous support over the years. They have helped me in many ways, especially with words of encouragement and, at times, financial assistance. For all of their supportive efforts, I am grateful.

P. Macia Richardson, archivist and Head of Public and Technical Services, at the Archive of African American Music and Culture, deserves special acknowledgment. Macia has been a joy to work with and assisted in identifying and securing many of the photographs in this book. I thank you, Macia, for all of your help.

Preston A. Blakely, Willie Mustafa and Karen Cathey, my graduate students, helped with the research for this book. Thank you for your help.

Last but certainly not least, I wish to acknowledge the support of my children, Malik and Janelle, and my wife, Kimberly. Without their patience and understanding I could not have written this book. I am forever grateful for all your kind words and encouragement.

◆ 1 ◆

Introduction: On-Air Power—Legendary Pioneers of Black Radio

"The radio disc jockey wakes us in the morning, puts us to sleep at night, and in between, his time, weather, and music announcements take us through the day."[1] African-American disc jockeys, however, have been more than announcers. They have transcended their jobs as radio station employees, often to become cultural heroes. By being admired and respected in the African-American community, they have also brought about changes in society.

This chapter explains how and why African-American disc jockeys communicate with their listeners. It analyzes the music African-American (and some white) disc jockeys play and examines the language patterns and personalities of prominent and representative DJs. The performance styles of black radio DJs developed and evolved as their communities changed during the twentieth century. Sometimes this change reflected rural to urban migrations. At other times, it reflected dislocation and disorganization in African-American communities. For example, black DJs of the 1940s and 1950s often used the clash of rural and urban cultures as grist for their programs.

Over the past seventy years, the fortunes of African-American disc jockeys have risen and fallen for several reasons.

Some have argued that the widespread use of uniform radio station formats, that is, formulas used to determine musical and nonmusical elements on a station, brought an end to "personality" radio. In "personality radio" style, a disc jockey's own personality is the main attraction. As a consequence of this shift, African-American disc jockeys say their influence on thought and action in their communities is weaker than it used to be. They feel unable to fulfill their role as purveyors of cultural symbols. Many complain that the radio format is similar to a straitjacket, denying them an opportunity to express themselves in a language other African Americans can relate to and understand.

According to Norman Spaulding, noted communications scholar, another reason for the loss of stature of black DJs was that African-American communication style, language and cultural symbols changed between 1930 and 1970. For instance, by the late 1960s, younger African Americans no longer related to the language patterns of African-American disc jockeys who began working in radio in the late 1940s and early 1950s. As Spaulding put it, these men and women no longer "talk the talk or walk the walk" of this new generation of radio listeners.[2]

In fact, this group not only accepted African-American disc jockeys who sounded "white" but also white DJs who played black music. Although white DJs had appealed to African-American listeners in the 1940s and 1950s, they had done so by imitating the black communications style. However, by the 1960s, African-American listeners accepted white DJs who simply played black music but used few, if any, black idiomatic phrases or language. By the 1960s, pure black dialect may have lost some of its appeal, both to station management and to the listening audience.[3] To a certain extent, then, cultural changes in African-American communities explain the fluctuations in popularity and influence of black DJs over time.

African-American disc jockeys exemplify the essence of African-American culture. What follows is an analysis of their work at the radio station and in the community and explanations of their power, popularity, and status.

AFRICAN-AMERICAN CULTURE

Improvisation is a defining characteristic of African-American culture. It is a defining and identifiable feature in the music African Americans create—blues, gospel, soul, spiritual, or rap, for example. Moreover, it is found in the music of West Africa. This aspect of African-American music is what Melville J. Herskovits, in his *Myth of the Negro Past*, calls a "cultural survival" in our contemporary culture.[4] Additionally, according to musicologist Tilford Brooks, improvisation "is found especially in songs of derision or allusion in the United States but it is used in similar songs in West Africa."[5]

While improvisation is easily identified in African-American music it is also noticeable in other aspects of African-American culture, including popular dances and even in formal dance repertoires such as those of Alvin Ailey and the Dance Theater of Harlem. Moreover, "most elements or motifs characteristic of African dancing, such as the shimmy, the crawl, the shuffle, the strut, and the jump, remained an integral part of American black dancing."[6]

Language arts, how African-Americans speak English, for example, also reflect improvisation. In addition, the griots, or storytellers of

Africa are known for their ability to use language. Indeed, griots have gained such a reputation for honest appraisals that some individuals have paid them to withhold parts of their stories: They collect tribute from tribal members for what they withhold and for what they say. African-American disc jockeys are often said to be the griots on this side of the Atlantic Ocean.

The most important aspect of the griots' performance is audience participation and reaction. Therefore, the griots' goal is to both entertain and instruct the audience. Audiences react to oral performance by establishing a relationship with the griot. This relationship is referred to as "call-and-response." It is an aspect of African culture that has survived as part of African-American culture.

Examples of this relationship include the interaction between a preacher and his congregation in African-American churches, and between a soloist and the ensemble in jazz performances. Some black DJs have achieved this level of interaction with their audiences. In each of these situations, the individual strives for technical perfection, in playing an instrument or speaking ability, for example. Additionally, they strive for originality. Their audiences support them throughout their performance and urge them on to reach ever greater heights.

Black DJs used radio broadcasting as an opportunity to perform their art. Radio is a more personable medium than print and that is why black DJs used it effectively. Black DJs become aware of what their audiences are interested in and keep them entertained while at the same time teaching valuable lessons of honesty, generosity and self-worth.

African-American disc jockeys are masters of improvisational conversation, which is by no means the same thing as spontaneous speech. When black DJs perform, they are often calling on a reservoir of material borrowed from others. They spend years simply listening, absorbing, and analyzing. Disc jockeys adopt and modify phrases, ways of introducing music, and techniques used in selling products in commercials. "When this is done adroitly, the performance" is the disc jockey's personal approach to announcing. It may sound spontaneous, but it is really masterful improvisation—variations on a theme.[7] In their roles as griots, black DJs act as the society's moral police using instrumental music, songs, words and their own voices.

"Griot" is a French word for an expert in oral performance. Other names are also used for this artist. To the Xhosa, this person is "imbongi," and the Hausa refer to the village storyteller as "maroka."

Griots tell stories to teach morals, preserve history and rituals, and keep traditions alive. Griots have a great deal of freedom when they tell their stories. Thus, they are allowed to denounce social misbehavior, regardless of who is involved. In this way, griots provide a release for pent-up anger and resentment by "telling it like it is."

AFRICAN-AMERICAN COMMUNICATION

African Americans recognize cultural symbols by "recurrent patterns" of use and their "shared interpretations" of these symbols. The patterned use and interpretation of symbols and messages are simplified by the radio disc jockey. For example, through the years, black DJs have provided answers to such questions as: How do we (the audience) make sense of our world? What symbols are important? Who are we as people?

Sharing, uniqueness, positivity, realism, and assertiveness are five core symbols that define African-American communication style. African-American disc jockeys use these symbols to affirm a sense of affinity with their audiences.

The call-response patterns of preaching, speaking, and singing are examples of sharing. One disc jockey explained the call-and-response communication ritual this way: "Take 'C'mon' . . . the deacon say 'C'mon son,' if you're singing or if you're testifying. It's an encouraging thing." Testifying is the act of professing a commitment to a spiritual being, feeling, or music. Moreover, African-American disc jockeys have testified on the air about how certain songs make them feel. Lee Garrett, who called himself "The Rocking Mr. G" on WGPR in Detroit, made this comment after listening to Willie Hightower's song *It's a Miracle.*

Yeah, I wanna testify, I wanna tell the world how I feel. Oo mercy, I feel so good children, I feel so doggone good. Little Bobby's in the back there shoutin'. He's standing up with his hands on his head and he say "Burn, baby, burn" cos I feel so good. Aw my goodness, the soul is in me chillun. Lord have mercy! Good God almighty! I say it, I say it, I say it, I say it, it's a miracle what love can do. I know, I know deep down in my soul I know, that it's a miracle." [8]

Uniqueness focuses on the individual and individuality. Upbeat words and phrases used in everyday language and interactions reflect the core values of positivity and emotionality.

"Telling it like it is" expresses realism, another core symbol of African-American communication style. African-American disc jockeys point out that the music they play reflects genuine feelings and tells the truth as well. "Alright, there you heard it. He's telling you nothing but the natural truth," said Chicago's WVON disc jockey Ed Cook after he played a particular tune. Other disc jockeys underscore their sincerity with such phrases as "You'd better believe it;" "ain't that the truth;" "tell the truth;" and "tell it like it is."[9] Realism is "reflected in blues lyrics and gospel music that portray the difficulty of life and advise a cool, steady and persistent toughness . . . to overcome this difficulty." In other words, "being real" tells an individual to be genuine and not to "have a hole in one's soul." "Being for real" on the air or in any setting is a positive act. Listeners perceive this act by the black DJ as expressing "sincerity and true conviction."[10]

Finally, assertiveness is the process of standing up for oneself and letting others know that you have as important a place on this earth as the next person. African-American disc jockeys display this value by being "intense, outspoken, challenging and forward," expressing their assertiveness through "loud, strong voices, threats, insults, manner of dress and use of slang or street talk" on the air.[11] Whites sometimes interpret this style as hostile.

Through these five core symbols, disc jockeys show solidarity with their audience. Hecht et al. conclude that "engaging in rituals . . . is a way of showing allegiance to the group and communicating an identity." Among the communication rituals created with these symbols is jiving, "a style developed by African Americans based upon *improvisation* and accentuation of behavior that is highly acceptable."[12]

Six groups of "jivers" have been identified.[13] One group includes entertainers "who perpetuate the racial myth that all African Americans have rhythm, can sing, dance and act silly." A second group is characterized by its slang language, dominated by black English idiomatic phrases. Hecht et al. believe that "this type of jiver may gain immediate and positive feedback from other African Americans."

A third group of jivers consists of African Americans who use talk to develop nonserious reputations. These are individuals who participate in small talk just to hold conversations or have someone buy them a drink at the tavern. A fourth type is the "hipster," who is very intelligent, resourceful, and creative—a good or superior talker who "can think, act and talk circles around the average person." A fifth type of jiver uses words to belittle others or make them appear naive, often making others the butt of their jokes. Finally, swing is a sixth form of jive. African Americans who use swing enjoy congregating among themselves after working all day among European Americans. Swing is a "vigorous, vibrant, ostentatious and often graceful act in a nonserious environment" such as a bar or social club.[14]

Besides jive, another African-American communication ritual is "playing the dozens." This folk speech is "an aggressive contest often using obscene language in which the goal is to ridicule and demean the opponent's family members, notably the mother."[15] According to some scholars, this ritual is a means of "socialization and learning to compete with other males."[16]

The communication ritual called "boasting" is often heard at black radio conventions and just about every time certain groups of African-American DJs get together. Humorous exaggeration is the major feature of "boasting," but its impact is "to bring harmony and cohesiveness to the group." As the public boasts occur, people crowd around to listen, laugh, applaud, and otherwise encourage the boasters.[17] Besides their boasts, most DJs have unique gaits and accoutrements, which also set them apart from the crowd.

Another African-American communication ritual is the "toast or epic poem." Examples include the ribald versions of "Shine" and "The Monkey and the Baboon." Sexual assertiveness, "use of taboo four-letter words and scorn for sentimental verbiage" characterize the "toast."[18]

AFRICAN-AMERICAN MUSIC

The music African-American disc jockeys have traditionally played and the music currently heard on black-oriented "urban contemporary" radio stations throughout the United States (and many other parts of the world) reflect African-American core values. The disc jockeys' close ties to this music and their sense of what this music means to their listeners further demonstrate DJs' knowledge and understanding of the African-American community.

Some disc jockeys have become musicians and singers (B.B. King and Sly Stone are examples), while others have tried but failed. Nevertheless, the act of music performance forms a symbiotic relationship between disc jockeys, entertainers/musicians, the music, and the audience. Each benefits from this relationship, but in different ways. For the DJs and entertainers the relationship is a paying proposition, the way they earn their living. The audience's reward is the pleasure—even catharsis—experienced when listening to the DJ's and entertainer's performance (the music). The audience identifies with the singer's experiences, which may include falling in and out of love, poverty, racism, or other aspects of life. Audiences feel what the performer feels and believes that the singer is "expressing true and innermost feelings and emotions."[19]

Thus, African-American disc jockeys endear themselves to the community not only because of their verbal skills but also for the music they play. In many ways, the DJs become associated with this music, the values and feelings it expresses, and even with recording artists who create it. Additionally, the music unites the audience and encourages greater involvement and participation.[20] Disc jockeys, for example, "anticipate" the lyrics by saying a line before the song is played and "confirm them by repeating and paraphrasing it afterwards."[21] Through their shouts and testimonials, DJs reinforce the message in the music.

BLACK ENGLISH

African-American disc jockeys have historically used black English in their broadcast presentations and in personal appearances, for example, at dances and as masters of ceremonies at concerts. They quickly recognized that black English was part of the socialization process for many African Americans. In addition, black English, with its West African syntax and sentence structure and its vocabulary of old and new words, is a form of improvisation, since elements are combined to create unique cultural artifacts that vary from the main theme or language. When African-American DJs use black English, it endears them to their listeners because it proves, among other things, their ability to improvise in a white occupational setting. Quite often the black English includes phrases with double meanings. One disc jockey explained his manner of speaking this way: "It's definitely a difference in communication because there are certain ways that we say things to each other that we don't say when we're talking to a white person."[22]

Hence, African-American disc jockeys often create phrases that reflect the social reality of their people. These words and phrases are "coded to mean something other than what they would mean to the non-Black listener."[23] When the outside culture discovers the true meanings of these words or phrases, African-American DJs are among the first in their communities to stop using them.

A similar phenomenon exists in African-American musical creations. Keil points out that "each successive appropriation and commercialization of a Negro style by white America through its record industry and mass media has stimulated the Negro community" and its musical spokesperson to generate "new music that it can call its own."[24] This "appropriation-revitalization process" may explain why some African-American DJs lose their "edge," whereas others remain "fresh" by creating new words or phrases and dropping the old.

THE FIRST GENERATION: 1924–1960

The popularity of early African-American radio disc jockeys is partly related to the migration of southern blacks from rural towns, hamlets, and farms to northern urban centers. African-American migration from the south began after the Civil War, but the most significant increases occurred after World War I and World War II, with the numbers of blacks in the nation's largest cities increasing dramatically after 1945.

For instance, in 1940 African Americans made up 8 percent of the population in Chicago; by 1960 more than 23 percent of Chicago's population was black. In Detroit African Americans were 9 percent of the population in 1940; by 1960 they made up nearly 29 percent. New

York in 1940 had a 6 percent African-American population; by 1960 it had grown to 14 percent. In 1940 African Americans in Philadelphia were 13 percent of the city's population; by 1960 that number had doubled to 26 percent. Los Angeles had a 4 percent African-American population in 1940; however, by 1960 blacks made up 12 percent of that city's population.[25] Even in Memphis the black population grew from 41 percent in 1940 to 48 percent in 1960.

With these population shifts came changes in lifestyles and culture. The new migrants changed their respective cities' neighborhoods and the way neighbors and communities interacted. African-American residents who had moved to these cities in the decades before World War II sometimes looked down on the new residents; nevertheless, they intermixed with them and together they created a new urban culture.

It was in this new urban milieu that African-American disc jockeys gained popularity, power, and status. Disc jockeys used music, language, and other forms of cultural communication to help the new urban residents adjust to their surroundings. In this way, they made the newcomers feel that some of what they had left had mysteriously reappeared with a familiar sound and nuance. Although the world view of black migrants had probably undergone a paradigm shift, their favorite DJs reassured them that they could still hear music "with a little chitlin juice on it."[26] They also gave advice. For instance, DJs told their new listeners how to make contacts with new institutions and helped the new migrants understand the concrete jungle they had moved into.

A SHORT HISTORY OF AFRICAN AMERICANS ON RADIO

African Americans have been on the radio, mainly as singers and musicians, from the early 1920s, where they sang or played everything from blues to jazz, spirituals, and ragtime music. By the late 1920s, listeners easily recognized the distinctive sound of Noble Sissle, the Pace Jubilee Negro singers, and other black musicians. In the 1930s Cab Calloway, Duke Ellington, Art Tatum, Fats Waller, and Paul Robeson were often heard on American radios.[27] Black entertainers were on all radio stations that played music.

African-American comedians also participated in the country's early radio broadcasting story, usually as stereotypical "uncle toms, mammies, and coons." For example, Eddie Green and Ernest Whitman acted as "coons" in a production of the famous musical "Showboat." Hattie McDaniel had "mammy" roles in the "Optimistic Doughnut Hour" and was also in the "Showboat" series.

Later, black actors attempted to establish themselves in dramatic roles. A few managed to achieve dramatic acting roles. However, the majority of black actors who worked during radio's so-called golden age had to settle for stereotypical acting roles.[28]

Sometimes black newspapers joined forces with black actors and civil rights organizations to denounce racial stereotypes. For instance, *The Pittsburgh Courier* petitioned the Federal Communications Commission (FCC) to remove "Amos and Andy" from the air. Neither the newspaper nor the National Association for the Advancement of Colored People (NAACP) had been able to convince CBS to cancel the stereotypical *Amos 'n' Andy* radio show; the FCC petition also failed.[29]

Meanwhile, African Americans did find work in soap operas such as "Our Gal Friday" and "The Romance of Helen Trent," but these roles were stereotypical also. On the other hand, in Chicago, Richard Durham produced "Destination Freedom" and other radio programs that presented positive perspectives of black life and condemned America's racism.

Radio woke up to the blues and rhythm and blues in the 1940s, as stations realized the music's potential to reach black listeners. By the late 1940s and early 1950s, radio stations began playing so-called race music, which later became known as blues, rhythm and blues, and gospel, which attracted African American audiences. Moreover, station owners, who were mostly white, soon realized that they needed black DJs to present this music to listeners, and a new era of radio announcing emerged.

These radio stations are distinguished from mainstream stations that played Ellington, Calloway and the Pace Group. Stations in the mid-to-late 1940s and early 1950s that played "race" music were black-oriented and employed black DJs to introduce the music. By contrast, stations that had played Ellington, Art Tatum and other black jazz artists catered to white audiences and utilized white announcers.

CULTURAL HEROES

The early (1945–1960) African-American disc jockeys were considered role models and heroes because their audiences admired them. These men and women shared a similar background with that of their audiences and showed an appreciation of their needs. Additionally, they gave their audiences a sense of identity as the music they played expressed the joys and pains of the African-American experience. Further, these DJs were prominent during a time when few African Americans, with the exception of some sports stars, had achieved any recognition on the local, state, or national level.

For the recent migrants, the city was an alien and bewildering environment. They needed to find ways to connect with old friends and relatives. Black DJs played an integral part in making those connections, for they created an electronic village in this new urban setting using the familiar sounds and words that the migrants were accustomed to. If the newcomers could not have face-to-face conversations with friends and compatriots, they could at least listen to the words of the DJ and the music that reminded them of their old homes and neighborhoods.

In this way African Americans were no different from other immigrant groups, who recreated, "in modified form, the institutions from back home."[30] For this reason alone, one could make the case for hero status for black disc jockeys: They fostered a sense of community—"something familiar and therefore secure . . . after the break in lifestyle, customs and climate."[31]

As far as the new migrants could see, black disc jockeys had entered the white world but managed to maintain their own identity, humanity, and community spirit. Further, the black DJ allowed his listeners to "share and imitate him."[32] From a cultural point of view, these men and women were considered entertainers—one aspect of life where African Americans still maintained a sense of identity, dignity, and other cultural traditions. Keil explained the significance of "entertainment" in African-American culture in this way.

This domain or sphere of interest may be broadly defined as entertainment from the White or public point of view and as ritual, drama, or dialectical catharsis from the Negro or theoretical standpoint. By this I mean that certain Negro performances, called "entertaining" by Negroes and Whites alike, have an added but usually unconscious ritual significance to Negroes. The ritualists I have in mind are singers, musicians, preachers, comedians, disc jockeys, some athletes, and perhaps a few novelists, as well.[33]

African-American disc jockeys invented and used such styles as "riding gain" and "talking through" in musical presentations in the late 1940s. Specifically, the DJs would "ride gain" when they boosted or lowered the power on the audio board to accent various parts of a record. To "talk through" a record, the DJ lowered the volume of the music and spoke while the record played, a common practice even today.[34] Philadelphia disc jockey Joe "Butterball" Tamburro described how his co-worker "talked through" a record:

And Lord Fauntleroy was not to be believed. He'd come on and do this thing over James Brown's 'Out Of Sight.' He'd say, Lollipops, carrot tops, my extremely delicate gumdrops. This is the Lord of Rhyme bringin' the sound from out of the ground to your part of town.' Then he'd scream and do all these things as the record would climax and peak. He'd scream and ramble through this two-and-a-half minute record. People would go crazy.[35]

African-American audiences, and many white youngsters who listened out of earshot of parents, embraced these styles and the language patterns the disc jockeys used. Because the DJs spoke to them directly, audiences were attracted and flattered. In addition, DJs who could "rap" and speak eloquently were immensely popular— cultural heroes, in fact.

The oral tradition in the African-American community places a high premium on individuals who speak well and greatly admires the best orators. Keil observed, "In White America, the printed word—the literary tradition—and its attendant values, are revered. In the Negro community, more power resides in the spoken word and oral tradition—good talkers abound and the best gain power and prestige."[36] Black DJs mastered timing, sound, and the spoken word, all of which "are defining features" of African-American improvisational culture.[37]

As African-American disc jockeys developed entertainment skills that appealed to new listeners on black-formatted radio stations in the late 1940s and early 1950s, stations programmed for white audiences lost audiences. Several other factors contributed to this decline. The first was television. The major broadcast networks decided to put substantial time, money, and energy in this new medium. As a result, their radio station affiliates had to scramble for programming, promotion, and financial support. When popular network radio programs migrated to network television, so did the advertising dollars, as national advertisers lost interest in network radio as a viable advertising vehicle. Indeed, between 1945 and 1955, air time purchased from ABC, NBC, and CBS radio networks declined from $134 million to $64 million.[38] Radio station owners looked frantically for ways to stop the loss of revenue and audiences.

Advertisers had searched for effective methods to reach the huge black consumer market and they quickly recognized the marketing potential of black disc jockeys. Station managers promoted these disc jockeys, using billboards, on-air announcements, newspaper ads, and other means. Many black DJs participated in advertising and marketing promotions at various retail outlets. When an advertiser bought radio air time, the "buy" often included using photographs and other promotional items with the disc jockey figured prominently. In some instances, the disc jockey endorsed the product and became the dominant sales figure for it.

In Chicago, for instance, Coca-Cola bought time on the great Al Benson's show(s) and also featured him prominently in their print-media advertisements. Similarly, Seven-Up purchased time on Richard Stams' ever-popular radio program. Stams also participated in many of the bottler's retail store promotions. In addition, these businesses expected the disc jockeys to represent them at social and political functions. Advertisers believed that black DJs gave them additional positive exposure in communities as a result of the promotional appearances.[39]

As advertisers became aware of the African-American consumer market, radio stations all over the United States scrambled for ways to reach it. Broadcast historian J. Fred MacDonald observed:

While in 1943 only 4 stations throughout the country were programming specifically for Blacks, 10 years later, 260 such stations were attracting national and local sponsors to their broadcasts. And throughout the country many stations that traditionally had been directed toward White consumers now switched their formats and became all-Black outlets. Among these stations were WMRY (New Orleans) in 1950, WEFC (Miami) in 1952, WCIN (Cincinnati) in 1953, and WNJR (Newark/New York) in 1954.[40]

In addition to these stations, at least one black-owned radio station, WERD (Atlanta), was formatted to African-American audiences in 1949. Other major market radio stations with black formats included WWRL (New York), WDIA (Memphis), KUDL (Kansas City) and WGES (Chicago). However, although African-American disc jockeys had increased opportunities to work, jobs were precarious, competitive, and highly pressured. Moreover, even though these DJs performed communication rituals using the cultural symbols and language of urban America, they never forgot that their primary function at the radio station was to sell. Disc jockeys sold air time to advertisers, and commercial products and the station to listeners. As Spaulding stated, "The prime requirements for success as an early Black disc jockey was to be a good salesman."[41] Usually these disc jockeys bought air time from the radio station and then found businesses that would repurchase it at a higher rate. Of course, the enterprising DJ kept the difference.

THE PIONEERS (1924–1960)

The first African-American disc jockey with a commercially sustained radio show was Jack L. Cooper, a former vaudevillian and ventriloquist who got started in broadcasting on WCAP in Washington, D.C., in 1924.[42] Cooper had complete control over his show and introduced several innovative programming concepts. For instance, he was the first black sports announcer and he started a daily newscast that highlighted news of interest to the African-American community. National advertisers supported Cooper's shows.[43] Cooper's speech reflected a middle-American dialect and enunciation pattern. He avoided black dialect and used none of the African-American "jive talk." His announcing style is more aptly compared with that of Martin Block.

Al Benson began his broadcast career in 1943 on WGES in Chicago. WGES told him to get his own sponsors. Before long Benson had almost more advertising sponsors than he could handle. He had 12-1/2 hours of daily programming on three Chicagoland radio stations. As his popularity increased, Benson's salary hit six figures. Later, he diversified his investments to include ownership of a newspaper, a record shop, a restaurant, and a boutique.[44] At first, he was known as the Reverend Arthur B. Leaner. Later he changed his name to Al Benson and became a legend in black radio. Benson's broadcasting delivery differed completely from Cooper's. Benson spoke with a southern accent, often mixing "lower class street language" and black English idioms in his broadcasts. Contemporaries said Benson killed the "King's English," played the blues, and was a master showman. "He was the first black guy," said Herb Kent, a.k.a. "The Cool Gent," "who had a massive audience." Kent and Benson both worked at WGES-AM (now WGCI-AM) in the 1950s. Kent remembers Benson as an announcer who broke all the rules of grammar. "He didn't have that polished speech, but he certainly talked to folks. You'd come home and turn on the radio to that familiar sound [that] would just be soothing."[45]

Benson's announcing style is legendary. Calling himself the "Ole Swing Master," he said he spoke so eloquently and persuasively "that he could sell hair straightener to a bald headed man."[46] Benson credited his huge success to the music he played. He maintained that "because white disc jockeys refused to give black artists airplay, I played music that had a little chitlin juice on it."[47] Chicago's black listeners completely embraced his programming innovations and announcing style.

Benson and those who imitated him had moved far away from the announcing styles of whites, whom they sometimes mocked. Benson's delivery came closer to that of Arthur Godfrey, on the Martin Block (smooth) and Godfrey (folksy) continuum. His down-home speech patterns and huckster style of delivery made the newly arrived rural migrants feel right at home in their urban environment. Benson's power and influence extended far into the African-American community and to a new generation of black disc jockeys that he introduced to Chicago. His innovative style created a sensation in his adopted hometown, mainly because the "urban blues music" he played "revolutionized Chicago's Black radio programming."[48]

Benson was also admired for his strong stand against racial discrimination. Thus, he personally integrated several nightclubs that had previously refused to serve black patrons. A native of Jackson, Mississippi, Benson hired an airplane in 1956 to drop 5,000 copies of the United States Bill of Rights on this hometown as a protest against the state's white racism against African Americans.

Al Benson influenced many DJs with his inimitable style. Other disc jockeys created their own identities and styles and they also embodied the qualities of a cultural hero. Herb Kent is a good example. Recently inducted into the Radio Hall of Fame, Kent began his career in broadcasting in 1944. He has worked as a disc jockey at Chicago radio stations WBEE-AM, WJFC-AM, WJOB-AM, WGES-AM, and WVON-AM. Kent said he first got *paid* at WGRY in Gary, Indiana, in 1949. Kent is an announcer on WAV-FM in Chicago.

Kent's style is characterized by the music he played, "dusties" or old R&B favorites, his efforts to keep the peace during the explosive 1960s, and now a campaign to reduce the number of school dropouts. "A guy told me," Kent remembered in a recent interview, "an old record is like an old movie—it's always good. It's stuck with me down through the years. Maybe that was my salvation in this market."[49] Kent says he was the first "truly contemporary announcer who crossed all lines." Several announcers and personalities influenced Kent, among them Al Benson and other Chicago DJs, Sid McCoy, Sam Evans, Ric Ricardo, and the Magnificent Montague. Kent pointed as well to "the whole WGES/Chicago crew . . . TV talk show host Hugh Downs . . . listened to my tape . . . and told me I was naturally talented." Kent also commented, "My high school buddy . . . came up with 'It's time to get real sent with Herb Kent the "Cool Gent"' back when I was on WBEE."[50]

Another pioneer was Eddie Saunders, who was listed among the top 25 black DJs by *Color Magazine* in 1951.[51] Born in Covington, Kentucky, in 1909, Eddie Saunders graduated from Garnett High School in Charleston, West Virginia. Later, he attended West Virginia State University and Wagner Vocal School. For a while, Saunders sang with the Kings of Harmony, a gospel group. In 1937, he moved to Columbus, Ohio, and continued to sing gospel music with a group he founded—the Gospel Trumpets.

Saunders began his career in broadcasting at radio station WHKC (later WTVN) in 1944, where he created two radio programs, "Helping Hand" and "Swanee Hour." When Saunders accepted a job at WRFD radio station in 1947, he became the first black DJ in Central Ohio. At WFRD he spun records during his "Chatter Platter" show.

Saunders moved from WFRD to WVKO in 1948, which offered listeners Columbus' first and only black-formatted music. AT WVKO, Saunders played rhythm and blues music and was the first DJ to do so in Central Ohio. In addition, he also played gospel music. Saunders worked at WVKO for 22 years. In 1953, Saunders hosted "Get Ready with Eddie," an early morning program. On weekday afternoons his "Jump and Jive" program entertained listeners with the latest rhythm and blues music. Saunders hosted "Sermons in Song" and "Helping Hand" on Sundays.

Eddie Saunders received so many awards for his work that they are too numerous to list here. According to a program guide from WVKO-FM, Saunders was most proud of the Urban League of Columbus Award for "Outstanding Negro of the Year" (1955). He was also recognized for promoting gospel music. Additionally, the Ohio Senate applauded Saunders' longevity, tenacity, and professionalism. Moreover, the mayor of Columbus gave Saunders a citation of appreciation. At the time of his retirement in 1974, the Governor of Ohio and the Ohio Senate issued a proclamation and resolution praising Saunders for his outstanding achievements.

Eddie Saunders became a cultural hero because of the music he played—gospel and rhythm and blues—and his hobby "was people." Saunders broadcasted live remote at health clinics to promote vaccinations for youngsters; visited the sick and shut-ins; and actively participated in his church's activities. Finally, Saunders achieved cultural hero status because he was an excellent salesman. He made personal appearances and live broadcasts from retail stores to sell merchandise.[52]

Jack L. Cooper had established himself as the pioneering leader of the first generation of black DJs and had helped many other African Americans get jobs in radio. By 1947, *Ebony Magazine* reported that Cooper had started an advertising agency and his programs were heard on four Chicago area radio stations: WSBC, WEDC, WAAF, and WHFC. Sponsors paid $185,000 to advertise on his programs.

Moreover, *Ebony Magazine* reported that sixteen African Americans were working as radio DJs in 1947: Ed Baker (WJLB) and Van Douglas (WJBK) in Detroit; Al Benson (WJJD), Jack L. Cooper (WSBC), and Jack Gibson (WCFL) in Chicago; Bill Branch (WEAW) in Evanston, Illinois; Ramon Bruce (WHAT) and Sam Price (WPEN) in Philadelphia, Pennsylvania; Jessie "Spider" Burkes (KXLW) in St. Louis; Bass Harris (KING) in Seattle; Eddie Honesty (WJOB) in Hammond, Indiana; Harold Jackson (WOOK) and Emerson Parker (WQQW) in Washington, D.C.; Sam Jackson (WHIN) in Providence, Rhode Island; Norfley Whitted (WDNC) in Durham, North Carolina; and Woody Woodard (WLIB) in New York City. Finally, the *Ebony* article stated that Duke Ellington, the famous band leader, became a DJ in 1948 on New York's WMCA.

Cooper and most of the early black DJs had come out of entertainment and show business. A few were college educated and some had received training in radio announcing. The majority of the pioneers worked at midwestern stations.[53]

MacDonald observed that the African-American disc jockeys of the 1950s and 1960s "were a new breed" who played and promoted blues and rhythm and blues. They attracted attention in urban markets throughout the United States. These individuals created phrases and used language that the masses of black Americans understood. Additionally, these new DJs offered unique perspectives on life, mastered the fine art of improvisation, and effectively used African-American communication rituals. It was this combination of factors and the way these individuals put them together that catapulted them to cultural hero status.

The 1950s group included Al Benson, Richard Stams, Daddio Dailey, and "Lucky" Cordell in Chicago; Eddie Castleberry in Birmingham (Alabama), Miami, and New York; the Magnificent Montague in Los Angeles; Enoch Gregory in Detroit; Tommy "Dr. Jive" Smalls and Jack Walker "The Pear-Shape Talker" in New York; and Jim Randolph in Los Angeles. Other announcers who became well known in their communities during these years included Harold Jackson, Ruth Ellington James, and Cecilia Violenes in New York; Carrie Terrell, Helen Lawrence, and Jack Gibson in Atlanta; Roberta Polk in Birmingham (Alabama); Jessie Morris in Atlantic City; Nat D. Williams, Hot Rod Hurlbert, and Willa Monroe in Memphis; France White in Washington, D.C.; Mary Dee in Homestead (Pennsylvania); Ken Hawkins in Cleveland; Gino Baylor, Fred Quinnie, and Gladys "Gee Gee" Hill in Houston; and William "Boy" Brown in Beaumont (Texas).

By the 1960s, Yvonne Daniels, E. Rodney Jones, Ed Cook, Roy Wood, Sr., Pervis Spann and Norm Spaulding had attracted attention in Chicago. Others of note included Eddie O'Jay in Buffalo and New York City; Frankie Crocker in New York; Martha Jean "The Queen" Steinberg in Memphis and Detroit; George Woods, Joe "Butterball" Tamburro, and Jocko Henderson of Philadelphia; Ed Love, Jay Butler, and Ernie Durham in Detroit; Shelly Steward in Birmingham (Alabama); Rick Roberts in Houston; and Rocky G. in Miami.

The music they selected for their audiences consisted of jazz, rhythm and blues, and blues. Many of these DJs had southern accents or a hybrid style of a "cool northern accent" with a generous mix of black English idiomatic phrases tossed in. Sometimes they used street slang and sometimes they rhymed phrases and talked about favorite foods, rituals, and practices that made black residents feel welcome. The black DJ was a "major agent of socialization for the newly urbanized Blacks. (S)he told them what to buy, and stores at which to buy them."[54] The new migrants identified with these DJs because of the music they played, information they presented, outreach activities they performed, causes they supported, and rituals they practiced.

THE FORMAT AND PAYOLA

"Personality" radio began to lose its popularity in the late 1950s and has continued to do so. Instead of promoting disc jockeys, radio stations promoted their own call letters, dial position, and formats. As personality radio faded as a prominent feature on radio stations, so did the popularity of black disc jockeys. Many black DJs had perfected their roles in personality radio and their success was tied to it. Additionally, by the 1960s, broadcasting schools began producing young people for jobs in radio, many of whom were trained as disc jockeys. Because the applicant pool was so large, radio station owners could hire and fire at will.

The payola scandal of the 1950s also had a negative impact on personality radio. "Payola" is the payment of unreported money to disc jockeys for including certain records on their shows. Disc jockeys, black and white, once had the power to choose their own records for broadcasts. That is how they "broke" new music and, indeed, made certain songs into hit records. White DJ Alan Freed, for example, had the power to decide which songs to air and Al Benson once boasted, "Nobody has ever told me what to play on my radio shows. I picked the music and artists I liked."[55] The disc jockey in such a situation is vulnerable to bribes. Most disc jockeys accepted payola as a way of doing business. They often earned meager salaries, and payola from record companies helped make ends meet.

George Woods of WDAS in Philadelphia made more money than most disc jockeys from payola. According to one report, Woods received at least a penny in royalties for 80,000 single records. Although Richard Stams, Alan Freed, and Tommy "Dr. Jive" Smalls were convicted of income tax evasion because they failed to report money paid to them by record companies, Woods, who some called the "King of Payola," was never prosecuted because he paid taxes on all money he earned from record companies.

Foster observed, "The one indisputable fact was that if a DJ was prominent enough and wanted to make extra money, there was ample opportunity. It was quite possible for DJs in a major market to add from $50 to $150 thousand dollars to their annual pay."[56] Black disc jockeys did not take as much money through payola as whites, but they certainly participated in the practice. "Some [record] companies," wrote Spaulding, "kept certain jockeys on the payroll and regarded them as a promotional expense deductible from their income tax. . . . In exchange for the payoffs, a record company would ask for a certain number of air plugs during the day, six days a week."[57]

Congressional hearings on payola exposed the practice and, although it had been legal, it was outlawed after 1960. Several prominent black disc jockeys were called to testify before the congressional committee investigating payola, including George Woods. "They wanted to know how much they would pay me," Woods recalled. Woods agreed to testify but only if he could condemn "racism in the broadcast industry—how it's impossible for a black person to get a job on a station that's over 200 or 300 watts."[58]

Woods had been smart enough to keep an office memo encouraging him to take money from record companies. That, along with the fact that he paid income taxes on monies received, and his strong stance against institutional racism in the broadcast industry, convinced the congressional committee to leave Woods out of their deliberations. He did not testify at the hearings.

Some white disc jockeys, such as Tom Clay, received payola and made out like bandits. As an announcer for Detroit's WJBK radio station in the late 1950s, Clay received more than $3,000 a month in cash and checks from record companies to play their music. In addition, Clay got vacation trips, free landscaping, a swimming pool, fur coats for his wife, diamond rings, and other products. However, Clay failed to report his additional earnings to the IRS. He was fired from WJBK, along with "nearly every jock at the station," once the payola scandal became public knowledge.[59] Clay argues that the managers at WJBK knew record companies paid him undisclosed sums of money but distanced themselves after the federal authorities identified him as a violator.

As Clay, George Woods, and many other disc jockeys knew, taking money from record companies was perfectly legal. Payola only became a federal offense after the U.S. House of Representatives Special Subcommittee on Legislative Oversight held hearings on the matter and Congress decided to put a legal end to the practice.

In addition to Clay, the House Subcommittee investigated several other prominent white disc jockeys, including Richard Wagstaff Clark, better known as Dick Clark, host of American Bandstand. Clark testified before the congressional subcommittee but was never indicted. Clark maintained he "never agreed to play a record or have an artist perform in return for cash or other consideration."[60]

According to some accounts, white disc jockey Alan Freed received the harshest punishment for his role in the payola scandal. A prominent DJ in many cities, Freed held on-air positions at one time or another in Cleveland, Miami (where he was indicted while working at Todd Storz's WQAM), Los Angeles, and New York. Freed, like Tom Clay, did not report money record companies paid him. Freed lived the good life in Long Island, New York, on his unreported income. Freed's "posh Long Island home had been completely furnished by record companies."[61] Freed was indicted on charges of commercial bribery (1962), fired from several jobs for taking payola, and died a "penniless drunk in 1965."[62]

Payola has taken on many forms over the years. Disc jockeys have received sexual favors, drugs, record royalties, cash, vacations, household appliances, jewelry, clothes, and just about every other thing of value so they would agree to play or push a particular record. The practice continues today but in different guises. Nowadays it is program managers, station managers, or music directors who decide which records are played, and record companies find creative ways to pay them for adding the company's records to the music rotation. In an interview with *Pulse* magazine, Tom Clay said that although payola is illegal, it is "as rampant as ever," even in today's world of music formats.

I won't mention any names, but I knew it as a fact that at a major, major market radio station, a major manager owns an art gallery that has little posters on the wall. They ask the price of a poster, and the manager says $25,000. They're worth about $500 a piece. That's payola.[63]

The combined impact of the Congressional hearings, radio station managers' attempts to control payola, and broadcasting industry investigations into the matter led to disc jockeys losing control over record selections. When radio station management took control of the payola issue by allowing program directors to determine music selection and rotation, record selection became part of the managerial process. Radio station managers achieved two goals: (1) they diminished the power of the disc jockey; and (2) they made sure that record promoters' money went into the program manager's pockets rather than the disc jockey's.

Meanwhile, the music format emerged as a means of creating a consistent sound throughout the broadcast day. "The development of the 'Boss' radio format," argued Denisoff, "formalized every segment of air time, dictating what was to be played when."[64] Program directors created playlists and DJs were told to select music from those records. (See Figures 1 and 2.) The DJs could not choose their own records with the format.

The Drake-Chenault format, devised in the 1950s, "compressed program elements so tightly that DJs did not have the opportunity to express their personalities." Routt noted that disc jockeys were told to "play the music and shut up."[65]

Formatics, as it came to be known, greatly affected black formatted stations. African-American disc jockeys not only lost their power to select music but they could no longer express rituals, words, and sentiment that reflected "a distinctive Black value system." In addition, radio stations promoted their call letters, dial positions, and so on, more than they did the names of their DJs. And with good reason. A disc jockey who left a radio station could conceivably move to another station within the market and take a huge slice of the audience along. Thus, while the disc jockey's power and influence faded, the program manager's star climbed higher. The black DJs lost much of their clout as guardians of the community's culture, often to be supplanted by versatile music and a program director as "cultural gatekeeper."[66]

Figure 1
WJLB "Superadio Survey" July 22, 1968

1. You Met Your Match	Stevie Wonder
2. Eleanor Rigby	Ray Charles
3. I've Never Found a Girl	Eddie Floyd
4. Grazing in the Grass	Hugh Masakela
5. Hanging On	Joe Simon
6. Love is Like a Baseball Game	Intruders
7. Girls Can't Do What the Guys Do	Betty Wright
8. Stoned Soul Picnic	5th Dimension
9. Love Makes a Woman	Barbara Acklin
10. Good Old Music	The Parliaments

WVON "The Good Guys" Playlist July 12—July 18, 1968

1. Grazing in the Grass	Hugh Masakela
2. Stone Soul Picnic	5th Dimension
3. Never Give You Up	Jerry Butler
4. The Horse	Cliff Nobles
5. A. Here Comes the Judge	Shorty Long
5. B. Here Comes the Judge	Pigmeat Markham
6. Slip Away	Clarence Carter
7. Here I Am Baby	Marvalettes
8. A. Yesterlove	Miracles
8. B. Much Better Off	Miracles
9. Workin' on a Groovy Thing	Patti Drew
10. Love Makes a Woman	Barbara Acklin

Michael Haralambos, *Right On: From Blues to Soul* (1975), pp. 14, 98.

The separation of the sales function from the black disc jockeys' main responsibilities further eroded their power, prestige, and status. As large corporations purchased several radio stations, managers tended to streamline or compartmentalize functions within stations. As early as the 1950s, corporate managers assumed responsibility for

Figure 2
WWRL "The Soul Brothers" Playlist

1. Private Number	Judy Clay & William Bell
2. Message from Maria	Joe Simon
3. Don't Chance Your Love	The Five Stairsteps & Cubie
4. Cadillac Jack	Andre Williams
5. Gonna Give Her All the Love	Benny Gordon
6. Little Green Apples	O.C. Smith
7. Nitty Gritty	Ricardo Ray
8. OH	Jay Lewis
9. Who Was That	Tina Britt
10. Soul Drummers	Ray Barretto

KUXL Radio "Rhythm & Blues Hit List" February 24, 1969

1. Baby Baby Don't Cry	Smokey Robinson & the Miracles
2. Give it Up & Turn It Loose	James Brown
3. Every Day People	Sly & the Family Stone
4. There's Gonna Be a Showdown	Archie Bell & the Drells
5. Can I Change My Mind	Tyrone Davis
6. I Forgot to Be Your Lover	William Bell
7. Good Loving Ain't Easy to Come By	Marvin Gaye & Tammi Terrell
8. I'm Gonna Make You Love Me	Diana Ross, Supremes & Temptations
9. Riot	Hugh Masakela
10. Take Care of Your Homework	Johnny Taylor

Michael Haralambos, *Right On: From Blues to Soul* (1975), pp. 13, 15.

various functions such as programming, sales, and promotion. Moreover, when corporate America discovered the buying power of African Americans, these companies bought large amounts of air time on black-formatted radio stations. Corporate advertisers demanded "formats" where their advertisements would play in "consistent and professional" environments. Format radio became preferred over personality radio.

As mentioned earlier, the first generation of African-American DJs could sell as well as they could talk. They usually worked on commissions of 10 to 35 percent. In the late 1950s, radio stations continued to hire black disc jockeys but employed whites for nearly all sales positions. Eventually, almost all sales accounts were controlled by corporate managers.[67] This change, perhaps more than any other, curtailed the black DJs' power within the radio station, as sales, program, and station managers assumed more power. As the disc jockeys' responsibilities in sales were severely cut back, or eliminated, their professional roles were significantly diminished too. Their names came down from outdoor billboards, and their status as cultural heroes diminished also.

Naturally, African-American disc jockeys were disappointed, disturbed, and angered by these changes. "Personality radio has been deleted," lamented the great E. Rodney Jones. "You're supposed to *communicate* with your audience. That's next to impossible when you're sitting there and there are only two or three lines you can read at a certain time during the hour of any merit to the community. I think that's starving the community of what it needs to know."[68] Another black DJ noted, "The politics of the country are right wing now. There is no white person, however, who knows what black people want to hear."[69]

George Woods observed, "Personality radio began to lose popularity when the personality got bigger than the station. The call letters are more prominent now; the personality is put in the background." Woods, a long-time on-air personality in Philadelphia, said, "Small record companies have been hurt most by the situation. Format radio has been detrimental to the industry as a whole." Woods criticized format radio because "disc jockeys lack freedom of expression to choose the kind of music people want to hear. Radio station management wants to control the disc jockeys. Black radio is kinda sad; it can't use the power it has."[70] Another disc jockey at a black radio conference expressed a similar view: "Listeners are being robbed and cheated. Record companies are hurting most as a result of format radio."[71]

As radio stations change with the times, various programming innovations are attempted. One approach allows "the on-air personality enough freedom to be innovative, free form expressive, and creative."[72]

Perhaps Joe "Butterball" Tamburro best summed up the concerns and feelings of disc jockeys when he said, "Radio today is not as much fun for an air talent as it was back then. Talent today can only do what the PD [program director] says they can do—back then there were no lines and no Formatics per se. Radio is about talking to people. If you can get everybody listening to feel like you're talking to them, that's the key to successful radio."[73]

CULTURAL HEROES OF 1980s AND 1990s

George Woods is to black radio in Philadelphia what the Liberty Bell is to Independence Hall: Both are symbols of freedom. For more than thirty years, "Georgie Woods, The Guy with Goods," has worked for WHAT and WDAS-AM/FM—top stations in the hearts and minds of black Philadelphians. During these years, Woods has hosted a morning talk show from 8–11 a.m. (Monday–Friday), been an afternoon personality, conducted voter registration drives, raised money for the poor, and collected donations for such worthwhile groups as the United Negro College Fund. Woods is recognized by the African-American community as a concerned individual, interested in the welfare of those less fortunate than himself. His listeners have witnessed Woods' efforts to open up educational and employment opportunities for them. They have seen his strong determination to fight for freedom, dignity, and human rights.

Another example of Woods' community outreach activities occurred during the Christmas season, when he helped raise money to feed, clothe, and pay rent for 5,000 needy families.[74] A close associate of the Reverend Dr. Martin Luther King, Jr., Woods is a firm believer in nonviolent protest as a catalyst for social change. Because of his commitment, Woods has been elected (and re-elected) to the Board of Trustees of the Martin Luther King Jr. Center for Non-Violent Change. African-American citizens of Philadelphia admire those and other qualities in Woods and recognize his value as a role model.

Woods is a cultural hero in Philadelphia. Although he is recognized for work in the community, he is primarily known for his abilities as a disc jockey. Woods played music that listeners enjoyed and his distinctive announcing style reflected many aspects of the African-American oral tradition. "I didn't want to sound like anyone else," Woods admitted in a 1993 *Radio and Records* interview. He said, "I always tried to be original. If you try to sound like someone else, you'll just be another voice in the wilderness. When they heard me they had to know they were listening to 'The Guy with the Goods.'"

The Magnificent Montague is a cultural hero in Los Angeles. Renowned for his positive and uplifting rapport with listeners as a disc jockey, Montague also owned and then sold KPLM-FM in Palm Springs, California. Although he no longer delivers an on-air monologue to listeners, Montague is well remembered and revered by those who heard him in Chicago, San Francisco, or Los Angeles. Montague gained widespread respect because of his announcing abilities and, he said, "because I was able to get into the lives and lifestyles of my listeners."[75] Montague is recognized as a black man who used his talents and finances wisely, so much so that he was able to buy and operate a radio station. Montague says he "left an imprint on listeners and they still regard me as a hero."

African-American disc jockeys recognized for their contributions in the 1990s include Martha Jean "The Queen" Steinberg, Jack Gibson, Kenneth "Doc" Kilgore, Tom Joyner, Donnie Simpson, Frankie Crocker, Rosetta "Rose" Hines, John Mason (Mason in the Morning), and E. Rodney Jones. Others who have made names for themselves are Ken Webb (WRKS), Greg Mack (KJLH), and Cliff Winston (KKBT) in Los Angeles. Stan Bell is well known on Memphis's WHRK; in Miami, James Thomas announces for WEDR and is widely recognized; and Barry Stephens is heard on WMBM in Miami. Further, Bob Law, National Black Network, is a "top-rated talk show host" whose comments and concerns deal with serious topics affecting the African-American community. Richard "Onion" Horton at WGNU in St. Louis, Missouri, is also well known for his discussions of serious topics that keep listeners informed.

These individuals continue a tradition established more than seventy years ago.[76] Each of them continues to make unique contributions to this rich cultural legacy of black radio. Countless other African-American disc jockeys and commentators are using their own unique approaches to reach their listeners. Much of their work goes unnoticed; this book attempts to bring some recognition to these men and women.

BLACK RADIO TODAY

There are 256 black/urban-formatted radio stations in America today, representing 10 percent of all currently used formats. Although contemporary hit radio, sometimes referred to as CHR/TOP 40, is now the most popular format, found on 16.8 percent of the nation's radio stations, the black/urban format has continued to enjoy popularity. Black/urban-formatted stations continue to attract listeners. Since 1977 these stations have witnessed a 53 percent increase in their audience share. According to Duncan's American Radio, the 10 best markets for black/urban-format stations are in the south. However, stations using this format with the highest quarter hour listening are found in major urban areas.

To be sure, part of the increase in black-formatted stations is because the number of black-owned radio stations continues to grow. In 1977 there were 56; this number had increased to 125 by 1982, in 1984 there were 131, and in 1997 there were 189 black-owned radio stations. However, not all black-owned radio stations have adopted the black/urban format.

African-American disc jockeys have continued to evolve and change. Many of the changes have been forced upon them by the dynamics of the radio industry. Still, black DJs have made positive changes themselves, using new and old ways to communicate with their listeners, helping solve their listeners' problems, and speaking for their listeners when they had no voice. Format changes, deregulation, and ownership patterns will no doubt continue to influence how African-American disc jockeys do their jobs. Nevertheless, black DJs' commitment to their communities will determine how well they complete their tasks.

CONCLUSION

African-American disc jockeys are cultural heroes because they keep oral traditions alive. In addition, many have made major contributions to American society.

Some white disc jockeys imitated black speech and other improvisational techniques to "create an identity." For example they played rhythm and blues, blues, and other forms of black music. And they used catchy phrases and lyrics from black music and essentially copied the style of black DJs.

Alan Freed and Wolfman Jack (Robert Smith) are two of the best known white disc jockeys who borrowed from African-American oral traditions to create their own identities. Black DJs knew of the white imitators and most resented them, not so much because of the imitation, but because the white imitators often made a lot more money than their black counterparts. They understandably resented the fact that whites used improvisational culture to receive far greater financial rewards than the original creators.

African-American disc jockeys reacted to white appropriation of black music—for example, when white artists Pat Boone and Elvis Presley "covered" blues and rhythm and blues tunes—by not playing the white version on their shows. They reacted to the appropriation of their announcing styles by "reexpressing American Negro identity and attitudes in a new revitalized way."[77]

The revitalization process involves a synthesis of new experiences—political, social, economic—and a restructuring of the "old mazeway." Thus, black DJs use urban experiences, politics, humor, and religion as features of their dialogues. For instance, Tom Joyner uses humor. Martha Jean, "The Queen," brings a religious fervor to her announcing style. Frankie Crocker's black stream-of-consciousness conversations are laced with references to music, politics, racial matters, and other aspects of life in the urban scene that his listeners are familiar with. As black DJs create new styles, it has become more difficult for whites to imitate them.

Hip-hop culture—its music, clothes, and speech—is a reaction to white imitation of black culture. The "gangsta rappers" and the disc jockeys who play their music are well aware of white imitators. Their hard-edged music and unique phrases are attempts to re-create oral cultural traditions that have not been appropriated by whites.

Hip-hop and gangsta rap came long after the institution of format radio, which started in the late 1950s and early 1960s. Payola scandals initially occurred at about this same time, as record companies tried to find ways to get their products played.

White disc jockeys, such as Alan Freed, Johnny Otis and Wolfman Jack, started imitating black DJs since the time they (black DJs) first began to become popular announcers—the late 1940s and early 1950s. White station owners, managers and advertisers reacted negatively to this imitation, especially the "personality" radio of the late 1950s and 1960s. As radio formatting became more widespread in the late 1950s, disc jockeys were increasingly told to essentially "shut up and play the music." The payola scandal further contributed to the widespread use of radio formats. Eventually, the uniformity of formats caused disc jockeys to almost completely reverse from whites imitating blacks to black DJs discovering they had to "sound white" to announce on some radio stations.

Nevertheless, African-American disc jockeys who stayed close to their roots managed to survive and thrive as cultural heroes in the 1990s. They constantly revitalize improvisational cultural traditions in their on-air performances. Many still use black English and several forms of "jive," and they play blues, soul, and rhythm and blues music. As the interviews that follow reveal, black disc jockeys are gatekeepers who protect the African-American community from "impure" music, language, and thoughts. They were African Americans' first voices in the electronic village and made the transition from rural to urban society easier for their people. These disc jockeys continue to perform a valuable service to their listeners.[78]

NOTES

1. Williams, Gilbert, "The Black Disc Jockey As a Cultural Hero," *Journal of Popular Music and Society*, Summer, 1986, pp. 79–90.

2. Spaulding, Norman W., "History of Black Oriented Radio in Chicago, 1929–1963," Ph.D. dissertation, University of Illinois, Urbana-Champaign, 1981.

3. Spaulding, op. cit., pp. 122–125.

4. Herskovits, Melville J. (1958), *The Myth of the Negro Past*. Boston: Beacon Press, originally published in 1941.

5. Brooks, Tilford (1984), *America's Black Musical Heritage*. Englewood Cliffs, NJ: Prentice Hall, p. 29.

6. Brooks, op. cit., p. 29.

7. Haralambos, Michael (1975), *Right On: From Blues to Soul in Black America*. New York: Drake, p. 100.

8. Haralambos, op. cit., p. 100.

9. Haralambos, op. cit., p. 111.

10. Hecht, Michael, L. Collier, and S. A. Ribeau, (1993), *African American Communication.* Newbury Park, CA: Sage, p. 104.

11. Cheek, J. M. (1976), *Assertive Black . . . Puzzled White.* San Luis Obispo, CA: Impact Communications, passim.

12. Hecht, et al., pp. 100–101.

13. Hecht, et al., p. 99.

14. Hecht, et al., pp. 100–101.

15. Abrahams, Roger D. (1964), *Deep Down in the Jungle.* Hatboro, PA: Folklore Associates.

16. Ibid., p. 100.

17. Ibid., p. 111.

18. Abrahams, op. cit., p. 112.

19. Haralambos, op. cit., p. 27.

20. Haralambos, op. cit., pp. 57-60.

21. Haralambos, op. cit., p. 110.

22. Ibid., p. 100.

23. Smitherman, Geneva (1994), *Black Talk: Words and Phrases From the Hood to the Amen Corner.* Boston: Houghton Mifflin, p. 5.

24. Keil, Charles (1966), *Urban Blues.* Chicago: The University of Chicago Press, p. 43.

25. Williams, G., "Black Disc Jockey as a Cultural Hero," *JPM&S*, p. 87.

26 "Black Radio Pioneer Al Benson Dies at 70," *Jet*, Vol. 55 (September 28, 1978), p. 57.

27. MacDonald, J. Fred (1986), *Don't Touch That Dial! Radio Programming in American Life, 1920–1960.* Chicago: Nelson Hall, pp. 327-350.

28. Hine, Darlene Clark (1993), *Black Women History.* New York: Carlson, pp. 955–958.

29. MacDonald, op. cit., p. 334.

30. Haralambos, op. cit., p. 30.

31. Haralambos, op. cit., p. 30.

32. Keil, op. cit., p. 15.

33. Keil, op. cit., pp. 15–16.

34. Spaulding, op. cit., pp. 122–125.

35. Walt Lover, "Legends of Black Radio," *Radio and Records*, No. 998 (June 25, 1993).

36. Keil, op. cit., pp. 16–17.

37. Ibid., p. 17.

38. Sterling, Christopher, and Timothy Haight (1978), *Mass Media.* New York: Praeger Publishing Company.

39. Spaulding, op. cit., see Chapters 4 and 5.

40. MacDonald, op. cit., pp. 327–370.

41. Spaulding, op. cit., p. 47.

42. Ibid., p. 72.

43. Ibid., p. 72.

44. *Jet*, Vol. 55 (Sept. 28, 1978), p. 57.

45. "Cool Gent," *Chicago Sun Times*, December 3, 1995.

46. *Jet*, Vol. 55 (Sept. 28, 1978), p. 57.

47. *Jet*, Vol. 55 (Sept. 28, 1978), p. 57.

48. Spaulding, op. cit., pp. 78–79.

49. *Chicago Sun Times*, December 3, 1995, p. 13.

50. *Radio and Records*, June 25, 1993, p. 46.

51. Edmerson, Estelle (1954), "A Descriptive Study of the American Negro in United States Professional Radio, 1922–1953," MA thesis, UCLA, pp. 337–338.

52. James Edward Saunders Collection, Ohio Historical Society (MSS 422).

53. "Disc Jockeys," *Ebony Magazine*, December 1947, pp. 44–49.

54. Spaulding, op. cit., pp. 115–116.

55. Ibid., pp. 110–116.

56. Foster, Eugene (1982), *Understanding Broadcasting*. Reading, MA: Addison-Wesley, p. 100.

57. Spaulding, op. cit., pp. 65–66.

58. *Radio and Records*, June 25, 1993, p. 48.

59. "Thirty Years of Payola: The Inside Story," *Pulse Magazine*, Vol. 3, No. 13 (April 11, 1988), pp. 1, 13–19, 24–29.

60. *Pulse Magazine*, Vol. 3, No. 13 (April 11, 1988), pp. 1, 24–29.

61. Ibid., p. 24.

62. Ibid., p. 26.

63. Ibid., p. 26.

64. Denisoff, Serge (1973), "The Evolution of Pop Music Broadcasting, 1929–1972," *Journal of Popular Music and Society* Vol. 2, No. 3, pp. 202–226.

65. Routt, Ed (1978), *The Radio Format Conundrum*. New York: Hastings House, pp. 20–24.

66. Spaulding, op. cit., p. 62.

67. Ibid, pp. 47–48.

68. *Radio and Records*, June 25, 1993, p. 42.

69. Black Radio Exclusive Conference, Houston, TX, 1981, made during panel discussion on "Format Versus Personality Radio."

70. Ibid.

71. Ibid.

72. Ibid.

73. *Radio and Records*, June 25, 1993, pp. 32–50.

74. Gould, Harry M., Jr., "The Sound and Soul of Black Radio," *Philadelphia Inquirer*, August 13, 1983, pp. 13–33.

75. Personal Interview, September 27, 1984.

76. "Black DeeJays, Paid to Flaunt their Personalities," *Ebony Man*, January 1992, pp. 44–46.

77. Keil, op. cit., p. 45.

78. Spaulding, op. cit., p. 113.

◆ 2 ◆

William T. "Hoss" Allen

William T. "Hoss" Allen was born in Gallatin, Tennessee. After a stint in the U.S. Army, Allen enrolled in Vanderbilt University, in nearby Nashville. Upon graduation from Vanderbilt, Allen pursued a career in theater but decided that acting was not the vocation for him. He returned to Tennessee, and in 1948 he began his illustrious career in radio broadcasting at WHIN, in Gallatin.

Allen left WHIN to work for WLAC, which was located in Nashville, Tennessee. WLAC is a 50,000 watt clear-channel radio station and is received throughout much of the lower southern part of the United States. "The Hoss man," as he was called, became a popular disc jockey at WLAC. African-American listeners appreciated and liked his announcing style and the music he played. Allen became friends with all of the popular African-American disc jockeys, often attending the same conventions that they did, such as Jack Gibson's Family Affair in Atlanta.

During his long career at WLAC, he played all kinds of black music, including gospel. Listeners recognized his voice and a phrase he used to sell a hair pomade, which was "just a touch means so much." Allen's deep and gentle voice had an air of authenticity and trust about it. Moreover, Black listeners ordered records from a local record store, sponsor of Allen's show.

On WLAC, Allen spoke to listeners every night. They loved the new rhythm and blues tunes he played, ones that they could not hear on local stations or buy at the stores. So, they ordered through the mail.

APRIL 26, 1991
WLAC, NASHVILLE, TN

How did you get started in radio?

Well I started after graduating from Vanderbilt University. I got a job up in Gallatin, Tennessee, which was my home town. It was a little radio station that was just going on the air, September 1, 1948. I started working there helping to set up the music library and programming and whatnot. We were 1010 on the AM dial. I really had been interested in the theatre and had been working towards that end at Vanderbilt. I had an opportunity to go to Summer Stock up in Plymouth, Massachusetts, but my grandmother said, "You know you've been play acting all your life, time to get down to doing something."

I didn't know much about the blues but I liked big band music so, of course, this was going on at WLAC in '46. Gene Noble was the night-time disc jockey and he played records such as Glenn Miller, Tommy Dorsey, that kind of thing until midnight; we signed off at midnight. We were a 50,000 watt station and weren't doing anything different than any other CBS affiliate around the country. They had a signal that went about 800 miles in every direction. In late '46 a couple of guys, black dudes, came in with some boogie woogie and blues records and they got upstairs to see Gene. They went in and asked him if he would play some of their music and gave him some boogie and blues records. Now Gene Nobles was an old carnie, he worked in a carnival before he got into radio and he was just a real swinging, wonderful man who was very small and had been crippled since a young boy when he had polio. He had a hard time getting around and I guess he was only about 5'2" but he had a heart as big as the world and so he said, "Sure, I'd be happy to." So he started playing them once or twice a week and all of a sudden he started getting mail from all over the south, east, southwest and from as far north as Detroit and Chicago and as far south as the Bahamas and New Orleans. The sales manager at the time was a guy by the name of B.G. Blackman who they called "Blackie, Blackie, Black Man." He had been hired because we had that kind of coverage, you know. We reached so far and so he said, "Well gosh, why don't you play some more of that?" Then came the problem of finding more records by black artists. Gene had worked at one time for a guy named Louis Buckley who was a juke box operator and had a little used record shop on the side, so he went down to see Buckley. Buckley had a lot of boxes in the black area of Nashville and so he had a bunch of records and Gene started playing these. Now about this time a guy named Randy Wood and another fellow came back to Gallatin and decided to go into the electrical appliance business. They bought a little store, inventory and all. After they bought it they were going through the inventory and in a back closet they found 3,000 to 4,000 old 78 records, all brand new, all by black artists. Someone told old Randy, "Now there's a guy down at WLAC playing black music, maybe you can get together," so Randy met Gene and they came up with the idea of possibly selling these records by mail, C.O.D., like five records for $2.98 plus C.O.D. and handling charges. So he approached the powers to be at the station and bought one spot to run at midnight every night, six nights a week. I think they paid $6 or $7 and offered five of these boogie and blues records and that's how it all started. The first couple of weeks nothing happened and so he cancelled it. He said, "I've invested about $70 and I just can't afford it." So they cancelled it and lo and behold on the third Monday morning in the mail they got a whole sack of mail, all C.O.D. orders for this particular offer. So that started a big money-making project.

Were you aware of payola at that time?

Yeah, there was no law against it. I'm sure that Leonard Chess, owner of a black nightclub on the south side of Chicago, was more than generous to Gene as he became more successful. There were three places really that records broke out and now John Richburg comes into this in a minute in '47. Actually, Gene was doing all three shows. He was doing Buckley's, he was doing Ernie's Record Mart and he was doing Randy's Record Shop. He went on vacation in 1947 and old man Ernie Young who had Ernie's Record Mart always thought that Gene did more for Randy than he did for him, but anyhow that particular summer John Richburg, who had been with the station since '42, went into the navy in '43 and then came back in late 1945 or early 1946. He was our newsman. John had extensive dramatic training too and was in New York for many years trying to break into the theatre and did soap operas and stuff, but he was starving to death driving a cab and everything else trying to live, so finally he came back south to Charleston and went into radio, in his hometown, and then he came over to Nashville. He was big-voiced, beautiful voice and had a vocabulary from here to Buffalo, New York. I mean he was anything but a blues man. One summer, he worked all three records shops while Gene was gone, so then Ernie Young asked management at the station if John could do his show instead of Gene. Gene continued to do Buckley's and Randy's, and John began doing Ernie's.

Was personality allowed to come out at this time?

Yes, and no, but John Richburg developed into such a fantastic mail-order pitch man, big voice and very believeable in his delivery, and he was selling everything from baby chickens to gutted mufflers, besides the records.

Did you all have to brokerage time, buy time from the station and go out and sell it?

No, the station owned all the time. Everybody was on staff. I was playing from my own collection and I was playing these big bands — all the records I had. Like I say, Erskine Hawkins, Duke Ellington, Count Basie, things like that. But soon after I went on the air, we were a daytime station and I was on from 3:30 until we signed off, and in the summer I was on until about 6 o'clock and in the winter I'd be on until around 4:45 or something like that. I started getting mail and they wanted to hear Bull Moose Jackson, Wynoni Harris, people like that.

What were your call letters? I mean what was your ferequency?

WHIN, and it was 1010. 1010, WHIN. Through Randy I started coming down to WLAC and I met Gene Noble and I met this guy Blackman who was sales manager and had taken an interest in the nighttime. Oddly enough, management was a little embarrassed about this whole thing because they didn't perceive themselves as a black station. And then people were sort of kidding them about it and at the country club and people sort of gave them a jab about their playing . . . a negro station. They were making so much money out of it they couldn't change.

Were there any black-owned stations during your time?

There were no black stations to speak of on the air and that is one of the big things that WLAC did, was to prove that the black music was viable and more. Now WERD went on the air with Jack Gibson. Zenas Sears, "Daddy Sears," and Stan Raymond opened up WAOK. While Zenas, the general manager who owned the station, was white, all the rest of the staff was black. They had a white guy named "Poppa Stopper" on the air, but he had black fellows sitting right beside him telling him what to say, giving him all the expressions to use but the black guy wasn't doing the air work. Jack's station was the first black-owned, black-operated station to go on in 1949 in Atlanta. Of course, there were two or three stations on the south side of Chicago but you couldn't hear them. . . . Al Benson was awful big at this end. Al Benson goes back to the early '40s. Of course, the first station to play black music at all was over in Helena, Arkansas, with King Biscuit time, it just had 15 minutes.

What about Sonny Boy Williamson?

Sonny Boy Williamson, Robert Junior Lockwood, Robert Johnson, and B.B. King got their start over there. There were so many artists out of Mississippi, Arkansas and Texas, including Bobby Bland, that first got their start on this station in Helena. They were the early, early blues artists that made such an impression. King Biscuit was a flour company that had a festival and they used to take a truck out and have Sonny Boy and some other blues artists on the back of it. They would go around to little towns and have these blues artists play and they'd have signs like KING FLOUR. This is how they sold their flour, how they promoted their products.

Did you do any of that, promotion like that?

No, we were all just working for sponsors, such as Randy's, Royal Crown, and Ernie's Record Barn.

Who did new artists see to get their records on the air? Was it the DJ or the program director?

These guys came to see the disc jockeys, there was no program director. If you could get in to see John or Gene, that's where you did business.

Did you guys do platter parties?

No, we didn't go out and do anything like that. John would go on the road now and then with James Brown. He'd go out with him for a week and M.C. and James would pay him, you know, like $1,000.00 a night or something, which was unheard of. All the people wanted to see what John looked like and they were all amazed when they saw he was white.

What was the audience's reaction after they saw him?

Oh they didn't care. John had a big, deep voice; I compared him with Nobles. Gene didn't sound like a radio announcer. He was just funny and he had this great personality.

Did you play songs by white artists?

They had a great school of music out there and they had a lot of small groups and I was always interested in semi-jazz. I was cutting these groups for Randy so he called me and said, "I have this group of white boys that want to cut a record and they are driving me crazy and I'll send you a tape down there." I said "You send me a tape and I'll just do it. They can't sing but. . . . " So he said, "Well, they are going to Western Kentucky State University so I'll just go ahead and cut them. I might even start another label." He did and he called it Dot. The group turned out to be the Hill Toppers. They were white but they sang black and they were a big success. I just said, "Well, just send me my money. How much have we got in the bank?" I think he said "$1600." I said, "Send me my $800, I want to go to Daytona Beach or somewhere," so I missed out on Dot Records. Of course, Randy got the idea that he could sell a lot of records by getting white artists to cover these black groups. He found Pat Boone and he started doing everything that Little Richard and Fats Domino would do. Randy became tremendously successful, making lots more money from Dot Records than he was making on the Record Shop. While Little Richard sold 600,000 records of "Tutti Fruitti," which was unheard of at that time Pat Boone did a million and half on the same record.

So, what about the independent companies, did they start fading out at about that time because the big boys got in?

No, not at that time. In 1956 we were still going big. That's the time Gene made himself a little over $400,000, so he just quit. He retired. So I took over the show. My job was to call on the white stations and try to get black records played. I was fairly successful at it. Of course, I called on black stations too, but they were already playing them for the most part. I stayed out three years on the road just calling on disc jockeys, damned near killed myself because all I had to do was just entertain them, you know. You're up all night and then you have to get up early to meet a guy at 6 o'clock in the morning. We had a guy that came in during that time by the name of Hugh Jerrod and took over the show. He called himself "Big Hugh Baby." Now he did have some dances and things called the "Big Baby Hop." Hugh started playing a lot of white artists rather than black and he wasn't playing what Randy told him. Our policy was to call Randy's Record Shop and get a list of records to be played that night because they knew what was selling. We could play what we wanted to from 11 to 12 on Royal Crown, but on Randy's I played exactly what they told me to play every night. Hugh went over the line a little bit so the station came to me, and at this time I was sort of spread out on the road, and they said, "Would you be interested in coming back?" And I said, "Oh, Lord, would I?" So I came back in 1964. Things were still swinging.

At this time, was it more format radio than personality?

No, radio was format everywhere else, but we weren't. We were still just doing what we wanted to do. But there were a lot more black stations on the air, so we had a lot more competition. We were not unique anymore. We weren't the only place you could go to get black music and if you lived somewhere that didn't have a radio station, you could always get WLAC, no matter where you lived in the south. We were covering up the middle of the country from New Orleans to Chicago, including such places as Ohio, Illinois, Indiana and Michigan. Chicago and Detroit had big jocks by this time, so black people and white people were listening to the local stations. I mean they weren't listening to us like they used to. Some of the old-timers stayed with us and we started playing more and more gospel.

In 1971 I just really had seen the writing on the wall with the Motown sound coming in and the little independent stations and record companies being bought up by the larger labels and companies. John was getting ready to retire in '72 so they wanted me to take over his l to 3 o'clock show. I was working 7 to 1, so I told the boss, "Look, I don't want to stay up here until 3 o'clock." I'd had a problem with booze and in '71 I'd gone into treatment and gotten myself straight. John didn't drink but Gene would come to work with a fifth every night but I never saw him tight. He'd sit around and get to drinking. When I first came there I'd sit with him all night just to watch him work and meet the record guys that came in, and drink his whiskey. Of course, it was awful rough on the road too, because all I had to do was pick these jocks up and party with them and so it finally got me and I just bottomed out. I joined AA and they got me straight, so I told them there was no way I was going to stay up here until 3 o'clock and tempt myself. I said, "If you'll let me change from blues to gospel and tape it so I won't have to stay up here, I think I can sell it." They said, "Well, if you can sell it, do anything you want to." It became so very successful.

In the meantime, John retired, and we had to hire our first black jock just to satisfy the minority. We hired a guy named Spider Harrison out of Indianapolis. He called himself "Spider-Man." He started messing with it and was playing blues at night. Finally, Randy cancelled with us because this guy just wanted to play only what he wanted to. By this time, 1972, my gospel had gotten so big so he said, "Look, you give up the Royal Crown and let 'the Spider' do that and we'll let you lengthen the gospel show until 5 o'clock." So I started taping the gospel from midnight to 5, all gospel, and then that day I started working at an FM station from 2 to 6. We had had Royal Crown for twenty-five years and a black guy doing it always; we changed to another black guy and they cancelled within three weeks.

I was a gospel man from '71 until '78 when *Billboard Magazine* bought the station and on the advice of consultants, they decided to take all the black programming off. We had spent thirty years building this black audience and they just pitched it out the window. We made $400,000 a year on the gospel from midnight to 5. And I wasn't on commission, I'm sorry to say, because I sold it all myself. By this time Ernie's, Randy's and Buckley's, all the record shops, had gone to gospel because they had nowhere to play blues anymore. So I had all three of those record shops I was doing myself, as part of my gospel show. And then gospel got almost damn near as big as blues. I've still got a little black gospel show on tape. In 1978 I went over to a local television station and just did voice-over work. The radio station came to me, when they couldn't make any money on talk shows and white preachers and said, "Look, I think we made a mistake, would you be interested in coming back?" I said, "Yeah, but on my own terms; I'll take commission but I don't want any salary." So that way I came back and they started to enter the blues again from 11 until 2, and from 2 to 5 I did gospel, but it was too late. . . .

How did you come to meet Jack Gibson and all that crew?

Before there were any disc jockey organizations, there was the National Association of Record Manufacturers and the record companies would have conventions and always bring two or three important disc jockeys. It was just to let them have a good time. I first met Jack and Eddie Castleberry and a lot of other guys at these conventions, although I knew who they were because I had heard them on the air. Jack was instrumental in starting NATRA, which was the National Association of Television and Radio Artists, which was a black organization. John and I were active in it, well not active, but we went to the conventions. Jack had had these little conventions called "Family Affair" in Atlanta. In 1980 I went to my first one, and I've been going to them ever since. They used to be just wonderful fun because so many of the older black jocks that we had known over the years all got together; it was just a big homecoming.

Then it just got so big in the last 4–5 years. Last year I was standing out in front of the Alanta Hilton with Arthur Prysock, Hy Wise and Velvet Moore when all these young, hip, rap disc jockeys were walking around, coming in and out of the hotel with these baseball caps on backwards and sideways and everything. I was the only white guy there practically and I said, "Damn, I know how it feels to be black, I'm going to tell Jack to get some more damn white people or I ain't coming no more." So Prysock said, "Hell, if he did you wouldn't know them." So that's about the way it was, but Jack has got a very successful thing going there now and he's done so much for black people and he's done so much for the elderly black jocks, guys that have fallen on hard times. I love him, he's been a great friend to me. But time moves on and you know somebody's got to take over and you've got the younger guys in and for the most part they've never heard of WLAC, especially white guys playing black music.

Well, that's why I'm writing this book. I've already done stuff on black disc jockeys as cultural heroes and that's why I'm interviewing you, so I can get all of this into a broadcasting book.

Well, we weren't the first to play black music by any manner or means, but we were the first to give it national recognition. I used to come on the air and say, "Hey, I'm down for Royal Crown, America's favorite hair dressing—just a touch means so much!" I was out somewhere at a church, and somebody came up to me and said, "Just a touch means so much," and that's all he said but I knew he had to have listened to the Royal Crown show because he didn't say "Hello Hoss" or anything else; he just said, "Just a touch can mean so much."

◆ 3 ◆

Eddie Castleberry

I first met Eddie in the summer of 1991 in Birmingham, Alabama. I had spoken to him and interviewed him over the telephone several months earlier. Jack Gibson had given me his telephone number and I called him at his apartment in New York City. His voice was clear and he enunciated each word clearly. Eddie's personality quickly emerged as we talked about his love of announcing, African-American music, and African Americans. Eddie asked me if I had heard of Ruth Brown, the legendary rthythm and blues singer; he knew her and many other artists.

During his visit to Birmingham, Eddie's hometown, we hung out at a couple of night spots with some of his old friends. I had a great time. I learned a little about what it must have been like to party with black DJs in the "old days." I got back to my apartment sometime near 3:00 A.M. The next day I had a hangover and Eddie called and asked if I wanted to hang out again that evening. I had to decline his invitation. Even though Eddie had a few years on me, I just couldn't hang.

Edward J. "Eddie" Castleberry was born on July 28, 1928, in Birmingham, Alabama. After attending Miles College from 1950 to 1951, he worked as a disc jockey at WEDR and WJLD in Birmingham. Later, he became program director at WMBM in Miami, Florida; newsman and disc jockey for WCIN in Cincinnati, Ohio; disc jockey and news announcer at WABQ in Cleveland, Ohio, from 1961 to 1964; program director at WVKO in Columbus, Ohio, from 1964 to 1967; worked for WHAT in Philadelphia, Pennsylvania, in 1967 to 1968; and held disc jockey and news announcing jobs at WEBB in Baltimore, Maryland. Finally, Eddie worked for the Mutual & National Black Networks as anchorman and entertainment editor.

Eddie received the Newsman of the Year Award from the Coalition of Black Media Women in 1980, Newsman of the Year from the Jack the

Rapper Family Affair in 1980, and Outstanding Citizen Award from the Alabama House of Representatives in 1983.

FEBRUARY 13, 1991

Tell me how you got started in radio.

Well, when I graduated from Parker High School and I started going to Miles College, that's when they had just about a year before starting the idea of black radio stations, which were mostly white-owned, but with black operators.

What year was this?

Well, they started in Birmingham in 1949. And in '50 I had graduated from Parker and was going to Miles. Wiley Daniels was the big black male personality in the city at the time. He was one of them. They were on a station called WEDR, white-owned but black-operated. Wiley had seen me at the Parker school plays as a kid in a couple of our variety shows. So he came to Parker to speak one time (right after the boot cavalier) and he asked me, "Well look Ed, I've got to go do my army service, I've got to go do my two years. Why don't you come down and see about taking my place?" So I went down there and I took the audition and I was chosen and that is how my career started.

What was the first thing you said when you went on the air?

I can't remember, that was so long ago. Gosh, I have no idea. At first I had a show that was the movies. I did a 15-minute show about movies and I think I said, "It's Movie Time." That was the theme because we always had a theme.

Did you have a handle or something like that when you first started?

No, when I first started I used "Eddie Castleberry." But when I got to Miami, Florida, everybody on that station, which was WMBM, had to have a nickname. And so I took "Castle Rock" because there was a swinging song out called "Castle Rock" by Johnny Hodges. I took "Castleberry Castle Rock" and called myself the "Castle Rock Show."

Now, when you went on the air, did you see yourself as a radio personality who was a role model for the black community?

Oh yeah, I thought so; I mean, I would have liked to have been. I like to think that I was. As was proved by the big crowds we used to draw in whatever we did, I guess I was. There were times, not only in Birmingham, when parents would call us up and ask us "Would you talk to our kids?" Maybe their kid was going to quit school or something like that and we would talk to them and sometimes we'd win. The kid would stay in school or whatever.

Did you say certain kinds of things that helped you relate to your listening audience?

Oh Lord yes. I used to say things at different times, you know, mostly I was a smooth-type jock and I didn't use too much jive. But it depended on what market I was in because I've been in about twelve different markets.

In terms of your style, how did it evolve? How did you pattern yourself, or who did you pattern yourself after?

I patterned myself as the smooth Wiley Daniels, because Wiley was a smooth jock. In fact, all the guys on WEDR at that time, there were three main guys, Wiley, Frank Smart, and Ben Alexander, all were smooth. So I patterned my style after them too. I always tried to be the smooth cat. Of course, it would take you a little longer to catch on, but I always caught on. Sometimes, in other words, if you're on a station with a guy who is more flamboyant, it takes you a little time to catch up with him. However, I used to always do it. I'd manage to do it. In other words, people liked our contrasting styles. They didn't want every guy on the air to be flamboyant.

So after your first tour here in Birmingham, where did you move to?

Well, I went to Greenville, South Carolina. As a matter of fact, I thought I was hired for Miami. I was hired by a guy who owned four or five radio stations and he told me I was going down to Miami, but at the last minute he called me and told me, "You're going to Greenville, South Carolina, for a while. And then after you work up there for a while, then we're going to send you to Miami." I didn't know he was sending me to a white station and I was going to be the only black person on there.

Were you going to be doing news or did you have a show?

I had a show on the air and we were network affiliated. The radio network scheduled my program right after "Gunsmoke."

This was "Gunsmoke" on the radio?

On the radio. In fact, Matt Dillon was played by William Conrad, the man who plays "Jake and the Fat Man" now. And during the week my program used to come on right after "Art Linkletter's House Party." Also while I was in Greenville, I gave a young man his first-ever radio interview; he was about fourteen to fifteen years old then. And that young man was Rev. Jesse Jackson. I have Jesse on tape right now saying "The first interview I ever had was with Eddie Castleberry and I've been talking ever since."

How was your career affected by the Civil Rights Movement?

Well, when the Civil Rights Movement came I was in Columbus, Ohio, when the kids got killed in the bombing in Birmingham. Our station would always advertise and help organize rallies for Dr. King. Dr. King came to Birmingham; however, I never went home. I never got a chance to go to my home, which is Birmingham, during that period.

Was 1963 the year when the 16th Street Baptist church was bombed?

Yeah. And when they had the march on Washington, what they did was they assigned another person on the station to go to cover that story. I was aching to go but they assigned another person, rather than me.

So, do you think your career was enhanced by the Civil Rights Movement?

Now that's ironic. I don't think my career had anything to do with the Civil Rights Movement, except that I was on the air advertising about the Civil Rights rallies and interviewing Civil Rights people. After the Civil Rights Movement, and after Dr. King had been killed, I got a job in Washington, D.C.

What actually happened was, a bunch of black kids from Howard, and I think someplace else, were going around to all the radio stations in the city and they would ask radio owners, "Where are your blacks?" You see, very few stations had any blacks. This was in the beginning of the 70s. And so, it just so happened, me and my partner had a business over in Baltimore and I was between jobs on the radio, and one guy, a guy who was a record promoter, went into a station called WASH FM and said, "We've got to find a black announcer quick because these black kids are coming in and giving us a hard time because we have no blacks on the air." So this guy recommended me. Well, at that time I had already been in the radio business for about twenty years and so I was offered a very good job. After I got the job, the very same kids that were protesting about blacks not having jobs in these stations were saying that the management was pulling just anyone off the street to hire black people, which is what some people were doing. They were pulling just any black they could get. So when they came to my station they said, "No, we got Mr. Castleberry. He's been on the air for twenty years." I would say as a way of indirect affirmative action, I did get a job but that was after I had been in business twenty years.

How did advertising work when you first started out?

Well, we had sales departments. They went out and they sold the slots. Sometimes they would sell a 15-minute program for which we would get extra money, which was called "talent fees."

Is it true that at first disc jockeys had to buy their own time from the stations?

No, that wasn't true. Not necessarily. What it was, there were staff announcers. Now, they didn't have to do that. Sometimes you might work at a radio station where you had to be a salesman, an engineer, announcer, everything at once. This didn't happen at all black stations. At all the stations I worked I was a staff announcer, I had nothing to do with sales. However, if the station sold a 15-minute or one-half hour show, then I would have to deal with the sponsor. In other words, if Schlitz Beer was the sponsor and paying extra money for a time slot, I would go out to clubs and other events in my off-time promoting their product. Especially in Birmingham, if you sold like a half-hour or hour of time on the air, whoever sold it could get on the air and do what they wanted to do. They didn't have to be an announcer, they didn't have to be good, they didn't have to be nothing. All they needed to do was lay that money down and they got time on the air. You could go on the air and do whatever you wanted. Luckily, now most stations don't do that anymore.

If you wanted to get on the air to preach, could you?

Yeah, something like that. Of course, preaching is different. Nobody expects a good announcer to be a preacher. But a lot of these guys just get on the radio and sell products, you know. Or they plugged things but they usually had some kind of agenda. The key to making extra money was to pay the station just enough to get on the air and then undersell the time for less than what they paid for it.

How do you feel about formats versus "personality" within the structure of radio?

Well, I feel great about personality radio. I think personality radio needs to come back, especially in black radio. I believe it is something the audience needs; however, I can see why they don't have that much personality on the radio now. It's the same old thing. They don't want these guys to develop their personalities on the air to where they get too well loved. They want to be able to remove them without any problems. Some of us guys got bigger than the stations. Of course, that didn't stop us from getting fired.

Now, if you're bigger than the station, that means that if they fire you, you can walk across the street and start talking on the radio someplace else?

Yes, but in our time we couldn't do that because most towns, unlike Birmingham, had only one black station and if you didn't work at that black station, you didn't work, period. I don't care how good you were, how big a reputation you had, you were still black and no white station was going to take a shot at you. They weren't going to do it . . . that's why some of us moved around so much. We had to move from city to city, either to get some more money, or it just so happened that three of the stations I worked for were for the same guy and he kept transferring me because I was single.

Have you ever heard of the concept of "payola"?

Oh yes, it was simple enough. The record companies paid us to play records. They gave us money and sometimes they gave us checks and we took it until they put a law against it. See in the years we started taking it, there was no law against it. They'd give us $50 or $100, whatever, but then we got chump change, you know, upside the white boys. They got big . . . when the white boys started playing the records on the bigger stations, those guys got money that was out of sight. And that is why the government stepped in. For $50, $75, or $100, wasn't nobody saying nothing. You're talking about huge amounts of unreported cash that the government don't get any taxes on. Oh, they jumped on some guys, you know. Some guys were careless and things like that, but you know, if a guy is giving you cash, what are you going to do? We were getting mostly cash. You get cash and they can't track that down. But you see these guys, the white boys, when they got in the payola game, they started getting automobiles and all that, you know. You know the government is going to ask questions about that.

So what happened was, when the government got a hold of the quiz shows on TV, they said, "Well let's go get the radio stations while we're at it." So we all had to sign forms saying that we would not take any payola, that we would not take anything that smacked of remuneration. I mean nobody is going to come to you to break a record any more. What it did, record companies started giving out all cash with us. Before that, from time to time we'd get a check or something. What they did, for the most part, they stuck with the black jocks somewhat because they weren't getting all that much anyway. It was the big guys they couldn't deal with. A lot of guys who would tell you, "Well, we can't do it no more because the government stepped in," they were just saying that to keep from giving you anything. It was just a game.

In terms of format, did the format tell you when to play music?

We did not have formats until a few years after I was in. Each guy played what he wanted to play but it was usually the same thing. You know, with a little deviation.

How did you know which were the hot records?

Well, we made them hot. We were the ones that made them hot. The black jocks in the early days, they were the ones. See when white boys started playing our music, what they'd do is listen and see what the black stations were playing and then they would play it, unless it was a blues or something like that. Now they're acting like they discovered blues. Back when I started, there ain't no way you could get a white boy to play a B.B. King record. . . . And now they think he's God. In fact, in them days when you talk about black music they'd think you meant Nat King Cole. Those boys had never heard of Jimmy Witherspoon, Ruth Brown and Louis Jordan. Now wait a minute. I'll tell you what. There was a certain segment of the white audience that was hip to it. They would be at our dances, I mean they would be at the dances upstairs. You see in Birmingham you'd go to the city auditorium. If you have a black band, white people could sit up and watch from the third tier. They used to come out for people like Buddy Johnson's band and Louis Jordan. They couldn't dance but I mean they enjoyed themselves.

What would you consider to be the most significant changes in black radio from the time you got into it until now? The last forty years.

When we got formatted like the white stations. This thing about urban contemporary, see, we'd never play a white record. The majority of us would never do it.

Why wouldn't you play a white record?

Well, we figured our air time was needed for black artists, and not only during the time when the white boys started playing a few black records. I never played a white record until I got to WASH and, of course, they were a pop station so I had to mix it up. But I'm talking about breaking a white record. We would never break a white record.

But today I wouldn't say that that kind of solidarity exists between the disc jockeys, even black disc jockeys, and the community. That is, the sense that we have some kind of commitment to the community.

Well what they got, they got this urban contemporary. In other words, everybody thinks we are integrated now, in spite of all the racial problems we're having today that we thought were cleared up when Dr. King got killed. Despite all the racial problems we have today, everybody is still in the mood for integration. Got an illusion of integration. But the plain fact of the matter is, when it comes to a black station, especially down south, you are only going to have a certain amount of white people listen to you anyway and they're going to listen to you to hear black music. So playing white records ain't going to draw no more white people than you already had. And the ones that do listen to you are going to wonder what the hell you're doing playing a Rolling Stones record. Usually they say, "Hey, we've got eight other radio stations in town we could hear that jive on," and like I said, what they are doing is they're taking air time from good black artists that need it.

What would you prescribe if you could prescribe some kind of remedy for black radio?

They should have good black gospel and good blues and stuff which is our heritage—which is us. That is exactly what we need on black radio stations. And see, these guys can say all this jive about urban contemporary, you know, about how it works and all that but I just don't believe it. We've got to go back to our roots. Go back to what we're doing because we are who we are and we've got a very rich heritage. A lot of guys don't realize that.

What about this format idea?

Well I never like that, period. And since I very seldom had to work under formatting, it didn't affect me one way or the other. But what it is a lot of times with a format, is that one guy picks all the records. And you know what he is doing. Well, I'm not going to say it out loud, but you can guess. One man has control over . . . see when all of us did our own thing, we all got a little piece.

Do you think that owning more black radio stations is part of it?

No, because the trouble with owning a black station was that, like down in Birmingham, I ain't going to call the man's name because he's always been my buddy. Anyway, when black men with money had a chance to buy a radio station dirt cheap, they would not do it.

In 1954 we tried to get a certain person to buy WEDR and he wouldn't do it.

He didn't think it was a strong investment?

No, they couldn't see what it was about. As a result, the guys buying stations now are paying too much. There was a time they could have got the same station for $25/50,000 or something like that. Now they're paying a half million, three-quarters of a million, all that for this stuff. Of course, maybe some of the guys were too young to know about this, but I'm talking about the guys back then who had money. The black men who had money.

What about this problem of advertising though? Do you feel blacks get the same amount of money for the advertising when they have top-rated stations?

No, the only thing we can do about that is to let our people know that these sponsors aren't spending money on our stations. Therefore, we shouldn't buy from them. Meaning, don't buy their products, they're not spending money in the black city. Now Jesse [Jackson] managed to get the message out about some of the products our community shouldn't buy. But we need to hit all the products. The most shameful period was, I think you've heard about it, when Nat King Cole had his show. He couldn't find sponsors. People, even the southern stations, were supporting that. Running his program, sustaining as long as they could. And even when big-name guest stars were appearing on that show for union scale, which is much less than their going rate, the program still couldn't get advertisers. I blame all that on Madison Avenue. Still today, Madison Avenue does not support the Nat King Cole show. It boils down to this, the black community has gotten too complacent. They look and they see themselves on TV, "Hey, they got a black guy on TV and everything," and they swear everything's all right. But it isn't. We've got the same problems, of course, they don't lynch us any more. They don't lynch us anymore, instead we're killing each other by the dozens.

◆ 4 ◆

"Sir Johnny O." Compton

Jonathon O. Compton's broadcasting career began at radio station WOV, which was located in New York. Compton was only nineteen years old when he was hired, making him the youngest disc jockey at the station. Compton used the moniker "Sir Johnny O." as his on-air name when he worked for WWIN in Baltimore, Maryland, the radio station that hired him away form WOV.

At WWIN, Compton became very popular with the young listeners. He also became close friends with Larry Dean Faulkner, who was the program director. Faulkner was also a mentor to Compton, offering advice to him on how to make his way in the field of broadcasting.

Compton worked for WWIN for several years during the late 1960s and early to middle 1970s. A manager at WWIN told Compton that he could not operate an advertising business and work for the station too. As a result, Compton decided to leave the station and pursue his business ventures.

Today, Compton is the Area Coordinator for the Larry Dean (Faulkner) Memorial Fund. This non-profit organization is raising money to build the the Larry Dean Media Center in the Baltimore-Washington area.

JUNE 1, 1991

You worked with Larry Dean. How have you honored him?

We established a Larry Dean Memorial Fund upon Larry's death and we sort of put together some scholarships, especially for people who are in college with a major of mass communications. This is for anywhere in the country. Our first recipient was from Louisville, Kentucky, attending Morgan State. When Larry ended his career, he was teaching communications as well as being a news director at Morgan State's radio station. He had a lot of students that just loved him, so this is why we went that route to help youth that was trying to learn broadcasting. Larry's whole life was devoted to broadcasting. He had quite an impact on others, as well as myself, because he started me off when I was nineteen years of age. He was my mentor and then became my friend. He taught me the entire business.

What was your first announcing job in radio?

WWIN in Baltimore. Prior to that I was in New York at WOV, 1280. We transmitted between New York and North New Jersey. Larry at that particular time was just a regular disc jockey and then he became program director of the first 24-hour black radio station in Baltimore.

Which station was that?

WWIN. At that time the black jocks that were operating were on daytime stations.

Approximately what year was this?

Let's see, Larry became program director in 1962 or '63 at WWIN. Prior to that, the white stations would hire the black jocks like at night. You know, between the hours of 8 to midnight, something like that. So when Larry first came to Baltimore that's what he was doing. He was in Baltimore in the latter part of '59 or '60 at WITH, a 24-hour white station with the regular rock and roll. The Dick Clark-type of thing. The only black jock on the station at that particular time was Larry. Hot Rod Hulbert was there prior to him. He was doing the slot that Larry got from 8 to 12. Hot Rod left and went back to Philadelphia and they wanted to get a jock that would maintain that audience. After they put the search out around the country, Larry ended up with the position. He came from Detroit. He had worked in Cincinnati and other places.

Do you know how many years his career spanned?

Twenty-five years. Now prior to that he was one of the first black disc jockeys in the country. Also one of the first black program directors in the country and one of the first black managers of a station. We're so proud of that. He was the vice president of the first black network, which was Mutual at that time. So he has had all the firsts, you know, being the first black broadcaster of any note working for national stations. He was one of the originators of NATRA (National Association of Television and Radio Artists). Dell Shields was involved in that too.

What kind of air personality was Larry Dean? What was his persona on the air?

Oh man, voice-wise and as far as enunciation, he was just the guy that set the example for most of the younger guys of that period. He had the command of the English language and a great vocabulary and he had just a hell of a personality, man, he could do the okey-doke, as he called it— a little jive, slang for things. He just had the voice. There was just no way you could beat Larry Dean.

Do you know if payola had an impact upon his career?

Well, he kind of stayed away from that scene because it's one thing Larry always used to tell me. He said, "Johnny, stay away from this graft because it can tag you in this business." By him being a program director, naturally guys would approach him, but Larry was the kind of guy that would more or less want to be your friend. He had a lot of friends in the recording business. Berry Gordy was among them. In fact, he helped get Gordy started at one time. They were all out of Detroit and when Gordy first wanted to start Motown, Larry lent him $700. Larry was in with all the Motown crowd. He grew up with pushing the Supremes and all of those kinds of people. In fact, Mary Wilson was here at his tribute and in the book that she wrote, she mentioned Larry Dean and Eddie Castleberry. When they were teenagers Larry used to take those girls around in his car because he was one of the hottest disc jockeys in Detroit during that period. Naturally he'd go back when the Motown thing was trying to get off the ground, you know. So he and Berry Gordy and most of the guys from Motown, Smokey Robinson, you know all those stars. . . .

Were there others at Motown that he knew?

Marvin Gaye, I mean he goes back with all of them when they were just trying to get it together. Before Motown really developed into Motown, of course, they had to come to Larry to play the records because he was the hottest disc jockey. They used to appear at his record hops free of charge during that time. During that time we had what we called "record hops" and "cabarets" that the jocks would put on. We would sort of rent the halls. . . .

Did you promote your own radio programs too?

Yes. We were allowed to do it without any conflict of interest. In fact, the station welcomed our doing this type of thing because it was promotion for the station. Also, when we were out in the community doing something, we created more listeners and that sort of thing. So our popularity was shown through the different types of crowds we would get at these affairs. During that time the disc jockeys had more of an impact on the community; we were like family. Once they would turn you on in their homes, it might be in the bedroom, bathroom, anywhere, we were the only voices they would hear and we'd play all the hottest records and interview the stars, you know, the whole bit. So, especially in the black community, all the kids had was us to look up to. So whatever we said, that was it. During that time we would dress neat and nice, there wasn't no t-shirts and things like that, we were in suits and ties, monogrammed shirts. It was a beautiful period really. Now I see it as a more or less electronic-type disc jockey—ten in a row, station break, back to the weather report, back to the music, hardly any news—nothing back to the community. We used to have interviews, breaks in the show if something nice was happening. But now they have to have ten in a row, this thing and another thing. We used to back the records up, I mean play a record and have like an instant replay of the same record if somebody happened to enjoy the record, you know. They don't even do that any more. And that is how a lot of records would become the number one tune. All of the jockeys would select one record that we felt could go and use it as the pick of the week. Some jocks, like Billy Ware, they would play the same record for maybe twelve hours a day, lock themselves in the studio and play just the same record over and over and over again. They had gimmicks going on. Some of that might have been payola, it's hard to tell.

Did you guys have to sell time or were you staff announcers?

Well, Larry never liked to sell time. Now I, myself, at one time I wanted to sell, I wanted to come off the air at one time and sell time at WWIN. We had a white manager and part owner of the station, and I went into his office and asked him. During that period of time, we didn't have black salesmen, we had black stations as far as personalities but the sales managers and all the salesmen, general managers, all those were white folks. We were out front but they were the main administrative forces of the business and I'll tell you what this is all about. I used to be on the air playing the records and going through my little spiel and I noticed all these carts had these labels with these businesses, so I woke up one day and my mind had told me that hey, the real deal in this business is who you know . . . and nobody knew us, but he was the guy that had the swimming pool and the this and the that. So that's what started me leaning toward advertising, I'd do some freelance advertising. And I told Larry, he was program director, "Can I go in and talk to the general manager? I want to come off the air." Larry didn't want me to go off the air because he was the guy who started me off, so to speak, and he felt that we had a good team and the station was #1. He said, "Man you don't want to come off, you're doing a great job."

What was your time slot?

Well, when I first started I was working part-time on Sunday from 12 noon until 5 P.M. At that time you had a long shift. Well, what happened, we'd just changed the station over from all-white to the first 24-hour black station because, as you know, during that period the stations were daytimers, they were black rhythm and blues, they'd go off at sundown.

This is WWIN?

Yes. They were an ABC affiliate. We had a lot of prestige with the news coming down the line from ABC and that type of thing. We had a lot of large accounts and we had white and black listeners. So what happened, they were having white and black church programming on Sundays. They didn't have any type of rock and roll on Sundays.

I was doing production for the station. I was the voice of WWIN, all the station breaks, all the announcements, promos, contests, and all that type of thing, that was my voice. Larry decided to put me on the air as a personality. He talked to the management and we auditioned a little gimmick as to my approach to it and the manager said, "Fine, we'll put Johnny on." So what they wanted to do was to cancel everything that was on on Sunday, that was gospel, and start having all weekend with the format stuff. So they pulled the gospel off and that is how I got on. They made a role for me. The first month I was on, it was near the time for the ratings to come out. They got the rating book and the manager looked at the rating book and the rating was sky high. We were beating everything on the weekends. He couldn't believe it, he said, "Now we have to wait until another book comes out because we've never had a rating in the history of the station on a Sunday and we can't believe this." So it came out and it was there, we were beating white stations, black stations, it didn't matter. That's what gave me a little power. They felt in their mind that Larry had made the right decision. So it put a feather in Larry's cap and it helped me out as well.

How did you guys feel about playing the blues?

Oh, Larry used to play the blues. See, we used to mix it all up. You know Larry would play a little of everything, Little Milton, B.B. King, Screaming Jay Hawkins, Z.Z. Hill, mix it all up because we used to have a little saying, "A little blues never hurt nobody," and then we'd play some blues records, you know, in between times. Al Jefferson used to play some blues. After we got the rating there, then I went on the air from 12 midnight until 6 A.M.

I turned nighttime into daytime in Baltimore. Larry left his job in the morning and we made enough money to hire Fat Daddy, which was our competition at that time. That was Paul Johnson. He worked for Motown before he died. We hired him and what happened, the general manager told me, "Johnny, you're doing such a fine job. As a result of you being on from 12 to 6 we are able to keep the dial on 1400 for the morning man, which is very essential to us." In other words, they wouldn't turn the dial to different daytime stations because I was playing such good music and doing such a great job for the station. They felt that, hey, we don't have to worry about them switching back to the daytimer because when our morning man comes, you have already set it up for him.

Did you have a large audience already waiting for him?

That's right. So as a result of that, when Larry wanted to put me on from 7 at night until midnight, the general manager told him, "Hell no, you can't move Johnny. If you move him who will we put there to keep the dial on?" As a result, I got stuck into the show regardless of my power or anything. I did too good of a job and sold advertising at night which never could sell otherwise. That's the type of thing that happened.

How would you describe Larry's relationship with other jockeys?

Oh man; all you have to do is call any jockey in the country. They know Larry Dean all over the country, not just Baltimore. Larry had a business here in Baltimore with one of the originators of Atlantic Records, Lou Crevis. They started one of the largest record shops in the downtown area of Baltimore called the "Larry Dean Record Rack." Then when Larry Dean was put out of the partnership, he went out on his own. Eddie Castleberry and Larry started two or three record shops around town called the Larry D and Eddie C Record Shop and then the guy downtown just dropped Larry Dean's name and left it as the "Record Rack." It was one of the most popular record shops in Baltimore. The thing of it is, if you ask any of the seasoned people around the country, they would know Larry. Jockey Jack, the rapper, and Larry worked together. Jockey Jack could tell you, anybody in the country would know Larry Dean.

What kind of impact did he have on the Civil Rights Movement in Baltimore?

Larry used to have forums with the Civil Rights people, with Martin Luther King, Jesse Jackson, and people like that. He walked out of the station to create a union and all that kind of thing, and guys wouldn't even cross the picket line. Larry was a pioneer and an innovator in the business, in broadcasting for blacks. Larry would always say, "Learn the administrative portion, what they are doing in traffic." Larry knew all of it and he showed me a lot of things that happened in production on down through what happens in traffic. When I say "traffic" you know what I mean?

Yeah, you're talking about scheduling advertisements.

There you go. Then you go from there to find out how the script is written, who's writing the commercials, copyrighting, and check into what is happening with the FCC and the FCC laws. During that time we had to take meter readings of the transmitters . . . we had to log all that ourselves. We had to take a test for our license. It was a restricted license; it wasn't a first-class license but we had to take different elements at the FCC itself here in Baltimore and we were tested on the FCC law. We also had to show that we agreed to read the meters, what the diagrams are for, read schematics, all that kind of thing. So we had to keep the station together with bubble gum. We repaired our turntables, spliced our own tapes because we didn't have cassettes and all that. We would have an old Ampex reel-to-reel tape that was running off a machine; we had to hold it in our hand and all those sort of things. So it was an all-different ball game.

Do you know how and when he [Larry Dean] first started in radio?

When he was going to Fisk University, he was in the dramatic department. He really wanted to be an actor at one time. And then he also was a musician, used to play the saxophone in little bands and things. That, I think, led him to that. His uncle was the chaplain of Fisk and he knew some people, I think the Cox family in Atlanta, or one of the noted families; he knew them and I think they were starting to buy radio stations. That's how Larry got in.

At one time, Larry was part owner of the station in Detroit. He was in with Dr. Bell. I talked with Dr. Bell's wife after Larry died, and she attended the Family Affair when they gave out a Larry Dean award for different jocks who have died or whatever. That was 1985. He helped to build that station, WCHB in Inkster, Michigan. Joltin' Joe Howard was on the station with Larry.

How did you guys feel about formats versus personality radio?

I feel, personally, that the personality jock will always be successful. He is the guy that creates the power. But what they have done now, they want the station to shine. You don't get a chance to put on your personality. They want you to play ten in a row; they give you a play list, they have a consultant maybe in California to tell you what to play in Baltimore. Everybody reads from a script in a sense. You operate that way so you don't get a chance to really exercise any creativity.

Now we were personalities, so what happens in this case is that we create a power for ourselves and the public begins to identify with, say "Sir Johnny O.," Hot Rod, Larry Dean, Rockin' Robin, Fat Daddy, or whoever it is. If we had sponsors, we played the music, we did the commercials and they got some response; so then another station will want to steal us, like football players, when our contract runs out. Then management of the station would have to put some protection on themselves because if I left WWIN radio, I could take all the accounts with me. The audience is going to say, "I only listen to WWIN because of Johnny O." So WWIN is nothing without Larry Dean, Johnny O., Al Jefferson, or whoever, right? If Hot Rod goes over to another station, then people are going to say, "Where's Hot Rod?" You know they are going to turn over to his station. So this is why I feel that personality will always be the strongest thing. But in black radio they will not allow it anymore because you create too much power for yourself. And then, like you are saying, the payola can get involved. They used to make us sign these papers from the federal government that we would not receive this and that, yet the manager of the station, he could get all kinds of trade-outs legally, you know, under the counter. He'd get all the prizes, TVs, whatever he wanted to get, but the black jock, if we looked like we were getting anything, we'd be in trouble.

Did the station ever try to control you or Larry as far as you know, in terms of your own personality?

No, in fact at that particular time, they wanted the personality to build the ratings of the station. But what they did after you built the station, that's when they screwed you. In fact, they screwed Larry, to be honest with you. What Larry did after we made the money and became number one, he brought in all of our competition and made us all a family on one station. In other words, he grabbed Hot Rod, he grabbed all the jocks, anybody making any noise. He said, "You have no reason to listen to another station because they are all on our station and how are you going to beat all of us when we're the biggest thing in town?" With all of us on one station, other stations didn't have a chance. We even had the white stars coming to us because we were hitting the Motown sound and the young generation. During that time we had a little jazz segment. We could do shows in segments so he'd have a jazz segment and we'd put on some Nancy Wilson, "Guess Who I Saw Today?," and we'd mellow out with Aretha Franklin. You know we could mix it up. In other words, this is the kind of personality and creativity that we had.

So you guys had all these powerhouses?

Yeah, we had little promos and a way to introduce everything we were doing so it was acceptable. Then we had all kinds of station promos. Larry and I would create the promos for the station, the production. We would have all kinds of fanfare. We didn't just use the call letters, we made WWIN a hurricane, blowing all over town.

So the station had promised Larry a promotion?

What happened was this. The station had promised Larry that he would be the manager of the station if he made it become number one, because during that time, as you know, you didn't have any black managers. That was unheard of. Larry was a program director, and the owner of the station promised Larry, "If you make the WWIN #1, we will give you shares in the station;" profit sharing; in fact, he promised me profit sharing. It never came to light because what happened after we made the station #1, he physically ousted Larry in a sense. What he did, he double-crossed him and that is when Larry left. He promised Larry a bonus and then when Larry and him was supposed to renegotiate the contract he said, "Hey, Larry, really you're making too much money." When Larry went on vacation for a couple of weeks during the summer, he had fired him, so when Larry came back, you know, that was it. So then Larry went to WEBB and that's when he started the record shop with Lou Crevis. Then Larry went to WEBB and became the manager to give WWIN some competition. James Brown had bought that station.

Did you guys think about the insecurities of the job, was that somehting that bothered you or wasn't that something that really concerned you?

Yeah, it follows most of the jocks but during that time we had one protection. At least we could get a contract so you'd know you were good for three to five years. Some of it was on a handshake. If you had a guy like Larry Dean who was program director and he hired you, then you could do it on a handshake. With a different manager you'd better get a written contract.

What would you say was Larry's greatest contributions to black radio? It could be several things, but how would you symbolize his work?

Well, I would say that he had a helluva impact on practically everybody he met, especially the younger people who were aspiring to become what he was, a good broadcaster, a jock, or that kind of thing. In fact, his legacy is left with that now, in keeping things alive through the memorial fund.

With scholarships?

Right. And then, like I said in summing up his career, he ended up teaching youngsters in the college community that were interested in broadcasting. He wouldn't just show them the glamour part. He would show them this was a business. Larry was that kind of guy, he never let a thing go to his head. He would break it down and tell you the real deal about the business. He'd tell it like it is. And management didn't want that because he's supposed to be a part of management and his attitude was toward the underdog. So Larry would say, "Look man, you'd better see that those stations you go to have a union, you'd better join AFTRA, you'd better be sure that you've got this contract," or he would tell you "Hey, look into all aspects of the business." You know, learn the business and know that this is a business and not just fun and games. He would tell you what the record cats were about and when the record promoters would come to see you, he'd let them know what that was about. That goes back to the payola thing. Don't let these guys tag you, don't let them buy you no drinks or women. Don't let them buy you anything. Don't let them slip no money in your hand because it could be a trick. So that is why he used to tell me to stay away from the graft. One reason that I know this is true is because a friend of mine, Chuck Leonard, who used to be opposite me in Baltimore was considered for a job with ABC for the very reason I'm telling you now. Chuck hadn't been involved in no graft. The first thing they said was that they wanted to get some young guys that didn't have any graft because ABC would not touch anyone involved with payola. That's how Chuck Leonard got that job and started on ABC. So that goes back to your payola.

Was Larry a teacher and an activist?

Exactly. Larry was a teacher as well as a disc jockey or broadcaster. He knew everything from news to how to put the formats. He could write the scripts, little bits for the promos, he could edit, he could just do it all. Only thing he didn't want to do is sell. When I wanted to be a salesman for advertisements for the station, the white manager would not let me come off the air because he didn't want me to know what was really going on. The white guy knew where the money was and he didn't want me to know about that. He'd say, "Look, you're a successful disc jockey on the air, stay on. I'll pay you more money to stay on the air."

I left the station as a result of that. I opened up my own little advertising company while I was at the station, and guess what—the advertising agencies in Baltimore called him up and asked him why was he allowing his disc jockey to have an advertising business. We couldn't come to a compromise and this was at the peak of my career at the station. That's how I left the station. He told me he'd give me a sizeable raise and everything, but that I couldn't have this advertising business because he could not explain it to these advertising agencies. He said they were threatening to pull their accounts off the station because they felt that he put me in business. And I said, "You know you didn't put me in business. You're not paying the lease on my office. I work for you and do your job and then I go out and meet with the shops and different clients and bring some accounts in," for which he had to give me 15 percent legally. He said "No, I got to set a precedent right here and now that you can not do that and remain a disc jockey on the station." So he told me he'd give me a raise and all that. So I thought about it and just on principle I couldn't. I was disenchanted, I could never get on the air and be a happy-go-lucky disc jockey anymore. So I told him that I would have a letter typed up for him and I would give my two-week notice and that I was resigning.

Now, were you married with a family?

I was married with a family and I've suffered from it ever since. My marriage broke up, everything. I suffered as a result of it but I had to make that decision during that time because I just felt, you know, it was during the period right after the mid '70s, when we had that Martin Luther King thing in '68 and we started going into the feeling of black in principle and blacks going to take over the world, so to speak. Nobody could tell us what to do. Whites don't try to hold me down. I was hung up in all that, right?

So when the mid-'70s came, then I started getting the entrepreneur-type spirit and that's what made me want to go into the real deal business, so I started the advertising business and I got a few accounts. I got an entire shopping center to give me their account and that was the thing that killed me because a white guy had the account and they bounced him out of there and let me have it. And when they got to the station, this guy had a lot of power. He called all the other advertising agencies and they said, "Well, who is the guy that got that account?" They said, "Johnny O.," and they said, "Well that's the guy that works at WWIN." They called my boss up and he called me in on the carpet. Then I left the station.

What was Larry's view of that?

Larry had left by that time and had turned the reins over to Al Jefferson because he had brought Al in to work at WWIN anyway. Him and Al were friends and Al was also a distant cousin of his wife. So what happened, Larry groomed Al to become program director. That's how Al became program director. It was all because of Larry. Larry was the first, original program director and Al came later. He was a jock on the station so it was a choice between Hot Rod or Fat Daddy or me or whoever, and who ended up with the position was Al because Larry had groomed Al. He told the owner, "If you're going to have another program director, I recommend Al Jefferson." So that is how Al got the job. Al, at that time, felt that I was knocking myself out, shadow-boxing, and he said, "Well man, you don't want to rock the boat. You'll knock yourself out, Johnny, and nobody will bother you. I know you know what to do, so even as program director I'm not going to tell you how to play your records or anything. You know what to do, you've been here, the man's not going to fire you so . . . ," so it was a thing where I was younger, I had a hot head. . . .

But you had to do what the man told you to do?

I knew I had the ratings, I had the audience, so I thought, "Go to hell, I don't need you. I'll do what I want to do." You know, when you're young like that you've got a little power, you're ego tripping, so I just told the white guy. You know, during that time I wouldn't let whitey tell me nothing no way. He said, "Johnny I want you to stay, you're doing a fantastic job for us. I'll give you a sizeable raise," and they offered me $100! He hurt me, man.

How old were you at this time, 29?

A little younger than that because I started out when I was nineteen, going on twenty years old. We had the first teenage disc jockey because at that time it was unheard of for a young guy to be on the air. We had guys that were seasoned like Hot Rod, guys that had been in the business for years. It was unheard of; Larry was the one that broke that tradition.

What was your wife's reaction to your popularity from females and that kind of thing?

My wife was jealous because you've got to remember, being married young I kind of outgrew my wife because at that time my wife was just an average kid. She just wanted to be home with the kids. She couldn't get caught up into what my world was about. My world was out there, I remember seeing big shows, I'm on the stage with Aretha Franklin or I'm on the stage with Stevie Wonder, like somebody she listens to on the radio and I'm a part of this world.

You introduced them at shows?

Yeah. We'd have big-stage shows like "The Motown Review," that type of thing. We might have twelve different acts and all them people on the show has got a hit record. And you're out there introducing them to the audience, just like you see on television. So I was caught up in all that and the little old girls were naturally going crazy because you are the big-time disc jockey. I wore iridescent and mohair suits and silk shirts and ties. You know, that's unheard of. So to the girls it's like every day is Christmas.

Is black radio better or worse today?

In my opinion it is worse.

Why is that?

Well, the guys don't really have the power that they think they got and the stations are playing a game with them. There is no question about it in my opinion, they have electronic disc jockeys. One jockey is just as good as another. Another thing that the black jocks are making a mistake on, they're all trying to sound alike. We all had our own voices and our own little style. And the formats are similar on most of the stations. So they have no reason to listen to this station or that station. Now some of the white jocks are still doing personality, but the black jocks are strictly copying each other. Larry liked you to be original, as unique as possible. So I would say it is worse. And then the management is playing a game. Even some of the black managers are playing games. They're not doing it like they used to do where we were all caught in trying to really build up black people as such. Some of these people are building the stations up and they're selling the station. Some of the blacks are doing it. They'll build a station up to a certain rating and then sell it. And when you sell the station, you know what happens. Very few of the staff stays. During the riots we had certain little messages that went there and we went out on certain shows. Now I had a battle of bands during the riot times. I promoted a battle of bands in the Civic Center to get all the guys, instead of beating each other up and rioting, to beat their drums and perform and bring all their little friends to cheer for them. As a result of that we were able to get them off the streets and getting along.

◆ 5 ◆

Moses Lindberg "Lucky" Cordell

"Lucky" Cordell has been described as an urban-sophisticate disc jockey. Cordell, a graduate of the Radio Institute of Chicago, had a northern-sounding voice but used some black expressions in his announcing. Lucky won Al Benson's disc jockey talent contest in 1950. He then began working for the "Ole Swing Master" as a satellite jockey at WGES.

Later, Cordell moved on to WHFC and WCFL, both Chicago-area radio stations. By 1954, Lucky began announcing for WGRY in Gary, Indiana, where he created several innovative programs. For instance, his "House of Hits" show consisted of popular songs, poetry readings, interviews, contests and audience participation. His program entitled "Lucky's Airwaves Exchange" gave listeners an opportunity to buy and sell products. This program innovation was very successful. His show started out as an hour program but was later expanded to four hours because of Cordell's popularity.

By 1961, Cordell had returned to Chicago, again working for WGES, which had changed its call letters to WYNR. Shortly after that Lucky went to work for WVON as a disc jockey. Two years later, management promoted him to program and music director. In addition, Lucky was promoted to assistant general manager and then general manager in 1970.

He has received numerous awards for his outstanding public and professional service. The awards Cordell has received include Certificate of Recognition from the First African Methodist Episcopal Church (Gary, Indiana); City of Chicago "Reach Out Program" for Exceptional Service to the Summer Youth Program; Fred Hampton, Mark Clark Memorial Black Community Service Award for Outstanding Contributions to Improve Conditions in the Black Community; Fred Hampton Image Award, Black Panther Party, for showing the black man in such a positive image; and the National Association of Televison and Radio Announcers' (NATRA) Meritorious Executive's Award, 1970–1973.

Cordell became a cultural hero because of the music he played and the community activities he participated in. He used radio to teach, help and sell.

SEPTEMBER 11, 1991

Where did you start out working?

I started at WGES, Chicago.

Were you working as a satelite Disc Jockey for Al Benson or Jack L. Cooper?

For Al Benson. When I started it was not my own production, it was my show. I ran it the way I chose to, but it was under the auspices of Al Benson. In other words, I didn't work for the radio station, I worked for Al Benson. This was a situation where all of the time that was allocated for black programming was under Al Benson. It was up to him to say who would work and who would not. So it was a Lucky Cordell show and an Al Benson production.

Did that mean that he bought time wholesale and sold it to you retail?

No, it wasn't brokerage. He had the time, I don't know exactly what his arrangement was with the radio station. I don't know whether he paid them X amount for time sold. I doubt very much that he was buying all of the time. He probably had proven himself by being one of the most powerful forces in radio at that time. And they probably made a deal with him.

When you started working at WGES, what was your show like?

It was a basic rhythm and blues show, that is to say, I played the black sounds.

Did you play Ruth Brown and people like that?

Right. Ruth Brown, Brook Benton and, of course, at that time, Nat King Cole. And I would play groups like the Moon Glows, it was, like, pretty rounded. Not a lot of jazz.

Did you ever have to sell time yourself on some kind of brokerage arrangement?

Yeah, I did. It was like Benson had told me when he hired me, at some point he would want me to sell time, but he would tell me when I was ready to sell. Of course, it was like I was being used to some degree. I worked part-time for him at his newspaper and I'd do radio a couple of hours at night; then I'd work 4–5 hours at his newspaper during the day and he's telling me he'd tell me when I was ready to sell. I was never going to be ready because I was never going to have time. He was using me to show the station owners, "Look, see I've got this young fellow, this young hot shot here, and he's not selling." Because he was in a slump, he was not selling during this period, the early '50s. By that I mean he wasn't getting the accounts in the way he had in the past. And they were putting pressure on him because he had all this time locked up. So he hired me and another young fellow by the name of Tom Duncan to show the station, "Look, OK, I'm not selling, I'm going to show you it's not me."

What he was saying is that he has two hot shots and they are not doing any better than he would be doing, right?

Right. So I busted the balloon and got the shock of my life because I was a go-getter and ready to run, so I'd ask him every couple of weeks, "Mr. Benson, you think I'm ready to sell now?" "No boy, I'll let you know when you're ready." So one day on my lunch period I went out and sold my first account, a cleaner's. I came back and I was so proud and said, "Mr.Benson, I think you're going to be proud of me." He said, "Why, what's that kid?" I said, "I just sold my first account." He said, "You did what?" Man he went off on me and then you could see the light bulb go on in his head. He said, "Well, you know of course you don't work for the radio station, you work for Al Benson." "I know that, Mr. Benson." He then said to me: "So you can't turn any contracts in to the station." I said, "Well, if you notice, I didn't sign it." And what did I want to say that for. He said, "Yes, let's see if you wrote it, yeah, you wrote, yeah, that's right. Well, OK then, maybe I misjudged you. I think you are ready to sell. But, of course, you bring your contracts to me, do not sign them because it is an Al Benson production." So I started selling, bringing him my accounts. He would sign his name, made him look good upstairs, and that went along fine.

Were you getting a little piece of that action?

Yeah, I'd get a little piece of action, not much, you know; not nearly what it should have been for soliciting the account and for doing the commercials.

Did you do the commercials live?

Yeah. And what interrupted it was, there were some accounts that I got that Benson could not get. People that didn't want him to do their commercials.

Why was this?

They didn't like his presentation. There were those who looked upon Benson as a disgrace to radio. These were some of the middle-class entrepreneurs who were trying to get away from that sound.

Where did you go to school?

I went to radio broadcasting school. I did the four-year course in 3–1/2 years and taught for six months. Benson would do things like one night he came in and had some friends with him and before I went on the air he said, "Lucky, you can take the rest of the night off. I feel like working tonight," so he'd just do the show. And he did the show and he did this commercial and the next day these people called and said, "Look, I'm not paying for that commercial that Al Benson did last night." Now they are talking to the people upstairs. I say "upstairs" because that is where the offices were. "I didn't buy Al Benson to do it, I bought Lucky Cordell to do it; he agreed that he would be the one to do it, and I'm not paying for it." So Dr. Dyer, a smart old guy who had been around a long time, said, "OK, we won't charge you for it, and yes, Mr. Cordell will do your commercials in the future." He called me upstairs. Now Benson had told me specifically, you don't go upstairs. You don't work for them, you work for me. Dyer owned the station, so when I came in and Dyer sent for me, I thought, Oh, hell, what is this? Then it hit me, Benson said don't go upstairs, so I'm betwixt and between. The man that owned the station said he wanted to see me, it's important, but I decided not to go up. Before I could get out of the building, out to the parking lot, Dyer came down the steps and now I'm certainly not going to run away from the man. . . . So he said "Look Lucky, I'm glad I caught you. There is something unclear here about a couple of accounts and I just want to get it squared away for the production room or something." I said, "Yes sir, what is that?" He said, "Well you did sell the such-and-such cleaner account, didn't you?" I said, "Yes sir." He said, "Yeah, well, how many other accounts did you sell?" I said, "Oh, I don't know, five or six." He said, "So that we can give proper credit, would you just make a list of those for me?" He had this paper in his hand and said, "Did you do so and so?" and I said, "Yeah." He said, "I thought you did. What about the so and so, and so and so?" And I said, "Yeah, that was mine." He said, "OK."

Well, the shit hit the fan when Benson came in; Dyer and Benson had it out and so now Benson is really ticked. I came in that night and found a note to me saying, "As of tonight you are no longer needed. Thank you for doing a good job. Sometime in the future we might be able to work together again." He doesn't give me a letter that says, "I'm firing you because you told them you sold these accounts." So the next morning I went to see Dr. Dyer, as there is no reason for me not to go upstairs now. So I go there and I pick up my money and I ask to speak to Dr. Dyer. "Sure, Lucky, come in." I said, "Well, Doc, I just want to thank you for the opportunity to work at my first radio job." He said, "What are you talking about, are you quitting us?" I said, "Oh, no sir, Mr. Benson doesn't need me any more, and he let me go." Then I made my pitch for some air time. I said, "I would just like to know, is there any time on the station, morning or night, anytime that is available, that is, not under Mr. Benson?" He said, "Well no, Lucky, there isn't but I'll tell you what, you come on to work tonight, I'm going to speak to Mr. Benson. I have an idea that he might reconsider." They say after I left he called Mr. Benson in, you could hear them through the walls. You'd hear Dr. Dyer cursing like a sailor, calling him all kinds of names, telling him, "You're not selling, you got a couple of guys in here going to bail you out and you're gonna fire them. You'd better not fire them," or something like that. So I came in that night kind of sheepish and Benson said, "Well, I'm glad you came on in. You know, I've been thinking. You will continue on with your position until further notice."

How old were you at this time?

Well, I was born July 28, 1928, and this was in the '50s, making me in my early twenties. When I left WGES, I went to Gary, Indiana, to a station called WGRY. I had made a name for myself and was doing very well in Chicago. The only thing was I knew that I could never really grow unless I got out from under Benson's control. Because whatever I did he got the credit for it.

Were you president of NATRA for a while?

Yes, I was executive director of NATRA. That's the National Association of Radio and Television Announcers.

What was your work with that group, what were the goals you guys were trying to achieve?

Trying to get better representation for the black announcers, basically trying to get them better working conditions. You know, we had no representation. Just whatever they chose to do with a black announcer, you know; if they want to fire him, he's fired. Back then many disc jockeys didn't use their own names. The station owned the stage name. So like "Dickie Do," they got rid of him. Tomorrow another "Dickie Do" would be in his spot. Same kind of thing they do in soap operas today. So what we did was form this organization. I was not a part of the initial forming of the organization, I came on board later.

So you knew Jack Gibson and people like that?

Very well. What the organization did more than anything else was to create an illusion because we would have the meetings of black broadcasters from across this country and we would release little tidbits to the press and they'd kind of scare both the radio stations and the record industry. A guy wouldn't want to be blasted by any black announcer as being prejudiced. Initially, they did not stop doing it but then we'd hold a spotlight on this station. We would get the word out any way we could when an injustice was done to brother so and so at such and such a place. Little Rock, Arkansas, was probably getting more negative publicity than it ever had and did not want. Remember now, black announcers, black audience, they depended on the blacks for their business. So we'd get this story out down there and some of their accounts that didn't want to be identified with prejudice started dropping off and all of a sudden this guy gets reconsideration. Maybe gets rehired, a slap on the wrist, so we never intended to fire him, he just got some time off. So it was a good thing. I guess it was much like what happens in the sweat shops, places where people have no representation, they work them to death and pay them nothing.

Wasn't it quite a risk to stand up and take a step at that time, given the fact that your job condition was so insecure?

Oh yes, no doubt about it, because we blacks didn't own anything.

There was no black ownership?

No, none. Most of the guys in the earlier days, they didn't make their money on salaries. They made it because they would spin records in lounges and for dances. All of sudden it was like one of the respected positions. There were days in the early times when the jobs that got you the most respect in the black community were being a preacher, a lawyer, or a disc jockey, you know you were way up there.

Do you feel you guys were revered in the community then?

Yes, we really were. At WVON there was a time when I honestly believed in my heart that we were given credit by some organizations and some people for stopping the rioting on the West Side. You know, when they were burning the West Side up when Dr. King was killed. We went on the radio 24 hours a day and pitched for the people to be calm, and stressed what a shame to do this, burning up in Dr. King's name, and destroying our community. Although they burned up a lot of businesses that were not theirs, all these buildings had apartments over them, next door to them. So they also destroyed many homes and left people displaced, black people.

How did you establish rapport with your audience? How did people come to know who you were as a radio personality?

I would say if I did one thing, more than anything else, I always tried to teach, by public service. I was known for my public service work even after I went into programming and management. When they sold the radio station, our numbers were top numbers. At the time, I had twice, maybe three times, as much public service on the station as any other local station.

You would do things like what?

Well, I initiated a program called "Operation Crime Stop," which was like one-minute vignettes about how not to become a victim of crime. It dealt with rape, robbery, burglary. Sometimes we would have recorded voices and have people call me who were victims of crime and I would have the actual person put on the air and tell how they were victimized. "I was carrying some packages to the car and I set one on the hood and I was looking for my keys," well there it is. At night you should have had your keys in your hand. And you didn't make them feel like a dummy. "We advise you ladies, especially, out after dark, if you are carrying packages you should also be carrying your keys in your hand so that when you get to your car you don't have to search for your keys. The same applies to when you are going in your door at night." No telling how many people that may have stopped something from happening to. Then we had medical tips, just plain stuff that they didn't have to go to a doctor for, like ways of getting rid of headaches and keeping your system regular. Those kinds of things. Legal tips. Things that I could get out of a legal book that they wouldn't have to go to an attorney to find out.

Things about contracts or rental agreements, those kinds of things?

Exactly. Things they would run into in everyday life. Many of our unsophisticated listeners didn't know that they had rights just like their landlord. So we were telling them. After Leonard Chess died, the new owners of WVON called me in and wanted me to fire two disc jockeys. They didn't care what two. They just wanted me to fire two disc jockeys because they owned other radio stations and none of the other radio stations they owned had people working only three hours. Most of the stations they owned were in the south. They worked four or four and one half hours and our guys worked three hours, made all these bucks. But what he didn't understand and I explained to him, was for that the type of programming we did a man could not stay up for more than three hours. You put him on for three hours, he'll come on like a house on fire and go off still smoking, hand the ball to the next guy who'd run with it. But if he is working four hours, he is either going to come on slow and build to crescendo or he's going to come on smoking and before he is off, his show is going to fall. They didn't believe me. They did, in fact, let some people go after I was kicked upstairs. You know, I mean, it was like they couldn't fire me, I was too powerful in my community.

This was right there in Chicago?

Yes. So what they did was about two months after we had this conversation, they promoted me from general manager of the radio station to assistant to the president of the whole corporation. Big title, no power. They pulled me out and put someone else in. The whole idea was, we need to put somebody in there that will do what we want them to do. What I said to them was, "Gentlemen, you own the station. You can do what you choose to do. I cannot go back to that radio station and fire somebody without just cause. I live with and am answerable to the black community. I'll fire a man for insubordination, inability to make time, drugs, all kinds of reasons, but there's got to be a good reason. I can't go there and when the community comes to me and says, 'Why did you fire these men,' I say 'Well so that the station could make more money.' And we're already making more money than any station our size in the country." He said, "Am I to understand that you refuse to do it?" I said, "No, no, I *can't* do it. You can, you can come out there and fire anybody you choose to. You can fire me, but I cannot do it." Now they were smart enough to know that a white man could not come out in that community and fire this black leader, you understand? Or anybody else without my approval. We ran it, they owned it, they made the big bucks from it, but we ran it. So the only way they could get out from under me was to promote me. They were willing to pay me that top salary. They even gave me a raise, with the promotion. That's the only job that I had in my whole adult life. When I got out of the service I went into radio school and when I stopped there I went into broadcasting. So I knew nothing else, it was my love. So you see, they knew I wasn't going to stay here in this office and do these things, that I'd quit. They were going to have me working with the Atlanta Braves Roadyboat Company and Faultless golf balls and other companies they owned. It was a conglomerate, they owned a number of things. They owned seven radio stations but I was not going to be affiliated with any one of the stations. So, I resigned. I got an appointment with George Gillett, president of the company. I said, "George, this is your office so we should be able to talk freely because it's always your word against mine as to what was said here. But I want to be able to speak freely and I want you to speak freely." So he's saying, "What's the matter, you're not satisfied with your secretary?" I said, "No, no, my secretary is fine." I had two secretaries, big desk, big office. I said, "I'm just unhappy with the job." "What's wrong? You're assistant to the president." "I know, but you own seven radio stations and I don't have any affiliation with any one of them."

Who was that?

George Gillett.

They own several stations over here in Michigan right now.

Well, I'm sure that they didn't just get out. So he said, "What have you got in mind?" I said, "Look, I understand that you would really like to put someone in there who would do the things that you would want them to do." I understand that. I understand control and power. "But, you know and I know that the board of directors is not going to be happy with you paying me this kind of money for the next three years to be a glorified delivery boy." I said, "I can't be of any great assistance to you in these other ventures because I know nothing about them. I've got to learn everything, you know. Here's something I'm recognized as an expert in and you own seven of them and I'm not going to be affiliated with any of them." If they had said to me, "Lucky, you're going to be trouble-shooter, overseer of the radio stations; you'll travel around the country checking on the stations," I would have thought it was a legitimate thing. But when you take somebody who is recognized, who has received all kinds of awards for their work, and you own all these businesses that you could use him in, and you take him totally away from them and put him in something else? There's no logic to it. "So, what are you suggesting?" I said, "I am suggesting that you pay me for half of my remaining contract, lump sum, and I'll go on and try to get into something that I'll be happy with and you'll have control of your radio station."

Is that the kind of person you have always been, one to stand up like that?

Oh yeah. It's the only way I know, and I've made it OK. Whatever I do, whatever I did, wherever I worked, I did it the best that I could and I never did it to please anybody but me. I never asked for a raise or a promotion in my life. If I worked for you and you didn't see my worth, I'd move on. So I left and I went to work for Leonard Chess. He first promoted me to assistant program director, I didn't ask for it. I didn't ask him to promote me to the full program director or assistant general manager, or to my final position of general manager. I simply did my best no matter what position I held.

Is this when you came from Gary?

Right. So I'm saying that I just put my best foot forward. Never in my life did I look up and see the boss coming and then get busy. I also know there are times that you don't see him and he's seeing you so if you're doing your best, that's never a concern. When I was a disc jockey I prepared my show in advance. I never went on the air without a prepared show. I knew exactly how many records I was going to play, what records, and in what order. I'd balance the show. There were days when the forecast was for a beautiful, bright, sunshiny day and I knew people's spirits would be up. I might give them three fast and one medium, go back to two fast and a medium, three fast and a medium, just cheer them up. Another day it is a real gloomy day and I might go just the opposite, one up and one down, two down and one up, and you slow the paces but I'd give some thought to it. It wasn't just something that just happened.

How did you feel about formats?

Well, I had no quarrel with formats as long as they left room for a person to be a personality. I think one of the things that happened in the major markets is they went to overkill. You know, some of the jocks were going too far, talking too much, and wasting too much time, that kind of thing. So you tighten them up, but you don't make robots of them.

Did payola adversely affect black disc jockeys?

Oh, no doubt about it. Because payola was used to bust a lot of powerful black jocks across the country. How many white ones got busted? That isn't to say that payola wasn't happening, but I know that if it was happening with the blacks it was happening ten times as good for the whites. The disc jockey in some smaller market might have gotten a $25 gratuity or something, while his white counterpart in that same market would have gotten $100.

Why would the government want to bust a black disc jockey? Do you think it was because he was too powerful?

Well, I don't think it was really the government. I think it was the radio station owners who brought this pressure on and forced the government to do it. It's like the government didn't know anything about radio. So the owners got together and said, "Hey, fellows, I got a guy at my station who's so powerful I am afraid to fire him." "Yeah, I've got the same thing in one of my stations." Talking about this payola thing, "Let's put a spotlight on some of these guys. They won't know who did it." So you had guys that were so strong and so powerful in their communities that they'd dare not fire them. They would lose half their business. They'd like to get something on him and this was an ideal way because it was out of their hands. The government came to them saying, "We're investigating," and the guy who didn't do it was scared to death and the guy who put the spotlight there, not only did it give them the option, but the obligation, to get rid of the person. So they may say to the community, "Hey, we didn't want to fire so and so but look at this here," they got this big letter from the government saying you could lose your license.

How has black radio changed in the last 40 years? Is it better or worse today?

Oh, I have to say it's better. It's technically better. Better reception, farther reach, that kind of thing.

Do they serve the community in the same way?

No, that has changed, I think, for the worse. All I know is that every-one got out of the public service business, so to speak. It seems like what they do today is try to out-music each other. You know, they try to play more music than the other station. There's a certain same-ness. There are so few, like Herb Kent, who are so recognizable that even though they don't have the same kind of freedom you once had, he's already a personality. He's already recognizable, you know. But the public service is gone. I have some old tapes of what we used to do. On radio we gave the public what they wanted and played the music that they wanted to hear, but in between, we gave them something that they needed to hear. It was done tastefully and it was well ac-cepted. For example, you give them a record they really enjoy and give a couple of commercials that are tastefully done and go back to an-other record, come out of that record with, "Did you know that it was your right . . ." and so forth. I mean you give them something before they even know what happened. Or your could go into Operation Crime Stop with a big drum roll, Operation Crime Stop! Make their heads snap. You put it right on them. That's it and they are gone again to a record they want to hear. So it was done in such a way that we could feel good about what we were doing. I really felt good about the contribution I made.

What kind of ratings were you getting at the time?

We were #1 in the city for a period. We beat all the other radio stations in the city. The jocks that are on the air today do not endear themselves as much to the community as our guys did. We used to have fundraisers for the NAACP, Urban League, Operation PUSH, and other worthwhile organizations where our guys would stay in a trailer and we set up goals for raising funds. These guys would not sleep or shave for days until they reached the goal. People would drive up and bring us money out of their pockets. I mean, cars would be lined up, bringing us money. So our guys could reach their goals and go home and get some sleep. We did things. We were out there. Our guys could not go anywhere in our listening area and not be recognized. We had some dynamite people. Each had their own personality. We gave them enough leeway. They still had some confinements. A guy couldn't let all his commercials stack up. You know, play a bunch of records in a row, then have to play six commercials. There were certain restrictions that a guy had to deal with, but for the most part, as long as he kept within what we were trying to do, this is our sound. Now, you put your best foot forward and do it your way but stay within this boundary.

♦ 6 ♦

Larry Dean Faulkner

Larry Dean Faulkner was a trailblazer in every sense of the word. He helped or participated in the development of several black-formatted radio stations, including WERD in Atlanta and WCHB in Detroit.

Although he was born in Society Hill, South Carolina, Faulkner spent most of his early years in Wilmington, Delaware,and Flushing, Long Island, New York. During WWII, Faulkner served in the United States Marines. Later, he graduated from Fisk University, majoring in English.

He used the name Larry Dean on-air, dropping the Faulkner to facilitate the brevity of broadcast radio. His tall, slim frame caused others to call him "long, lean, lanky Larry Dean" when he first became an announcer at WERD in Atlanta.

After WERD, Dean held positions as radio program director at WCIN in Cincinnati, KSAN in San Francisco, and WCHB and WJLB in Detroit. In Baltimore, he became program director at WEBB and WINN. Additionally, he worked as a news reporter and anchor at WLIF and WITH, which are in Baltimore.

Dean's mellifluous voice and professional demeanor made him a likely candidate for jobs anywhere in the country. Nevertheless, he dedicated his later years to developing young journalists in Baltimore. In 1977, Morgan State University (Baltimore) selected Dean for its news director at the noncommercial WEAA-FM. He stayed at that station until his death in 1985.

JUNE 1, 1991
(AS TOLD BY GWEN FAULKNER, HIS WIFE)

Would you tell me about your life with Larry Dean?

We were supposed to leave here and go back to Detroit. Larry had had another job offer. I think I was a sophomore in college at the time and my family, oh they were in an uproar. They said, "You're not going to take our daughter out of college, she hasn't finished." So he said, "I'm going to enroll her in Wayne State. I'll take her to Detroit, over to Wayne and she'll finish. She'll get her college education, you know I'll take good care of her." In the meantime, we didn't leave, we stayed here in Baltimore. Mutual, over in Washington, contacted Larry and said they were interested in getting the first black network started nationwide with he and Eddie. That is when Larry said, "No, we're not going to leave and go to Detroit." He said we may move to Washington or whatever. I came from educators, a background of educators.

Was that about 1971?

Yeah, when Larry went to the black network. My family looked at Larry as being in show business and they said, "That's not the type of career we want our daughter to marry. We want her to marry a school teacher or doctor or something. Something stable or something where she'll be able to eat and everything." So Larry assured them, "Well, she's not doing too bad now." So eventually they really liked Larry. My family started to see that he was business-like and that he was professional and that he had come from a highly professional family. They gave him a hard time for a couple of years and then after that they approved of him. He started giving them tickets to all the shows and they were rubbing shoulders with Gloria Lynn, Arthur Prysock and the likes of them and we'd have barbecues out in the backyard. My parents would come over and say, "Wow, we never thought we'd meet these people." It was a very interesting life with Larry and I wouldn't have traded it for anything in the world. You know it had a lot of instability with it to a certain extent, but I guess by me being so young at the time, I could cope with it all. The blacks were beginning to feel powerful at the time and doors were beginning to open and Larry had been hollering all of this even before all that was fashionable. He wasn't like the usual husband at that time . . . trying to hold you back. Larry was all about me learning every part of the business and being everything that I could be. Because he had traveled so much, his first family really suffered because he moved from city to city. His first wife couldn't cope with this business like I was able to. Larry and I never moved. I'm still living in the same house that we were married in. Right there in Baltimore. Even since Larry passed away, when people come in our neighborhood they still point over and say, "Larry Dean lives there."

Larry had such a strong spirit.

Oh, God, don't even mention it. And Johnny (Johnathan Compton) was very modest in a lot of things he said to you, but in his own right, he was a real innovator because at that time it was unheard of for blacks to start an advertising agency and to even have the gall to go out and talk to white businessmen about coming with his company. That wasn't even appropriate at that time, especially here in Baltimore, because it was a Jim Crow town. Johnny would get dressed and we would laugh and Larry would really talk Johnny up. "Man, you can do it, you can do it. Go ahead, go ahead." He would go out and pick up accounts and then have the manager of the station try to hold him back because they had that subtle discrimination. The sad thing about it, the managers would make the disc jockeys believe that's all you need to be—a disc jockey. You have the fame. He wanted to dig into that pocket and get that big security that they had, making that $50,000 a year or whatever, which at that time was like a million dollars. That's when they began to suddenly put their foot down on you and say, "Well what more did you want? A black man with fame wearing silk shirts." And this is what kept Larry and Johnny in dutch all the time, because they would say to them, "We don't care about these silk shirts. We want to be able to send our children to college. We want security. We want a good retirement." And this is when they really would get on Larry and this is what got him into dutch around the country every time he would say, "I want part of the station" or "I want" you know . . .

He came from that type of background. His father had owned a little store in Society Hill, South Carolina. And as quiet as this has been kept, I think it is going to come out in the next couple of years because a lot of background work has been done through Larry's family, saying they really are relatives of William Faulkner, the writer who was from Society Hill. Some of his family lived on the Faulkner land. Consequently, I think you've got a lot of advance information and all because of them being interracially married. A lot of Larry's family left the United States and went to Europe. They went to England, they went to Hawaii. To escape, they married big white doctors and businessmen and things like that, and if you see them there, they're not going to be black. Now once the book comes out or whatever, the information that they are related to William Faulkner, they might come back to black culture. But Larry took the opposite approach. As light as he was, when you looked at him you would never even think he was black. He's even whiter than some whites. He looked like the Spaniards or Italian men, with his nose, thin lips, an Errol Flynn-looking kind of guy. That's the type of guy Larry was. He could have easily gone white. However, he chose to stay with the African blood. He was always, above everything else, a human being for all people, really. That always came out. He always preached this to me even during the Civil Rights Movement and everything, he would say to me, "Above all else, you are a human being, and remember that." He'd say, "You are no better or no worse than anybody else. You have to pay your dues just like they paid their dues and you will pay. You will not escape it because you are married to Larry Dean or because you are educated, or because of this. Just like they bleed, you'll bleed." All those things have stayed with me. And it's true. He always told us that we were all human beings and to respect one another's cultures and worries and religions. He said, "You may not want to be a part of it, but there is something about that individual that you can respect, and I want you to find that in the culture."

And that is the type of person that he was. Just a hell of a human being. And they don't come like that any more. Larry could sit down, as a matter of fact, he got a proclamation or whatever it was, when he was at Mutual from President Nixon. I know what happened. Eddie and the whole group that first came on the black network, Nixon gave all of them awards for being the first blacks, and Larry came home that evening and was out here cutting his hedges. You know he came home and took his tux off and people were calling and asking, "How was it meeting with Nixon and his wife?" and this and that. Larry said, "It was great man, let me get back with you. I'm out here trying to cut these hedges before it gets too dark." It may be a day later before he'd call them back. He said, "Yeah, man, I was glad to get out of that tux." He was in here listening to B.B. King because he said, "Hey, there's another thing going on in another day." And he would always tell me that. He'd say, "Hey, you out here in the kitchen cooking, they got to pay taxes and die just like we do." So he said, "Never think that these people are above you because they got to get out here and hustle and make a living just like you do."

He could really see things, couldn't he?

Oh, he had great vision. Great vision, and when you met certain members in his family, like he was very close to his uncle who was the chaplain at Fisk, he was a visionary too. When you talked with him, he had such a slow way of speaking. When I sat down with him I thought I was with the Pope and I would just sit there in awe, you know, at nineteen and twenty years old, and he would read to us. He would read to us in Wildwood, because most of his family owned homes there. They had their summer homes in Wildwood, New Jersey. And at the time you didn't have any blacks hardly even going to Wildwood. But his uncle had bought an old deserted army barracks for $20 or something and had it moved to his property and made a house out of it. When we went to Wildwood we'd stay with all Larry's relatives that owned homes and cottages in Wildwood. As a matter of fact, people would look at me with Larry because I was dark. I'm like middle complexion and at that time that was black. And they would look at us and say, "What is that white man doing with the spot?" Larry's kids were light. We'd all be walking down the boardwalk, riding our bikes, but they would not dare to say anything to me because Larry's uncles and aunts were all big in Wildwood. Finally, there was a young lady that came into the family that was darker than me who had married Larry's cousin, a doctor. She was very beautiful and we used to get together and walk down the boardwalk in Wildwood just to be smart. They'd see the kinky hair and look at us and say, "What are you ladies doing here?" And honey, Larry would show us off. He would take us out to dinner, he'd have her on one arm and me on the other. He'd say, "I've got the finest black berries in town." And he'd take us around town and we'd go to all the big restaurants. It's been interesting along with all the other things that have taken place.

◆ 7 ◆

Jack Gibson

Jack Gibson is the dean of African-American disc jockeys. He has done so much to preserve the rich legacy of black DJs, probably more than anyone else.

I first met Jack Gibson in a telephone interview. I had called him to request an interview and Jack graciously agreed. After our conversation, I asked if he could help me reach other pioneers of black radio. Once again, he obliged, giving me telephone numbers of most of the people I interviewed for this book.

A graduate of Lincoln University in Missouri, Jack first worked as an actor in an all-black radio soap opera. This show was about the difficulties of a black family called the Redmonds. Later, he became a very popular disc jockey at WERD in Atlanta and WCIN in Cincinnati. In addition, Jack established the Family Affair, an annual event that brought record promoters, radio personalities and recording artists together. As with everything else he touched, the Family Affair became very successful. Although I never asked, I believe "Jockey" Jack's name comes from an old blues tune that goes like this:

My father was no jockey
but he sure taught me how to ride
I say, my father was no jockey
but he sure taught me how to ride
He said, first in the middle,
then you sway from side to side. (Leroi Jones, *Blues People* 1965, p. 169)

MARCH 6, 1991

Could you tell me a little bit about how and when you started in radio?

I was an actor—soap operas in Chicago, Illinois. This was before TV came into being. The advent of TV and radio drama was very big and they used to do 15-minute soap operas, the same as today on TV when they do half-hour and hour shows. In my day, in 1945, we were doing 15-minute shows and I was doing a lot of them in Chicago. In fact, I was on the first all-Negro soap opera with an all-Negro cast ("Negro" was the word then, it's "black" now), "Here Comes Tomorrow." It was about a black family. We were like thirty years before our time.

Was that the Redmond family?

Yes, and I played the part of Rex Redmond, one of the sons of the family who was a ne'er-do-well, the black sheep of the family. It was a wonderful show; we lasted a year before we were cancelled, too controversial, I was told.

What kind of ratings did you get?

I don't remember. I know the show was very strong. Several times they had to take us out of the studio and take us down the freight elevator and out of the building because people were saying nasty things about us because of how the script was showing equality and so forth. Back in 1945, that was unheard of. That's how my career started. Then I moved into the music end of it. We were in the green room one time between shows and the managers of the station came and asked if anybody knew anything about music. I had fronted the band in college so I said, "Yeah, I know a little something about Jimmy Lunsford and Andy Kirk and Duke Ellington." So they said, "How would you like to play records and make announcements?," because they didn't even call them disc jockeys then. So I said, "Yeah, for $50 more a week." That started the music part of it, with a half-hour show.

What radio station was that?

That was WCFL, the voice of labor in Chicago, 50,000 watts.

Did you ever work in Atlanta?

Oh yeah, I opened the first black-owned and -operated radio station in the United States in Atlanta on October 4, 1949, WERD, on "Sweet Auburn Avenue," in the heart of the black business area.

What was it like working there?

Beautiful. It was brand new, nobody knew anything about what to do. We didn't have any guidelines, and nobody knew anything. All we knew was that you turn a switch on. We had a white fellow that came with the station when the Blayton family bought it. Mr. Blayton bought it on the courthouse steps from bankruptcy and the judge, I believe, told the chief engineer that if he wanted to collect the money that was owed to him, his best chance was to go ahead and be chief engineer for the Blaytons. So he reluctantly did. He found out that all money was just the same. Just cause black folks had it, it didn't mean it was less money. We looked at the old logs and we knew that you had to keep a log because that's what he told us. We had to type everything, and I remember we used to listen to WSB, a 50,000 watt white station in Atlanta, and everything they did on Monday the girl would write down on a pad and we'd do it on Tuesday. Everything they did on Tuesday, we did on Wednesday. In fact, I believe that we were probably the most diversified black radio station that has ever been. We had farm reports; we had what cattle was selling for and what cotton was going for. We had news, analysts, cooking shows, drama shows, just a conglomeration of the way radio used to be in the '40s.

Could you describe the feelings that you had in terms of working in a black environment instead of working for a white radio station?

Well, nobody else had worked for radio but me and I had been in the soap opera doing that, so this style of radio was new to all of us. We realized that we were serving our community because WERD belonged to the black community and that's what made us become very, very strong within the community. You know, being able to tell that Aunt Sally May was having a "chitlin" supper on Saturday night with spaghetti and cole slaw and announcing that on the air made Aunt Sally smile because she would have more people than she could get into her house to help her pay for her rent. So we found out that the community depended on us because they never had anything else like that in their lives—that they could turn their radio on and hear black voices. That's what gave personality to our radio station because we belonged to the community and the community loved us. That's how powerful black radio was back then.

How did that tie into the Civil Rights Movement, or did it have any connection?

This was before the Civil Rights Movement. This was 1949 and the Civil Rights Movement didn't really start happening until the middle '60s. The Supreme Court passed a bill 1954 about separate but equal education. I could say this, there would have never been a movement if it hadn't been for black radio. We told the community where the meetings were going to be held, the marches, and so on.

How was it working in Louisville?

Oh it was quite different, because Louisville had never heard of black radio stations. They had never heard personalities like us. We came into the market and completely destroyed it. Radio was very staid and they were used to nice, quiet radio instead of yelling and screaming and hollering and singing all through the records, as we did. Completely entertaining to our audiences, they had never heard anything like that before. It was something, the way we were accepted.

There were just a very formal type of announcers?

Yes, before, but we came in with personality and made every show different because we knew we were entertainers. I had my name as "Jockey Jack," so going into Louisville was a perfect setup, being the home of the Kentucky Derby. They took me to make real silks for me and I appeared daily doing a program.

Are you referring to your clothes?

Yeah. The real jockey silk. I remember they took me the first time to a little old guy that was about ninety years, old and had been making jockey silks for years—a hundred years, I bet you. When they told him he had to make some silks for me, he looked at me and he was grumbling, and finally they asked him, "What is wrong with you? Why you grumbling so much? You don't feel good?" He said, "No wonder the horses are breaking down, look at the size of the jockey you got here." I wasn't big but I was bigger than the little, bitty guys that ride those horses and he thought I was that kind, he didn't understand what a disc jockey was. All he knew was the word "jockey." So that was very hip; in fact, a young fellow who later became world famous used to carry my records for me when I'd go and do sock hops at the USO and all the different high schools and things.

Who was that?

Cassius Clay, who is now known as Muhammad Ali. In fact, he remembered it better than I did. He came to me one day when he was a champ and he said, "Jockey Jack, I remember you. You don't remember me. You had all of the women, boy, and I just loved to watch you work . . . all these women just bowing to you and kissing your hand and I said 'one day I'm going to have all the women.' " And he said, "And now you know what? Who's the greatest now?" I said, "Yeah you're the greatest now but I was the greatest then. And don't you forget it!" That was quite unique because, you know, I had forgotten who he was and then I put it together as we talked; this was the kid that always used to be waiting for me at the door to carry my records. That meant that he could get in free. I never even thought of it like that, I just kept thinking that all he wanted to do was carry the records and come on inside and hear the music.

When you set up a sock hop, how did that work?

We'd go fifty-fifty with whatever, like at the YMCA or the school or anything. Whatever they took in we just split 50–50. It supplemented our income.

What was income like back then?

Very little. Only $50 a week and then you had to hustle to make more money and that's when you did these hops and made appearances in night clubs and dances and things like that.

Now, did you buy time from the station?

No, I wasn't a broker, although I had friends that did that in Chicago. Chicago was famous for that. That was Al Benson's thing. I had worked for Al Benson in Chicago. He had bought a half-hour on WJJD for me and I did the program for him. I got, I don't know, $50 or maybe $40, I don't remember the exact amount and he'd get all the rest because he'd buy an hour for a dollar and he'd sell it for $2.00. He'd pay me a quarter and he'd keep 75 cents. He was on about thirty-some hours a week on stations all over Chicago. That's what made him so powerful.

Did you meet him and get to know him?

Oh yeah. That's how I really got into the music end of it. I had this little program and he heard me do it and he asked me would I like to do another one. So I said, "Yeah," and he said, "Well it will be an Al Benson production." I said, "Hey, I don't care whose production it is as long as I get on the air and play records and talk to the people."

So that was how some disc jockeys worked, how one disc jockey had a lot of different people working for him. Was that brokering time?

That's what they call brokerage, yeah. They were brokers. Small stations, that was the way that they could sell out their time. They made money, whatever their time was, you know, you paid card rate and then you went on and sold it for whatever you thought the popularity would bear. Al Benson was the big name in Chicago then and people were fighting to get on his show, merchants and things. Chicago was my hometown; that's where I was born and reared.

So you could make a killing if you had a popular name?

Yeah. But they wouldn't sell time in any other market that I know of in those days. It probably did happen but I didn't know of it. We went to work for owners, multiple owners.

Did you ever work for Motown?

I was Motown's first national public relations director. In fact, that's why I left radio. I used to work all of Berry's acts because I was in Cincinnati at that time. And Berry, every act he would sign, he'd think of me because I used to run a theater show once a month. I would get a record that I thought was hot, I could make hot, and then I would make it hot and then I'd call the record company and say, "Look, so-and-so," let's just for instance say I'm talking about (Chuck Jackson), and I took his record "Any Day Now" and I played the shit out of it in Cincinnati and people were crying for it and then I'd call the company and say "send me the kid (Chuck Jackson) for a weekend" and that would be how they would take care of business. They would give me the act and then Berry would augment my show with all his stuff. He'd add the Supremes and he'd have the Miracles and Stevie and the Temptations. He'd send them all to me because they were brand new acts and they had never worked anywhere before. I'd fill the whole show out with Motown acts and then you couldn't get near the theater, you know, once a month.

So you would play these records, let's say on a Thursday, and then they would have a concert on Saturday and Sunday?

Oh no, what I'd do is I'd know what I was going to do for the next month and I'd set it up. In other words, I'd start a record on the first and my show would be on the first so I'd have one show, like this past Saturday was the second, I already had a show so I knew what I was going to do my next show. I'd have a whole month to work on whatever show. So I'd close a show on say this Saturday and on the Monday, before the upcoming Saturday I'd be calling my record companies and saying, "Do you have an artist that you would like to have broken in the Cincinnati market?" and whoever had a record coming out and it sounded good, that was the record that I'd go to work on. Then I'd call Berry and say, "Berry, my next theater show is going to be on this Saturday. Whatever acts you've got, let me have them." It was always one of those things that if they made good we'd give them some money in their pocket and buy them a Greyhound bus ticket and send them back to Detroit. I remember giving the Miracles $25 apiece and a bus ticket, and the same thing with the Supremes. In fact, the Supremes, when they came to me, boy they had one little old jive record called "Buttered Popcorn" and they were scared. When they looked out in the audience and heard all these kids screaming and hollering, they had never played before an audience like that. In fact, they had never played before any kind of audience. They'd played like in a gym or something like that but not a crowd of actual paying people who were screaming and hollering and jumping up and down. They were scared to go out on the stage; I was emceeing the show and I remember going back and asking, "They're not here yet . . . the Supremes?" and the band would begin playing anthems. I did about three of these and I looked over in the wings and they were standing there, they were crying their little butts off. So I said, "Excuse me, you all, I've got to go find out where the Supremes are," and boy the people were booing and raising hell, so I went backstage and they said, "We can't go out now, they're booing us." I said, "Would you all come right out on the stage. Suppose I sing it with you?" So they said, "Well, we'll go if you stand there with us." I was really the fourth Supreme. The same movements they would use, I used and was going, "Ooh ooh" and so on.

Was this in Cincinnati?

Yeah. At the Royal Theater on Lynn Street. So when I got with Motown these were like my kids already and whenever there was a show to go anywhere I would be the one that would take them. Like the first time the Supremes ever sang on the Ed Sullivan Show, I took them. Yeah, we all went together. And you know it's a funny thing, this memory doesn't come up until I talk like I'm talking now. I used to have to get two rooms. They didn't give me enough money for everybody to get a room, so I'd get two rooms and the girls would sleep in one and I'd sleep in the other. I'd keep the door open so I could watch them to see if they were all right. There was a time when I'd wind up in the room with all of them. We'd all be in a room just laughing and talking and, of course, they looked at me like Uncle Jack. I had to give them my fatherly advice and whatnot.

When did you have time to get a family together?

Well, a family was born in my early years of radio. My first child came in 1945 and the next one came in '49 and finally after we'd made about six cities in the United States, my wife said, "Now you can go to some other city if you want to but I ain't going no places, I ain't moving no more. The kids will get a chance to graduate with some folks that they know in a high school that they've been in." She stayed in Cincinnati until they all got in college and I used to commute. I would go to Motown like on Monday morning and whatever I had to do I'd plan that week, go ahead and do it and then I'd fly back home on Friday night and spend the weekend with the family.

What about this organization called the National Association of Radio Announcers (NARA)?

Well, the first organization I formed when I was in Atlanta was called the National Association of Rhythm and Blues, Gospel and Jazz Disc Jockeys of America. I'd picked twelve guys and I was the thirteenth because I was born on the thirteenth so I thought that would be a good number. We had a summit meeting; this was like a meeting of the boys in New York City and I had a buddy who was a big disc jockey in New York at that time, Dr. Jive, that was Tommy Smalls. I told Tommy, "I want to have a meeting so we can know how to take care of this business." Tommy said, "Come on, use my club, Smalls Paradise, and I'll get you a rate at the Theresa." The thirteen of us met and I became the first president because it was my idea. When we met we said, "Hey, we've got to have some officers." "Yeah, we've got to have a president, a vice president and all that kind of stuff." So then I said, "Well, then I'm going to be president because it's my idea." So they said, "OK, you can be the president. Who wants to be the vice president?" Very democratic!

I remember when we had our first big convention, I should have said when we had our first big party. It was the most gigantic party you'd ever want to see. It was in Chicago. The Sutherland Hotel. And then the next one we had was in Los Angeles where we went to a big white hotel because we didn't know about no black hotel in Los Angeles. I reserved about fifty rooms, one big party suite, and I told them that we were National Association of Radio Announcers, and so they said "Oh, welcome to our hotel." We didn't realize why they were welcoming us so until they called me down on a Saturday morning and said to me, "You misrepresented yourselves." I said "What do you mean I misrepresented myself?" They said, "You told me that you all were the National Association of Radio Announcers," and I said, "We are." They said, "Well then, where is Huntley and Brinkley, John Cameron Swayze and Eric Severeid?" naming white announcers. They never knew there was a black announcer. I said, "These people are all in radio." Because they were not white, they'd never heard of any black in radio, other than Amos and Andy. So it was a unique thing and what they did was, when we went to a party at Sam Cooke's house they took all of our clothes and bags and everything and moved us to one wing of the hotel, with security guards not allowing us to roam the hotel, only to our rooms and the elevators.

In your opinion, how did formatting affect black disc jockeys?

Oh, it affected them greatly because it took our personality away from us and they did that to control us. See, how are you going to control a superstar when everybody in the town knows you, from the chief of police to the mayor? If you want more money, you say, "Look, I want more money," and he says, "I can't pay you no money." So you say, "OK, then I'm leaving." Everybody leaves and goes where you go. So they got together, the powers to be, and decided they was coming up with this formatted radio to keep us in line. What they did was take the personality away from us but they also took the "R" out of radio. And until it returns, black radio is going to be in trouble. To show you that personalities still live, a fellow named Tom Joyner, who is in Chicago, Dallas, and now all over the country with his Saturday morning show, is a superstar because he is a personality. He don't just say, "And now the next record is Aretha Franklin." He goes into a pitch about who made the record, why the record was made, and who wore polka-dot shorts when they was recording it and all that. The owners didn't want you to say that and all that bullshit you hear about less talking and more music, that's bullshit. Ninety-minute music sweep. First they went for what they call the "half-hour music, 30 minutes of nothing but music" and then they'd do commercials, and they said an hour of music and then somebody wanted to top that with 90 minutes, that's bullshit. You don't know what you're listening to.

So, in your opinion, formatting didn't have anything to do with economics and the selling of radio?

They claim that. How are you going to beat an advertiser who is pitching your product and all your station allows is for you to give the name, address, and telephone number of the store, and you pitch it. Whenever an advertiser bought a minute and we might talk three minutes because we were putting our own personality in it. When I was at my peak, I was in Atlanta. I was in with the chief of police. Anything happened in the black neighborhood, he'd call me on the phone. He'd say, "We're having some problems over there in Buttermilk Bottom, so you gotta get everybody quiet or otherwise I'm going to have to send my people in there." I'd stop the record, "Hold it, you all having some fighting over there in Buttermilk Bottom, you all know better than that. If you gonna do that the man gonna come in there and you're gonna spend the weekend over on Decatur Street," that's where the jail was. So I said, "You all be cool and just as soon as I finish playing some more of this good music so you all can get down, I'm coming over there to Buttermilk Bottom and I sure hope somebody's got my favorite; pig feet with some butter beans." And then when I'd get over to the area, the word would go down that "the jockey is on the turf" and boy the cats that had been fighting would say, "Let me tell you what went on Jockey Jack, he did this" and the other cat says, "No, he did that." Well, I would mediate the thing. I got to be known as the Dr. Bunche of Atlanta because I was the head mediator.

How would you say disc jockeys differed from this current generation?

Well, in the first place we didn't make as much money as they make. And we were into a brand-new field. Now it's the science of all new technology and the different kinds of equipment and stuff like that, and they can do different things with microphones and fades and voices and levels and all that stuff. We didn't have that, we just had an old beat-up control board that had three switches; one for the microphone and one for each turntable. I remember we had a wire recorder.

How did that work?

It was a piece of wire running the same way the tape ran. And when the wire broke, which it did all the time because it was so fine, we'd flip a switch and I'd say, "Hey, the wire broke, you all talk to each other while I go fix it," and I'd be across the room where the control panel was and I'd be talking over the microphone way on the other side of the room saying, "I'm getting ready to put a square knot in it because that's the only kind of knot that will hold. You keep on, keep on talking now, don't get lonesome, I'll be right back there in a minute with some more music as soon as I tie a knot in this wire." And I'd tie a knot in the wire and say, "OK, there it goes," and then you'd make announcements on there.

So you mean you recorded the announcement on the wire?

Yeah. Plus you could record the show on wire. It taped, only it was wire and Webcore made it.

Do you think that black radio stations should play mostly black artists?

Yeah, because white stations are not going to play it. That's always been my contention. They'll play a super black artist but what about all the little black artists that don't get a shot? So why do we have to break one of theirs? They always say, "If we play a white record every now and then that will get white folks listening." Hey, white folks listen to black radio because they hear music that they don't hear no place else. If they want to hear white artists they listen to their own station. So the disc jockey of today is much better off equipment-wise, but he's not much better off entertainment-wise because he don't know how to entertain. The only thing we knew was that the government, the FCC, told you that you had to make or break on the half and on the hour, two before or two after, either way, and then you'd be within limitation. And that's what we did. I used to make all kinds of funny station breaks, I'd do every kind of station break in the world. Whatever I thought to make it sound interesting instead of sounding like, "You're listening to WERD, Atlanta." I might say, "You're listening to the G O O D words station, WERD in ATLANTA, GA, the peach state of the world," or something like that. Each day it would be something different. Those were good days, I have fond, fond memories. And do you know there are only two of us left? Hal Jackson and myself. So I hope that you will write favorably and chronologically put it down so that people will understand what it is all about—how it started and how proud we are to be pioneers and to have opened the doors for the Oprahs, the Bryants, and the many others.

Al Benson. Photograph from the Indiana University Archives of African American Music and Culture.

Herb Kent. Photograph courtesy WAV-FM.

Hal Jackson. Photograph courtesy WBLS-FM.

George Woods. Photograph courtesy WDAS-AM/FM.

William T. "Hoss" Allen. Photograph from the Indiana University Archives of African American Music and Culture.

Young Eddie. Photograph courtesy Eddie Castleberry.

Eddie and Peggy Mitchell. Photograph from the Indiana University Archives of African American Music and Culture.

Eddie Castleberry today. Photograph courtesy Eddie Castleberry.

"Lucky" at the grocery store. Photograph courtesy Moses Lindberg "Lucky" Cordell.

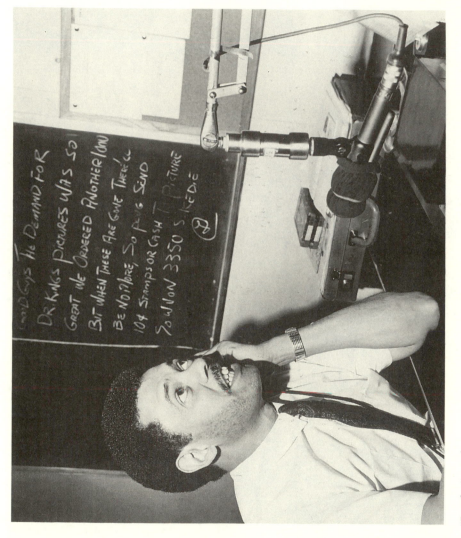

"Lucky" at the microphone. Photograph courtesy Moses Lindberg "Lucky" Cordell.

File photo of **"Lucky."** Photograph courtesy Moses Lindberg "Lucky" Cordell.

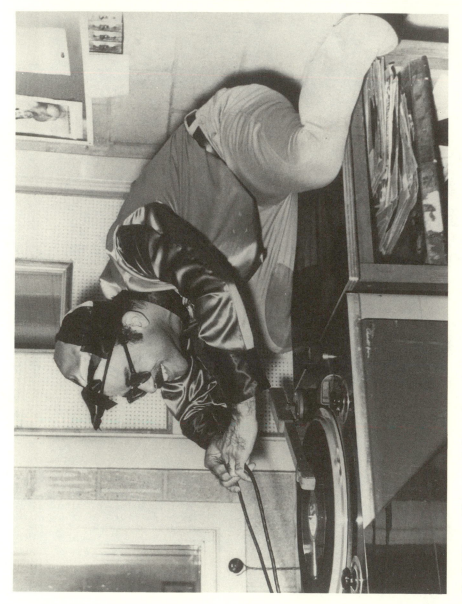

Jack Gibson. Photograph from the Indiana University Archives of African American Music and Culture.

Eddie O'Jay and **Eddie Castleberry.** Photograph from the Indiana University Archives of African American Music and Culture.

8

"Joltin' Joe" Howard

Joe Howard was born in Colorado but spent much of his early life in small towns in Texas. Eventually, his family moved to Waco, Texas. His first job as an announcer was at Houston's KNUZ, a radio station that played music for black audiences. Later, Howard found work at KYOK, also in Houston. By 1954, Howard had joined WAKE, a general-market radio station in Atlanta, Georgia. At WAKE, Howard read commercials, news and other announcements. Howard was known for his articulation and speaking ability, and WAKE's white audience never knew that he was an African American. Nevertheless, Howard was fired when a major sponsor found out he was African American and demanded that WAKE let him go.

Howard landed a job at WERD, also in Atlanta, and the nation's first black-owned radio station. In 1956, Howard left WERD to take a job at WCHB located in Inkster, Michigan. At WCHB, Howard was an instant success, as listeners liked his announcing style and personality. Later, he moved over to WJLB, another Detroit, Michigan area radio station, where he continued to make waves over the air.

APRIL 12, 1991

How did you get started in radio?

Quite by accident to be perfectly frank. I had just completed a two-year active duty stint in the army. I came home and was sort of getting myself reacclimated to civilian life and randomly called the local radio station and began inquiring of the guy who was on the air about job opportunities in that area. He said, "Well, why don't you come down Monday morning and talk to our program director." All the while I don't think the guy realized that I was black because I know that when I went in Monday morning and asked for the program director, he did a double-take when he came out and called my name and there I was.

Are you originally from Houston?

Yes, well in a roundabout way. Born in Colorado, spent my childhood in a little town up in central Texas, Waco, and moved to Houston with my parents when I finished high school.

Did you work on your articulation or enunciation or anything like that or was that something that basically came natural because of your upbringing?

Probably the latter. In school, throughout both high school and college, I debated and was engaged in public speaking. These were always my favorite endeavors but I never made any special efforts, it just sort of came naturally.

Where did you go to school?

I did my undergraduate school in Austin, Texas, at a private church-related college that was then called Samuel Houston. There were two black colleges in Austin at the time that merged after I graduated; it's Houston Tillotson College now.

Did you have any role models in regard to being on the radio, any black role models?

No, there was nobody for me to role model after. I was the third or fourth black on the air here in Houston and probably among the first eight or ten in Texas, and there weren't more than fifty throughout the country.

Were you accepted at that first radio station that you went to?

Yes, as a matter of fact I was. I mentioned that the program director, the guy whose name I had been given to ask for, did a double-take but he gave me a courtesy interview and then took me around to the studio and cut a tape. I didn't know a hill of beans; I had never been inside a radio station before in my life and he gave me some copy to read. Fortunately, I could read fluently and I read the copy. You know, he and I both felt this was a courtesy move and that neither of us would hear from the other for the rest of our lives. However, about two weeks later I got a call and he asked me if I wanted a job and I said "yes." I went in and he offered me a job doing a night show for an hour and a half, rhythm and blues is what it was called then. Race or black music.

What kind of records did you play? Can you tell me some of the artists? Did you play Ruth Brown?

Yes, Ruth Brown was just getting hot then. Ruth Brown, the Clovers, Joe Turner, blues records B.B. King was just starting out,

Muddy Waters, Chess records in Chicago was just getting warm then. It was called race music then, rhythm and blues. DJs had not been conceived yet.

What were the radio station call letters?

KNUZ.

After you left KNUZ, what happened?

I got a better offer because the dollars began; you know, that was the magic lure. There was another station here in town that was purchased by the OK Chain out of New Orleans, Louisiana.

You mean the record company?

No, it wasn't a record company, it was a chain of radio stations called the OK Chain. It was owned by Stanley Ray and Jewels Paglin and all of their stations ended in OK. They owned stations in Louisiana and then branched out to Texas and bought a station here and changed the call letters from KATL to KYOK. I left KNUZ and went over there because they needed somebody on staff that could read. As a matter of fact, if you are familiar with that chain, their practice was to hire blacks who had been in show business. Most of these show business people could not read fluently so they needed someone who could do production spots and read commercials and sort of teach reading skills to the other announcers, and I filled that bill. So I went there for the big bucks, $55 a week.

How did you get to Detroit?

By way of Atlanta. I had worked for a brief period for the Blayton family out of Atlanta. Mr. J. B. Blayton and his family were the owners of the first black radio station in the country. They owned WERD in Atlanta. They bought a little station here in the Houston area, and they thought they were buying the Houston market but they really didn't get into Houston. They bought a Bay Town station that only had fringe area coverage and I worked with them for a brief period. Then from KYOK I moved to Atlanta to work at a white station that was owned by the Bartel chain. I got fired from that station because I was black and while my voice did not sound black, one of the big sponsors found out that I was. He found it out when he came to bring me a Christmas gift and when he saw me, he did a complete reversal and demanded that I be fired or he was going to pull his advertising. So after I was fired from that station I went to work at WERD as program director, this was in 1955.

You had to be let go because you were black?

Yes. What had happened was that we had done some production spots for him; it was just before Christmas of '54 and he had a jewelry chain, his name was Jake Friedman. He had Friedman's Jewelers in Atlanta and he had bought a saturation schedule, running about thirty, thirty-five, forty spots a day and he loved the work that we did. I did the voice-over on the spots and he just fell in love with them and wanted to give me a gift. I was doing the 6 p.m. to midnight shift and the studios were in the basement of the Georgian Terrace Hotel, which at that time was located in downtown Atlanta on the corner of Ponce de Leon and Peachtree. When the office crew would leave at 5 o'clock, they would lock the doors and nobody could get into where the studios were. However, somebody inadvertently left the door unlocked and Jake Friedman gained entry. The people were there cleaning up and he asked somebody, "Where's Joe Howard? I'm going to see that announcer named Joe Howard." They pointed to the window and they said, "He's in there, he's on the air." And he said, "What? That nigger?"

Were those his exact words?

Yeah, so he stormed out the station and I didn't even know he had been there. This was on a Friday evening. Monday morning Joe Bartel, who was one of the owners, called me in the office. He and Cal Purley, the station manager with whom I had left Houston to go to Atlanta, apologetically informed me that Mr. Friedman had seen me and that he demanded that I be let go or he was going to cancel his package. The station couldn't afford to lose that kind of money as they was just getting into the market. So, they said, "We've got to let you go." I said, "Well," what could I say? They gave me a very generous severance pay.

Did you have any kind of bargaining power or anything like that? Was there a union to protect you?

Later I found that there was, but at that time I didn't know anything about AFTRA or ATRA or any of that. I didn't find out about that until I got to Detroit because in Texas being a nonunion state and Georgia being also a work-at-will state, you just didn't find out those things and especially as blacks we weren't provided that information. I went to WERD, the Blaytons took me in and I went over there as program director. Jack Gibson and I worked together. In fact, that is where Jack and I forged a friendship that is very close to this day. I stayed there for just a little over a year and a half before I moved to Detroit.

And you started working at WCHB?

Yes, I went to Detroit to work with WCHB. Larry Dean Faulkner was a friend of ours who had started in Nashville; he actually started in Atlanta, then he went to Nashville.

Larry Dean Faulkner is no longer with us, is he?

Right, he died about four or five years ago, about 1986 I think. But he was assembling the staff for Dr. Bell and Dr. Cox at their new station and he came to Atlanta and offered both Jack and me jobs in Detroit. Jack almost went but he changed his mind and decided he'd stay in Atlanta. I left. I said, "Well I'm going to see you buddy," so I accepted the offer to move to Detroit to work for WCHB. I was picked to do the morning show so I was the one that signed the station on at its very inception on November 7, 1956.

What kind of music did you play?

Here again, since the station was owned by blacks, the feasible kind of program to do to attract the clientele we were aiming for was to play black music, so I did. At this time the nomenclature had evolved from race music to rhythm and blues to rock and roll. This was just prior to the advent of the real rock and roll era. That started probably in the late '50s, around '59 or '60 just as Motown got started.

So you were playing the Platters, the Coasters, people like that?

Yes, the black artists who were very often then spinning over into the pop music. Most of the records were just a hairline difference. You could not tell, and I was doing morning drive and evening drive or afternoon drive and noonday news.

What was your on-air personality name?

Joltin'Joe Howard. I plagiarized that from Joe DiMaggio. He was the Yankee baseball player and was at the height of his popularity at that point in time and I thought it had a good ring to it. Larry and I agreed on it so he said, "Well, you're Joltin' Joe Howard from now on," and that caught on and reverberated through every hill and dale in the Detroit area.

What was it like working in Detroit?

At that time it was fantastic. Detroit was really the boom town. Everything was happening. That's why Motown blossomed so fast because Detroit was where the action was. That was the place to be, I mean, there was so much money to be made in Detroit. You could just stand on the corner and without even trying to hustle, bring in $200 or $300 a day. It was so different for me. I'm a country boy. I had never been to the big city before. Houston was not a big city then. Atlanta was a metropolis but you got to Detroit, that was the fourth or fifth largest city in the country and just booming. I mean the economy was at its peak and the people in Detroit received us with open arms. My name became a household word in less than a year's time. I was in demand for personal appearances and people would kick down doors and line up around the block just because I said I was going to be there. It really was hard to deal with, it was very difficult. Of course, when I went to Detroit I was only twenty-five years old. I'd never had a $100 bill that belonged to me in my hand in my life. So you can see what a tremendous revelation it was, all this money was just raining out of the sky.

Did you have anybody to "coach" you or serve as a mentor, to show you the ropes, or did you have to make mistakes and learn from them?

No one; I was there alone. I did not have the counsel of an older brother. My mother and father had been domestics all their lives. My mother was a cook and my dad had been a chauffeur and you know, $45–$50 a week was top salary, so they did not have the expertise with which to advise me and even if they had it would have been difficult for them to have done it long distance. I had to learn by trial and error and unfortunately there were more errors than successes. I just screwed up a lot of money, gave away a lot of money, got beat out of a lot of money, it's the age-old story. I know that it was the learning process and that was the only way that I could accomplish it.

You made personal appearances. Did you promote shows and artists too?

Later on, after I'd been there for about five years, I branched out into the promotion business and found out in a hurry that that business is very dangerous if you don't know what you're doing. I made good money in it, I was lucky. There was a ballroom called the Greystone Ballroom in downtown Detroit on Woodward Avenue and one of my big baths, I took in that ballroom. I stayed in the little clubs in Inkster and in the smaller clubs in Detroit but made good money. Then I branched out for this one biggie, this one big killing I was going to make but took a real bath.

So you had to put up money in order to bring in artists? How does that work?

Well, because I was in well with the record companies, I did not have to go through the same gyrations that the other promoters did.

They had to put up what amounted to a performance bond, a "deposit" it was called. I did not have to put up a deposit but I did have to pay the band and the entertainers even though I was getting them all for reduced rates. But I put together this mammoth show, I must have had eight acts and a big band and the whole bit. I promoted it on the air and my buddies promoted it on their stations. I had fantastic promotion.

Did you interview artists live on the air?

Yes, the whole bit. The show wasn't live enough for me, the artists that I had were mediocre and it did not have the pulling power that I anticipated. I had the competition of the clubs who were booking twenty grand, and booking big acts. Phelp's Lounge was booking big acts. Flame Showball was still going then. So I had all that competition and I just didn't have a strong enough package to fill the Greystone enough to make any money. So I lost about $8,000 in that one night. It took me a while to recuperate from that. Berry came to my rescue and guaranteed some people some money while they gave me a chance to pay them off at $300–400 a week.

Was that Berry Gordy?

Yes, he was just getting started. He didn't have any money then but he was beginning to make some noise and some of the people were working for him at that time and the band especially. So he rescued me.

Had you heard of payola at that time?

Oh yes, I was involved, I was deeply involved. Payola was something where the black jocks got the pittance and the white boys made the big money. They are the ones who got the swimming pools in the backyard and the wives got the 8–10 to 20 thousand dollar fur coats. That kind of thing. We'd get a couple hundred dollars when we went to New York or Chicago or wherever. It was the practice of the day. Record companies wined, dined, and got women for you, whatever.

It was not illegal, at that time, was it?

No, it wasn't illegal. The only illegal thing about it was not reporting it on the income tax, which none of us did because it was all cash or services. Incidentally, I got caught in that just as I was moving from Detroit to here in Texas in 1970 and got fined $10,000 plus penalties. While I was going through that investigation, I guess I really didn't do myself any good because I called this person a "little internal revenue investigator." He had found a $50 check that some little record company had given me and I didn't usually take checks but this one slipped through and I didn't report it. I remember a guy gave it to me one night when we were out partying and he slipped something in my hand. I put it in my pocket and didn't even think anything else about it. The guy says, "You mean you got a $50 check and you didn't think anything about it?," and I said "No, I sure didn't, I forgot about it." He said, "Well if somebody gave me $50 I would remember it," and I said, "Well, yes, that probably shows the difference between our earning powers." That didn't set well with the little fellow. About payola, record companies would send their reps out on the road with a bag of money to visit the key jocks in each key area and your payola was based on the level of importance of your area and the position of prominence you enjoyed in that area. Well, I got to be the #1 jock in Detroit, actually it was like a nip-and-tuck thing between me and another guy there named Ernie Durham, Frantic Ernie. When they came to town, the first thing they did was call me up and try to get me over and I got to the point. . . .

In Atlanta there was also payola going on but not to the degree it was in Detroit. In Houston, I was new and I wasn't kicking up any dust. I think I got one $25. Well, Don Robey called, I met Don Robey and he became like my dad. He put his arms around me and he's the one that coached me in my very early days of radio. He would give me $100–200—if Robey liked you, he was just like that, he was big-hearted—not necessarily to play his records, because he had good records and you were going to play them anyhow. He just knew we weren't making any money and were starving to death and he would help us out.

When I ran into the really big payola was when I got to Detroit and after my name hit. Then I'd open my mailbox and there would be $500 from a record company or I'd go to New York and make a couple of stops, one at 1650 Broadway which is the building right between Broadway and 7th Avenue on 52nd Street and that was a 14-story building. By the time we started at the top floor, 14, and came down to the bottom we'd have two or three thousand dollars in our pocket. Just stopping in offices saying, "Hi, how you doing?" They knew us and they'd be wondering, "Who's paying your bill?" "Where are you staying?" "Is there anything you want?" It was unbelievable, it was a real trip. You had to be very careful not to get caught up in the whole thing. Jack Gibson and I sit back now and reminisce about how we lived and we try to tell people now about it. My wife and I finally stopped telling because they can't believe it, they thought we were fantasizing and just outright lying so we had to stop even mentioning it. It was a fantastic life and talk about the fast lane. Of course, when the record owners would come to my town I would reciprocate. I got to be friends with a lot of them and they'd come in and I had a cadre of women and I'd fix them up and they'd still bring money with them but the dates were my treat. So it was that kind of brotherhood.

How did you become endeared to the black community? What were you doing during the riot?

Well, first we got on the air and we tried to get them off the street when it first broke out.

What station was this?

I'd just moved over to WGPR when this happened. It was 1967 and they called me at home, I lived out between 7 and 8 Mile Road on the west side. I had been out boozing it up or gambling or something that Saturday night and didn't get any sleep. They called me early Sunday morning and Sonny Carter, one of our announcers, said, "Man, you gotta get out here, they are burning up the town." I said, "Man, leave me alone." Finally, he got me up and when I was driving in, going down the Lodge Freeway, it looked like a battlefield. Our studios were still on East Hancock between Woodward and John R and we got on the air, stopped all our regular broadcasting and just started doing appeals, you know, trying to get them to go home. "Whatever your concerns are," we would say, "we'll march with you. We'll go down to Mayor Cavanaugh's office and we'll settle it, but please, please, stop looting, stop burning because you are burning up everything in the neighborhood." And then we got out in the car and started driving around trying to personally appeal to them but found out that wasn't a good idea. The brothers would want to know when they see you in the car is "Hey man, you shopping?" That meant were we getting ready to go into the store that they set on fire to loot and they were too fired up for us to do anything. So we went back to the studio and to answer your question, we just continually appealed on the air. In fact, all of the black radio announcers in Detroit started calling each other from station to station; Martha Jean the Queen was there and Bill Williams was out at WCHB and we started coordinating our efforts and trying to make one concerted plea. We touched bases with each other so we could all sing from the same page and do the same verse. And in a concerted effort we were trying to get our brothers off the street because we knew they would be killed needlessly or else they'd be rounded up and put inside a barbed-wire enclosure out on Belle Isle.

That's where they were taking our brothers?

Yeah, because the jail got overcrowded right quick like. We sort of like to believe that we probably saved a lot of our brothers'lives because we got some of them to listen to us. I was involved with NAACP and Voter Registration but as I look back in retrospect, I wasn't as involved as I feel I should have been. But when Martin Luther King came to Detroit I was right with him. C. L. Franklin and I were very good friends and C. L. was instrumental in bringing Dr. King there. So I used to do a lot of work with and for him on the air promoting things and I'd done a lot of promotion then so I was right down front with him marching down the Avenue to Cobo Arena with Dr. King. In fact, I was over to C. L.'s house on LaSalle Boulevard where he got shot and where he died. But the night before was the reception for Dr. King. But I was so caught up in all these big bucks and I was part owner of a club there, Phelp's Lounge, and I was caught up with that and was really just handling a hell of a lot of money and moving faster than I should have been moving. As I look back, I was not as civic-minded as I should have been or could have been.

How did you maintain any kind of personal life? Were you able to get married?

Yeah, more times than I should have. When I went to Detroit I was married. I was married when I left here, when I got in to radio really. I was married when I got out of college and my first wife and I divorced in 1959 about three years after I'd gotten to Detroit. Then I stayed single for two or three years and that was too hectic. I figured if I didn't get married I was going to kill my fool self. Trying to keep up with all the offers and I didn't have sense enough to turn any down at that time. So I got married again in '62 and that marriage lasted until '68. Then my present wife and I got married in '70 and that's when I moved back to Texas.

What is your sense of format radio? Is it a good thing for black radio to be involved or do you think we should develop more personalities?

Well, I think, and I guess it's because I'm from the old school, but you know when I was in the business we had personality radio and the jock was what the whole thing was built around. The records were actually an intricate part of the show but anybody could play records, anybody can push buttons. The humanistic part of it came from the relationship that the audience developed or perceived as having developed with that disc jockey. And I think the saving grace, if there is such a thing, for black radio is going to be a return to the basics, the basics being personality radio. That's the only thing that can save AM, AM cannot compete with FM music quality so unless it goes talk, it's going to have to resort to personality and strong personality projections. This, I believe, can save it and can make it the formidable entity that it was at one time. Back in our days you could tell when you had Joltin'Joe on the air. "That's Joltin'Joe Howard." We were getting into the area of more music, less talk but there still was that individualistic ingredient that made the show a personality show. I learned by listening to others. When I would visit Chicago I'd listen to E. Rodney Jones and to Ed Cook and I'd steal a little from E. Rodney and they would steal a little from me and take it back to Chicago. Jack was in Cincinnati so we all borrowed from each other all over the country and each of us developed a unique style that incorporated talking into records, talking over records, certain little idiosyncrasies that some of us had that others didn't that would involve the use of certain songs as theme songs or as break music, going from one segment to another. I did a show in Detroit for years on Saturday mornings called "Memory Time USA" where I played old records and told the story of the record because by the mid '60s everything that had come out in the '50s I either had possession of or knew the history behind the song. I knew how it was conceived and had met most of the artists and could talk factually and first-hand about them. Robey didn't have a big session that he didn't ask me to fly down and sit in on and critique. There were such people as Bobby Blue Bland, Johnny Ace, Willie Mae Thornton. You know Elvis Presley's "Hound Dog," Don wrote it. He paid a guy $50 for it so he said he wrote it but . . . Don made all the writer's royalties off "Hound Dog" and incidentally he didn't want to release that. That was a B side, he released the record on Willie Mae Thornton for the other side. "Hound Dog" just took off and King B. Smith and I tried to convince him that it was going to be a hit and offered to bet him but he wouldn't bet us. That was the kind of intimacy that was translated into our presentations on the air and went to the real depth of the personality radio.

Do you listen to any disc jockeys today?

No, well, there is one disc jockey here in Houston I listen to because he and I worked together at KNUZ back in '53, Paul Berlin, and he plays oldies. The contemporary jocks I can't listen to, it's an unpleasant experience, let me put it that way. If I'm not listening to Paul Berlin I listen to talk radio.

If you had to give any advice to a young person going into radio, a young black male or female, what would you tell them?

Well, I think my advice to them would be to look beyond the microphone. That's the glamour end of the business but that's not where the money is. The real grit of the business is beyond the microphone; sales and ultimate ownership and I think the market is right today for blacks who aspire toward ownership. Entrepreneurship, that's the name of the game. We didn't have the opportunity, the Blaytons and the Bells were few and far between. Things just happened to fall into place for Skip Carter in Kansas City. There had to be a lot of luck and a lot of initiative on their part but now it's wide open. The networks are wide open. The opportunity is there. I would definitely advise the young black going into radio today to not get caught up in the glamour end of it because that's all a facade and it will soon pass. The real lasting economic base in that business is behind the microphone. Get into sales and sales leads to management and management leads to ownership.

Are you still involved in radio or have you gotten out of it?

I am in human resources. I am a senior personnel administrator with the city of Houston. I've come full circle. I made the break from radio in 1980 and have not had anything to do with it since. I've had a number of offers to go back but that marked twenty-seven years for me and that was enough. I went to the mountain top, I did everything that I wanted to do in the business except own a facility and I didn't see that forthcoming so I went back and decided to use my degree and I got into personnel. So I'm in personnel management in human resource management.

Now you left Detroit in 1970?

Yes.

And you came to Houston and which stations did you work for there?

I, by this time, was in news and I worked at the NBC affiliate in radio and TV, KPRC from about '70 to '77, seven years. Then I went to work for KMJQ-FM, Magic 102, where I was news manager. I had a very serious automobile accident in August of '79 was not supposed to walk again. Of course, I overcame that. I still walk with one crutch but I'm very ambulatory and so after that I went back. It took me like six months to convalesce from my accident but after that I went back in February of '80 and then I saw that I didn't have the zeal anymore; it was getting to be a chore to go to work, so in May of '80 I hung it up after twenty-seven years.

If you had to say there was one particular thing or activity that symbolizes Joltin' Joe Howard's career in black radio, what would that be?

I think the one thing that I am the proudest of is the fact that I waged my own individual battle in an effort against the perpetuation of the stereotypes. I tried my best to erase the stereotypes that white radio and TV ownership had perpetuated when I came into the business and even tried to continue to perpetuate, that is, that blacks did not have the intellectual levels of their white peers and that in order to appeal to a black audience you had to sound stupid and "negroid." I never subscribed to that, I never did it. When I went to work for the OK chain here, they had names for all of their announcers. They only hired people from show business and they gave them names like Hotsy-Totsy and Hokey-Pokey and Zing-Zang. So when I went to work at the station they asked me, "What are we going to call you?" and I said "Joe Howard." We had a little tiff over that. "No, we've got to call you something like 'Sugar Throat'" and I said, "No, that's all right, you can have your job." So I was the first black to work with that chain and use my own name. I played blues music and talked jive but I never, ever, split verbs and left infinitives hanging and I felt that you could get down and be just as hep using correct English as you could just screwing up the King's English. Throughout my career I was very conscious of that and waged my own personal battle and that is what I am the proudest of.

9

Maurice "Hot Rod" Hulbert, Jr.

Maurice Hulbert, Jr., was born in Helena, Arkansas, in 1916. His first job in radio was at WDIA-AM in Memphis, Tennessee, in 1949. He became known as "Hot Rod" while at WDIA because of his fast talk and "jive" phrases. Hulbert created "good googa mooga" and the phrase "O-ble-doo-ba-blah-doo-lay-a-way," which was an improvisational ad-lib of a commercial for the E-Z Layaway Credit Company. Hulbert was one of WDIA's first fulltime African-American announcers.

While at WDIA, Hulbert worked three different shifts. In the morning, using his given name—Maurice Hulbert, Jr.—he hosted the gospel show "Tan Town Jubilee." Hulbert read scripture and played gospel music during this program. During the midday daypart, Hulbert became "Maurice the Mood Man." Here he played music that appealed to housewives. Hulbert also hosted the "Sepia Swing Club," featuring jazz and swing music, which came on prior to "Tan Town Jubilee."

In 1951, Hulbert left Memphis to accept a position in Baltimore, his adopted hometown. In Baltimore, he annouced for WITH-AM, where "Hot Rod" became one of the most popular DJs on the east coast. His popularity enabled him to find work in three major markets at the same time. By the early 1960s, for example, he was deejaying in New York City, Philadelphia and Baltimore.

In 1974, he decided to move out of announcing and into radio sales management. For example, Hulbert held sales positions at WBGR in Baltimorej and at other local radio stations.

Over the years, Hulbert received numerous awards for his community service and contributions to black radio. In 1991, he became a member of the Black Radio Hall of Fame and was inducted at the Jack The Rapper Family Affair in Atlanta. Warner Brothers presented Hulbert with the Living Legend Award in 1992. Quincy Jones presented Hulbert with the Musical Heritage Award in 1992. Moreover, in that year, he was the recipient of Morgenstern Broadcasting's Pioneer and

Radio Legend Award. In addition, the United States Congress pre-sented Hulbert with the Congressional Achievement Award for his out-standing contributions as a pioneer in black radio and music.

JUNE 23, 1991

How and when did you get into radio?

I got into radio in 1949 on station WDIA. I was born in Arkansas but I never lived in Arkansas, as I came to Memphis when I was a baby. Before going into radio I was in show business. I traveled with a show called the "Huntington's Mighty Minstrels" and also traveled with the F.S. Walcott show out of Port Gibson, Mississippi. Later I was with the Evan C. Brown Skin Models. That was something like a Ziegfield Fol-lies show, musicals where girls came out with all those pretty feath-ered hats and pretty things like that. That's the type of show it was, first-class show.

Could you describe yourself a little bit?

I am about 5'7", 154 lbs., brown skin. I don't have any hair. I cut my hair off one time, all off, shaved it off, when Yul Brynner won the Acad-emy Award in 1956 or '57. It's a part of my trademark. I did crazy things and during that time it was crazy. When all the people saw me with a bald head, it was laughter. I mean it was funny and you know, I always felt that you could make fun of yourself and people would still like you. You know, you can make fun of yourself instead of making fun of everybody else all the time. I shaved my head every day.

So, were you out of Port Gibson when you went on to Memphis, to WDIA?

No, I'd been with the Brown Skin Models, but I'd left Port Gibson, then I traveled with the Brown Skin Models and then in Memphis. Every year I used to produce, direct and stage a ballet for the school system. Once a year. This time when it was time for me to come back and do it I was in Oklahoma City. I'd been traveling with the band as a music director, conducting the band you know. We'd travel to differ-ent cities and we were out in Oklahoma City and then they left Okla-homa City and I stayed working in a night club. Good thing I did, because they had a terrible accident on the highway on the side of the bus where I used to sit and I wouldn't be here talking to you. Some of my friends were killed and some injured seriously. When it was time for me to get back to Memphis to stage my ballet, my annual play, I said, "I think I'd like to go into radio, I'd like to be the first black guy to go into radio, maybe it's time." But when I got to Memphis I was a little disappointed because they had a guy. His name was Nat D. Williams. He'd been on the air about a year.

Did they call him Professor?

Professor Nat D. Williams, he was a school teacher. Taught history I think. So I came back to Memphis and I was in production for my play, and he interviewed me in regard to the upcoming play; I think it was a ballet or a play I wrote called "Ballet Communicamaro" or "Ballet Illusion" or something like that. Those are a couple of plays I wrote and directed and I don't know which one it was. He said, "Well, come on over and I want to interview you about what the plays are going to be about." He asked me, "Would you like to do a guest disc jockey show, a 15-minute guest disc jockey?" I said, "Yes, I'd like that."

In the meantime I had been going to radio stations all over Memphis trying to get on and I couldn't get on. So I did the 15-minute interview with a girl I had taught to sing in Spanish and then she would sing it in English. They have a thing in Memphis called a "Cotton Carnival," it's something like the Mardi Gras in New Orleans and they have a Spirit of Cotton, Queen of Cotton, or something like that. Anyway, she was vying for the title for black people, see the white people had their Queen and the blacks had theirs. It was held at the Civic Center. The manager of the station where Prof. Nat D. was working was there and he had heard my interview and asked me if I would be interested in trying out for a show on WDIA and I told him "yes." To make a long story short, that was arranged and started out doing 25 minutes a day and that spread into an hour and then on into two hours. The next thing I know they had me doing a religious program which was early in the morning. I did that program which was different. My show was called "The Sepia Swing Club." Then I did the "Tan Town Jubilee," which was a religious show. Then they asked me would I do a mid-morning show, soft overtones. It was called "Sweet-talking Time." I was "Maurice the Mood Man" when I came to Baltimore and also on the "Sweet-talking Time."

Now when you were at WDIA did you have to sell time or find sponsors for your shows?

No, I didn't have to do that. Didn't any of us have to do that on that station but that did happen with some stations later and as you know Al Benson did a brokerage thing in Chicago. He bought the time on the radio station and then resold it, and he had guys working for him. He was on several stations at the same time in Chicago. So everybody was on the Al Benson show but he couldn't be on all those shows at the same time.

I did a lot of community work in Memphis and I had a great audience of people who had their radios in the cotton fields listening to me. They would invite me up there and I'd go up and see them and talk with them and they'd load my car up with vegetables, fruit, watermelons, meats and everything. It was fantastic. That's what I strived for, a great mutual affection with my audience. And I was successful in doing that. And then I did things like when people were burned out in Memphis, I got money, clothes, and furniture for them until they had more than they had before they were burned out. Then I started a program in Memphis, produced and staged the first one. It went on for nearly twenty years to raise money for people at Christmas time. And that went on for years after I left. In fact, they used to invite me back down there from Baltimore to visit for the big occasion. I worked with Stepin Fetchit (Lincoln Perry) too.

Was that after you had been on the radio?

Before the radio. Yeah, traveling with Stepin Fetchit, I emceed the show and I did an act called "Big Jeff, Little Jeff." I think this helped me become what I came to be in radio. The owner of the station walked in one day and said to me, "After a recorded commercial gets done, say something about a product or service, ad-lib, just say anything so that it gives you a chance to talk." It was my first opportunity to ad-lib so I had to say something. I would say something nice, something positive about the service or the product. And then I guess that promoted me to go on and say all kinds of things and I came up with a tongue-twister that Doug Henderson could not steal. He could not borrow that. It was a tongue-twister with nineteen syllables in it. Years later I put on a contest to my listeners and they said, "He must be crazy, knowing nobody can say that" but then I taught them how to say it, syllable by syllable.

Was B.B. King at WDIA while you were there?

Yes, B.B. King came there while I was there. He had a 50-minute show and from that show, he got a lot of jobs in and around Memphis. He could say, "I'm going to be at such and such a club tomorrow night." We all did that, you see we didn't get paid too much money but we could say where we were going to be appearing and make money on the side. That was our way and that happened in many cities at that time, but it can't be done now because there is the payola and the plugola[1] thing. I wasn't really involved but the government thought I was.

Couldn't you simply report any outside income and that would take care of any legal problems?

I did but you can't do it now even if you report it. Not today. Back then I was reporting mine. What I did, I recorded all the money that I received from record companies and whatnot. I wrote it into my little books and paid income tax on it. I was doing that trying to be a business man. I had no idea there was going to be a big payola scandal. You know I was just paying, so when the internal revenue investigated me, I called my account man and they went through my books and all my stuff. The record company said they gave me, yes, they gave me the money. In fact, I was so strong I used to bill them. They used to get a statement from me every month, some record companies. But I ran all that through my books. So, the government went through my books.

This was during the time that Alan Freed was on the air in New York. I knew Alan Freed. In fact, Alan Freed would go to various cities and recruit the top disc jockey and they would go do the show when it came to town. That's how big he was. So he and I did do some things together. The last time I saw him, he was a broken man and had lost everything, he was the light man in a night club. I saw this man who had been so big and so strong and so powerful, I saw him with the light and I acted like I didn't know him. I didn't want him to see me because I didn't want him to see that I'd seen how low he had fallen. It might embarrass him.

Were you married by the time you left Memphis and moved to Baltimore?

Yeah, these people sent for me and I came up and I worked at the station WITH for years before I found out that they had contacted a research company to find them a colored or Negro disc jockey, they didn't say black, who had the highest rating in the country. That's how I got to Baltimore but I didn't know that until 20 years later when they did a story on the guy who brought me here, a white guy, and in the article, that's what he said. He said "TV was giving us pressure at night and we thought we could bring a black personality in to kind of boost our night ratings" or something like that.

What was his name?

Jay Gimbrey. He's told it to me since then. He's the vice president and general manager of WITH. The owner was Tom Tensley. They got together and decided to do that. And that was a shocker, man, because I guess if I had known that I could have gotten a little more money. I started not to come to Baltimore because I didn't like Baltimore. I used to see motion pictures that had to do with slaves coming into Baltimore, the port of Baltimore. But economics brought me here and it's the best move I ever made in my life. So that's how I got to Baltimore and that's how the Rocket Ship show started.

You hit Baltimore with the Rocket Ship?

With the Rocket Ship. I transferred the Sepia Swing Club into the Rocket Ship and took Baltimore by storm.

Now, how many hours were you working? What were your shifts like?

I worked from 9 to midnight or something like that, then later on I did "Maurice the Mood Man Hour" in front of Hot Rod; I did that for about a year before Baltimore actually knew that Maurice and Hot Rod and Maurice Hulbert, Jr., were one and the same. I was doing three personalities on the station. I was doing a religious show on Sunday, under the name of Maurice Hulbert, Jr., and I did Maurice the Mood Man and Hot Rod, which were three distinct different personalities.

You mean, the black community accepted you as both a blues and gospel disc jockey?

I didn't mix it with my show, it was a different show alltogether. A completely different show. I did Sunday Jubilee, that's what it was called. That was my religious program. One other thing I did before I left Memphis, I did a dramatic play called "I Know My Redeemer Liveth," produced by Dr. Evart Brewston. It was a passion play and I played the part of Jesus Christ for two straight years until I left Memphis.

So you had this flair or talent for drama?

Yes, it's helped me. I did comedy, stand-up comedy. Then in Baltimore I did the same thing, I helped poor people. I was helping people so heavily until I had people write me letters from Jamaica to try to bring them into the city. They read some articles about me. It was so heavy until I stopped doing it because I couldn't handle it. I did it myself, you know, the station wasn't backing me. I had the freedom to do that kind of stuff. The station, you know, they didn't bother me.

Was this your commitment to the community?

Yeah. As I said before, earlier, before the Martin Luther King period, Parren Mitchell, crusader, and I marched in the city crusading for blacks, for the rights of blacks for better treatment. I spoke out on the air about anything that I thought was negative to the community.

Did you select your own records for your show?

Yes, I did.

Did anyone tell you what to play?

Nope. Not until in the early '70s when they had a little thing where they came out with a program and music director. They didn't have no music directors back in our day. You were your own music director. But then, it got around a little bit where a station would say, "We'll play . . . " I had a deal where I could play 50 percent of the music of my own selection. They would have a stack of records there that the station wanted, or thought you should play, so I'd pick out of their stack and then I'd pick out of mine, you know, because some of the things in their stack were things I wanted to play anyway.

Did you play the blues?

Yeah, I played them all. I played jazz, at one time I played a mixture of all of it.

Did you play them in a particular order? Like would you play so many fast, so many slow tunes? Did you try to create some kind of mood as you went through that or was that something that you felt?

I played my stuff in tempo. For instance, if I kicked off with a fast tune, I might follow with a good, fast tune behind it and then I'd drop the tempo down and then go back up. At times I used to tell stories with records, some Mood Man, Sweet-Talking Time. I used to get letters from people who were saddened at heart from some misfortune in their lives. Sometimes we're talking about people who could be suicidal and all that stuff. I'd talk to them and try to pull them back to normalcy. I feel like Baltimore is my home now. I'd rather be in Baltimore than any place. After I'd been here three or four years I felt like Baltimore had pulled me to its bosom and said, "Now you're my son." That's the feeling that I got, not only from blacks, but from whites. My white audience was as big as my black audience.

Were there white kids out there listening to you?

Oh yeah, I talked to some of them who were grown and parents who would give them hell about listening to me. They would have the radio on real low underneath or close to the pillow, dialed real low and they would listen to me and they'd hear their parents come and know the parents wouldn't allow it. They'd cut the radio off and act like they were asleep. I had some blacks that did that too. After a while it became popular to listen to "Maurice the Mood Man," he was a clown, he was on the backs of white guys and black guys.

Tell me about the payola scandal. How did that affect your career?

Well, I'll tell you. I was driving a big Lincoln automobile convertible. I could afford it with the money I made, with my salary. I even had an

Afghan hounddog, big beautiful blond Afghan hounddog. I remember one time I was going to Philadelphia alone and my hounddog was sitting up straight on the front seat with me and all of a sudden the police stopped me. The officer was talking to me standing up and then he decided to bend down because he thought the dog was a blond white woman. But anyway, back to your story, my management said, "We've talked to our lawyers in Washington and they feel that you should resign." I said, "Resign for what?" and they said, "The big payola scandal" and I said, "Well, I'm not involved in it."

What year was this?

That was '58 or '59, the first one. And so they had me in the office, and another white guy on the station, on in the morning, was doing everything, man. He even had offers across the street, had records all over the place. He was doing everything and they didn't say anything to him. I said, "Well, I have searched and searched and searched, and I cannot see where I have done anything that merits me resigning." He said, "Well, don't look at it that way, you're a good radio man and you can get a job anywhere." I said, "Well, would you hire Alan Freed? As soon as I resign it's going to hit the ticker tape, the news, and come across that I am no longer here because of payola. My community is going to think the same thing." They were hard against it. Then one thing hit me. I had had a, not a nervous breakdown, but I had a break out on my body that I thought was . . . it was sex-related.

Stress-related?

No, sex-related. Yeah, and I went to the doctor and he told me that it wasn't, so I went to another doctor and he told me the same thing. I thought they were crazy and I took all kinds of tests and came out negative. Then I went to another doctor and he told me it was my nerves and that I should go in the hospital. I went in the hospital for three days and the phones in there kept ringing and I took care of business but the doctor told me I needed to slow down. He didn't tell me how; I had my own office. I was getting into advertising, little advertising agencies, doing promotions.

Did you have a business on the side in addition to being on the air?

Yeah, I had a little advertising agency and was doing promotions and I was making money all kinds of ways. I was making money so I said, "Well, I'll tell you what, I will resign under one condition," and they said, "What is that?" I'm sitting in this plush office and these big white guys, one a billionaire and the other is rich, so I said, "You pay me until I'm re-employed. If you don't want to do that, fire me." They looked at each other, they went out and they came back and said, "Agreed." I thought "Damn, I sure have guts to do that, for a black boy to tell them 'you pay me or you fire me,' and they did it." Some people in the community said, "I know you were slick." I was still riding around in my Lincoln with my Afghan hounddog and still living my same life styles.

Were you still getting paid?

Getting paid, but they didn't know I was getting paid and the *Afro-American* newspaper called me and they wanted a statement. I said, "I have no statement, if you want a statement, call the station." So they called the station and it came out in the newspaper. When they asked them was I involved in the payola, they said, "Not to our knowledge. As far as we know he's as clean as a hound's tooth." I'm quoting, that's what they said. But it was never known that they were paying me. About three months later, I had a call from Philadelphia and they asked me if I knew of any DJs, they needed a DJ, could I recommend one and I named them two guys that I thought might be interested and I gave them the numbers. I told them how to contact them. I didn't name myself. Then they said, "Well, what are you doing?" I said, "Well, I'm not doing anything right now, just tending to a few little, small things." "Would you be interested?" and I said, "Maybe." "Would you like to come up and talk about it?" So I went up to talk about it and they were in the market for me. Well, you see if you are a black man, you have to be kind of sharp. See when they called and asked for jockeys I wasn't going to say, "Well, I'm ready, here I am." But I had it in the back of my head that they were calling for me and here's how I knew they wanted me. We negotiated the money, the salary, and I told them what I would come there for. They said, "Well, I'll tell you what, we'll pay you the same thing that WITH was paying you." They knew what I was making in WITH, so they had been talking. They had been talking with WITH and WHAT needed somebody and WITH was still paying me for nothing, so I'm getting off their back, going with WHAT. They're selling me, telling how great I was and all that. So then I said, "Oh, you'll pay me the same thing that WITH paid me. OK, I'll tell you what I'll do. If I don't bring your ratings up in three months, let's call it quits." They went out of the office and talked and came back in and said they agreed. My ratings beat those of the morning man at WDAS radio station (in Philadelphia). And they came with the money I wanted and paid me in retrospect, you know for the weeks I'd been there, brought all that up to that so that's how I got to Philadelphia.

So how did I get to New York? A guy named Jack Bart, program director at WWRL, called me up and told me he wanted to come down and talk to me. We made a deal to work at WWRL in New York. And then I had a call back from Baltimore, another station WWIN, but Jocko was doing a tape show there. My base at that time was Philadelphia.

Was that radio station WHAT?

Yeah, WHAT during the morning, doing the morning show. Doing an evening show in New York at WWRL. WINN back in Baltimore wanted me to do a tape show and they had Jocko on doing a tape show, so I said "Well, I'm not going to do it. I'll do it but not if you are going to have Jocko, Doug Henderson, on doing my show and me too." So they dropped Jocko and gave it to me. So that went on for a while.

Now on a word about first in commuting. In Baltimore way back in the 50s, I rode a jackass while wearing a high black hat and tails, patent leather pumps, white pig skin gloves, a zebra saddle and this is how I rode into a big arena with black and white folks. This jackass carried me straight through this audience, had to have police to lead me and the jackass on to the stage. In Baltimore, I used to have an annual affair at Cars Beach on the Chesapeake Bay and I used to come in there in a space suit, by helicopter, and come down and land on the pier. Sometimes I would come in on a yacht with girls representing the eight planets of our solar system, and come in with fireworks announcing my coming in at night and then when I land, a big explosion would go off over the bay. *Jet* magazine printed all that kind of stuff. They had me in several stories.

What were you doing during the riots in Baltimore?

They just did a documentary on that in Baltimore. They had me on Channel 13. What I was doing was trying to quiet the town, I was trying to quiet the city, that's what I was doing.

Did somebody ask you to do that? How did it come about?

Yeah, they called; I mean, somebody called.

The Mayor's office?

It was higher than the mayor, it was from the state. The government was all involved and, in fact, I went down there. I could get through, and I talked to the people, trying to sober them up because people had gone mad. So that's basically what I did, I mean I think many jocks did that all over the country.

How do you feel about formats?

Well, I just think it killed black radio. I think it killed it.

That's a powerful statement. Could you elaborate?

Well, when they started to format it took out the flexibility that DJs had. It disallowed them the opportunity to be creative. In disallowing them that, it took out the culture, in my opinion, of black radio. You see, just a few words mean a whole lot.

Do you think it had anything to do with payola? That is, if you have a format you have less opportunity for payola?

No, I don't think that because, you see, they came out with rules that all disc jockeys had to sign, statements that "I will not accept payola." Later on the plugola came in, "I will not participate in payola nor plugola." So every disc jockey, when he takes a job, still has to sign that form.

You say "plugola." What does that mean?

There used to be a time when some disc jockeys would throw a little plug for a guy on the air. "I went down to Johnny's Steak House the other night and, man, I had a fantastic steak in Johnny's Steak House and they treated me royally" . . . that's plugola. "Plugola" is announcing a business or service without the radio station being paid for it. But the guy who made the announcement could have gotten paid under the table. They can get free dinners, they can get a few bucks because they got a little plug.

How do you think black radio has changed since you first started?

It has changed for the worse, I mean basically based on what I said. Music seems to be the star of radio now. There is nothing, they have little ways of doing community services which involve the station. A lot of stations do promotions, which is good for these days but it doesn't hit the heart of things. It doesn't hit nerves. I mean that is something that came about from somebody else, it didn't come from the station. The station is participating in something, you understand, but when you originate something or you are the beginning of something, then you stand out. If you start a particular drive, then it's you but when you are doing certain things that all the other stations also do, for example, the Negro College Fund. All the stations get in on that. But if I wanted to do something individually, by myself, and say, "Well, I'm going to do this for the Negro College Fund," you probably won't find that.

If you had a free hand to change something about black radio today, what would it be?

I would give disc jockeys more flexibility. I would get good jocks that I thought had a gift of gab and could speak well but yet be fun and serious. He is the type of guy who can be funny and the audience knows he's being funny or the audience knows when he's serious about something. That, to me, is the epitome of being a good jock; when you can have such a love affair with your audience that you laugh together and then you settle down and be serious together.

Have the experiences of black females in black radio been significantly different than those of black males?

There weren't too many black girls in my day; Martha Jean was an exception. There are some exceptions but today they are the same thing as the other guys, on the same track with the black DJs, they are the same format. You had girls like Martha Jean, like Mary Mason in Philadelphia, Mary Dee out of Pittsburgh, Novella who was out of Texas somewhere, and a lot of girls I probably don't even know that was into things like we were into things. They would get on things that were very, very important, that touched nerves in the communities, but not today, unless it's a talk show or something like that.

NOTE

1. Plugola is the illegal practice of including material in a program for the purpose of covertly advertising or promoting a product without disclosing that payment was made.

◆ 10 ◆

Al Jefferson

Al Jefferson was born in 1919 in Baltimore, Maryland. He attended the public schools in that city and graduated from Douglass High School in 1937. Jefferson's radio career began at WMID in Atlantic City, New Jersey.

After several years as an annoucer at WMID, Jefferson was hired at WOOK-AM in Washington, D.C., in 1955. He worked at WOOK until 1963. In that year, Jefferson landed a job as a disc jockey at WWIN in his hometown of Baltimore. He was an on-air personality at WWIN for several years, and he eventually became the program director at the station, when Larry Dean Faulkner left that position.

Jefferson was known for his "ear" and ability to pick hit records. Among the many hits he broke were Aretha Franklin's "RESPECT" and the Dells "Oh What a Night."

JUNE 17, 1991

How and when did you get started in radio?

I got started in radio in 1952 in Atlantic City. A fellow there had a radio show called "The Young Fellow Show." His name was Thomas Young. He called himself the Young Fellow and the Young Fellow Show. I was working in Atlantic City doing the usual things that everybody had to do in Atlanta City at that time, working in a hotel. I lived in the hotel that Young's girlfriend managed so he used to come by quite often and once during a summer month he was looking for somebody to take his show for a couple of weeks while he took a vacation, so I just jokingly said that I would do it but I didn't think anything would come of it. He asked me to come down to the station and audition. So I said, "Well, OK, what's to lose," and I thought I'd just take a shot at it and see what happened. He had it arranged when he took me down to the station for an audition. I thought I was just going to sit there and get a voice test and see if I could read copy and stuff like that. I didn't know too much about radio at the time. When we got to the station he put me right on the air with him so it was a very frightening experience in the sense that I'd never been on the air before. I got on the air with him and we did a two-man show. We talked a little bit and played a couple records. He only had 15 minutes. After that he started getting some phone calls, "Who's that guy you had on with you?" "I like his voice," and so forth and so on. He decided, from the reaction that he'd gotten from the audience that night, to let me try his show until he got back from vacation. It was a unique experience for me because I'd never had to pull records, read copy, or anything like that, but I guess it was just something that God had directed my way and I did it pretty well. My selection of music was a little different from his because he was an old-timer and he didn't know too much about the things that were happening at that time record-wise. He used to play a lot of blues so when I came on the show I started to bring some of the more up-to-date things and in 15 minutes you've only got time for about a couple of records and a couple of commercials and then you're gone. But anyway, when he came back everybody was talking about how well I had done and so he asked me would I stay on with him and so I said "sure." No pay involved, just experience.

Would you tell me the extent of your schooling?

I just had a good education as far as public school was concerned. I was a high-school graduate. I graduated from Douglass High School in Baltimore in 1937. I had a pretty good voice and I used to sing a lot and stuff like that and I said, "Well, maybe I should get into radio," but I never really seriously intended to do it. Sometimes I would cut ads out of the paper and I would practice at home but I was just fooling around with it. I stayed with Youngs for about two years doing a two-man show every night. It gradually built up from 15 minutes to where we were on the air at least two hours a night. As I told you, Youngs didn't know too much about the music so I'd pull all the music and this guy was amazing in that he was practically an illiterate, he couldn't read and he could just barely write.

Was he a black man?

Yes, but he had the desire to do this and, of course, his grammar wasn't the best, being illiterate. There were people who would buy time on our show who wouldn't want him to do the commercial because Tom couldn't read so he would ad-lib the commercials. Some sponsors would ask that the commercials be read, well he couldn't read so I'd handle those.

What were the call letters?

The call letters at the station at that time were WMID in Atlantic City. We made a two-year run of it and we had a segment in the show where he'd do some gospel music. I would let him do that because that was his, quote, unquote "strong point."

Did you ever have to brokerage time yourself? Did you have to buy time to get on the air?

Yeah, we had to buy time. We used to go out and sell spots in the daytime and, of course, that would legitimize our being on the air at night. So we would sell time.

Your show was sold out in terms of sponsors?

From Memorial Day until Labor Day. That was Atlantic City's season. After Labor Day everything would shut down. Everybody went home. The businesses closed up, so you had to make it in those couple of months, you know. After those two years another company opened up a station in Atlantic City and they approached me about coming over and doing my own show with them. But I said, "Well listen, this is a golden opportunity for me," so I decided to go with this new company, which was WJLB, owned by Darcy and William Bremmer, I think. When I started with them, of course, it didn't leave a very good taste in the guy's mouth who I was leaving because I was now a competitor, so he began to bad-mouth me.

Weren't you under a contract then?

No, no contract. We just had a handshake you know. We were just good buddies. But after I decided to go for myself, it created a little animosity between the two of us but it wasn't that important and I did pretty well at this new station with my own show. I had a 2-hour show every night and it got to be pretty popular; I had a mixture of the pop tunes and some jazz.

Did you choose your own records?

Yeah, I had the choice of what I wanted to play but the irony of it was that was no library there at either station for black music. We had to pick up our records from a record store. We, in turn, would give the record store a plug for using their records.

Were promoters coming by to see you at that time?

Promotion was out of the question. The promotion men were in Philadelphia, who's going to come all the way to Atlantic City? They didn't consider that market important enough to promote any records, so we had to get most of our stuff from record stores. If you damaged or scratched a record, then that was your record, you'd have to buy it. It was a very strange situation as far as getting the music was concerned. That went on for a couple of years with me doing an independent show on WJLB. Then one day an engineer from Washington, D.C., was in Atlantic City vacationing and he heard me on the air and he said, "Where are you located?" I told him where we were located. So he said "Well, I'm coming on down" so I said "OK." He was black too, a black engineer, and he came down and said, "So this is what your operation looks like. Man, you sound good. How would you like to come to Washington?" I immediately said, "Hey, I'm really getting into the big time now if this happens." So he said, "Well, make me a tape and I'll take it back to Washington and we'll get in touch with you and we'll see what happens." So I made up a tape, just to give him an example of how I handle commercials, introduce the records, close down the records, open the show, and how I close the show—just bits and pieces of the show. He took the tape back to Washington. In about a couple of weeks the guy called me and said, "Hey man, we would like to have you come to Washington and get on the station with us."

Now the station that they were talking about at the time was here in Washington and was owned by Richard Eaton. Richard Eaton, at that time, owned about five or six different stations and this station in Washington was called WOOK. It was 1400 AM at the time. So I came down and got to be a member of a staff that included Cliff Holland, the morning man, Thelma Green, who was the gospel lady, and Tex Gathing, who handled all the jazz. Tex was something of a snob and he wouldn't think about playing B.B. King, blues and all that kind of thing. He played jazz. He would sit in on a show if he had to but he wouldn't be happy about it. There were a couple other guys, including Al Clark. So I came down and joined their staff and immediately they put me on the air and in those days you put in a lot of time on the air, as much as forty-eight hours a week.

Your shift would be for about five hours?

I would come on in the morning after Cliff Holland. He was on from 6 to 10 a.m. Then we had split shifts too. I would come on at 10 o'clock and stay on the air until 12. I would go off at 12 and Thelma Green would come on and do gospels from 12 to 2. Cliff Holland would come back at 2 and he'd stay on until 6. I would come back on at 6 and stay until closing down time and at that time we had a daytime license that we had to be off the air at 2 o'clock in the morning, so that is the way that went. Cliff Holland was considered the program director. There wasn't a whole lot of program directing to do because the station pretty much operated by itself. There was not a lot of discipline, we didn't have to worry about formats. No such thing as a format. You came on the air, you brought your own records and you did what you wanted to do. There was no set stops and things like that, you just got on the air and you did commercials and you played records until your time was up.

You could open the mike and chat and talk when you felt like it?

Yeah, you could open the mike.

Your personality, you could express yourself?

If you had a personality you could use it. At that time this station was the only black station in the market. So, you can understand that we were loaded with commercials. You had to get the commercials in. You could select your own records and stuff like that. It gave you a chance to build your personality in that you had freedom of expression. I got the job on WOOK in 1955 and I stayed there until 1963.

Did the payola scandal affect your career at all?

No, it didn't. In fact the payola didn't really surface until after I had left WOOK. I developed a teen show on Saturdays for young people that we called "Teen-o-rama." The young people would come in on Saturday and I would assign certain duties to each young person. There was a young guy named Calvin Hackett who really wanted to get into radio and he had the talent for it, so I made him the announcer for the two-hour show. I had another young guy who would do sports. A little teenage girl would do social events and stuff like that. It was a show made up with the young people.

Where was WOOK located?

We were located at 8th and I streets, North West. That young fellow that I selected to be the announcer on the teen show, Calvin Hackett, he went on to be a pretty good announcer and he cut out quite a career for himself. When I left WOOK, he took my slot. Luckily for me, anywhere you put me I could make it go because I was pretty well rounded music-wise. At one time on this station I did not only the current popular things, but also gospel and jazz. I was doing a jazz show and called it "Jazz after Midnight." It was one of the most popular shows in Washington. I used to have cab drivers and the all-night people and the post office people and everybody tuned in. The cab drivers would come by and bring doughnuts and coffee and stuff like that. It was one of the best shows that ever originated out of that station, but you know in young radio at that time all black guys had problems with making money. We just didn't make any money. I think I was making about $70 a week and putting in all that time. It was worth it for me from the standpoint that it opened up an avenue for me to do something else besides being a porter or something. I just stuck with it because in those days you could do a lot more with $70 than you can now. I got married in the meantime and we were raising a family so it wasn't easy.

At that time, was Washington a segregated city?

Very segregated. You couldn't go downtown to the theaters or to the restaurants, you couldn't shop in the downtown department stores. The blacks had their own theaters and their own stores and whatnot, you know, and they were basically owned by whites, Jews or whatnots.

Were you on the air when the March on Washington took place?

I was on the air but I wasn't working in Washington. I had moved to Baltimore then and I was on WWIN in Baltimore. That was quite an eventful day when the march took place and I was also in Baltimore when the riots broke out.

How did you deal with that, being a radio personality?

Well, when the riots broke out here in Washington I was working in Baltimore, but the riots at that time were contagious. It started here in Washington and then the riots broke out in Baltimore so the powers that be enlisted the disc jockeys'aid because black jockeys were very influential at that time. We were to come into the black community and try to tramp down the blazes. So we did that in Baltimore, we went on Pennsylvania Avenue, the main black belt, and we tried to get involved with the guys who were causing the problems and tried to get them to cool it because they were doing the same thing in Baltimore that they did here in Washington. They destroyed their own businesses but didn't do anything to the people who had caused them the problems.

Were you successful in getting them to listen to you?

Well, I think we did help to some degree. Black jockeys were very popular, they were more popular then than they are now. People just felt that they knew us as friends. People used to tell me in Baltimore, "I always know when you are on the air because every radio on my block, the volume goes up, and when you go off the volume goes down." So it was a very personal thing that we had with the listeners, and we would get out and we would do hops and we would emcee shows and stuff like that and people would get to know us like that. It was just great for the kids to walk up to you and say, "Hi, Al Jefferson, how are you?" and talk to you and touch you and get a relationship with you. They would write you letters requesting songs and stuff like that and I very diligently tried to answer all the requests that I could and I would elaborate on the records and stuff like that. That sort of one-on-one relationship, even though you were talking to thousands of people, a lot of people just felt like you were just talking directly to them.

The best part of my career was in Baltimore. I started in Baltimore in 1963 and I stayed on the air until 1977. During that time WWIN began to grow as a monster station because the general manager was able to get out and recruit some of the top jockeys in the area. At one time, Fat Daddy was on WWIN. His real name was Paul Johnson. He came up out of West Virginia and tore the town up for a while. Rocking Robin was on the air, Hot Rod was on the air; you know, these guys were giants. Back to back you had some of the greatest black personalities in radio on one station so the station just knocked out everybody. WBAL was carrying baseball at the time that we were there and we even beat them at night, and Baltimore is a baseball town. So WWIN ended up being what WOOK used to be in Washington. It was the giant, but then as will happen in all things, and especially in radio, after a while you peak and then the management gets a little antsy about the personalities and whatnot and it feels like the formats ought to be changed and all that kind of stuff. So gradually they just slipped away from their prominent position in Baltimore and now it's just another station. Some of our personalities moved on. Fat Daddy got a job with Motown Records and he left us. Hot Rod was about the oldest guy on the station. He still had that reputation of being a hot personality because a lot of jocks who came on the air after Hot Rod got on the air were imitating him. He was a very influential jock but mechanically he was not good and so the records would run out on him and he never was ready. He'd have to ad-lib and say a whole lot of dumb stuff trying to get ready. He would not stay on the microphone, he would be all over the studios trying to find something and it got so bad that eventually we put a lavaliere mike on him and hung it around his neck so that anywhere he went he would be on the air. So in other words, radio outgrew him because after a while radio got to be formatted and you had to do this at a certain time, a time check here and a weather cast there and so forth. You had to follow the format and he couldn't follow a format because he was so used to freelancing and ad-libbing; therefore, he was no longer an asset because people began to notice how ragged his show was. The ratings began to slide and when the ratings slide the management gets panicky, and then they want to make changes. So they began to bring in people that they thought would boost the station's ratings and bring it back to its former prominence. I was the program director there so there were a lot of things that I disagreed on with management.

Were you kind of forced to go along with them because you were outvoted by the general manager and sales manager and other folks?

Well, you could say that I had to go along with it if I wanted to stay there, because they even talked about cutting my time. That was in 1977, so I said, "Well, listen, I see the way you are going, I see the youth movement coming in," you know, because they were going out and getting young guys and bringing them in. But I had brought a lot of young guys in who are still on the radio today. At least I got credit for bringing in some people who were very stable and who really had brought something to radio.

Could you name any?

Don Brooks who is now the operations manager of WWIN, Lee Cross, a white kid that I selected, is still there at the station. I brought in Anthony Davis. He was a young kid just out of Morgan and he had a very soft, romantic approach to the things that he did on the air. This kid came on the air and he upset the town, especially the women. The management couldn't understand what he was doing and wanted to fire him. I said, "No, listen, you don't know what this kid is doing. You don't understand this kid. You're white and he's black and he's coming at the audience from an angle that you'll never be able to understand. Leave this kid on." This kid was beating WBAL with baseball at night. I look back on them and I say, "Well, I did make a contribution." Don Brooks right now is one of the most astute radio programmers and managers that I think you will find anywhere.

Was he on WEEB for a while?

He was on WEEB for a while, he went up there as a general manager and stayed until WWIN called him back to take over the general managership and right now he's the operations manager of the station. He is very talented.

What was your relationship with record companies?

My relationship to the record companies was the best. I didn't get into payola but I had an integrity about what I did with record companies. Atlantic Records were big at the time and there were a lot of companies that were big at the time.

Did Atlantic have Aretha Franklin at the time?

Yeah and I'm going to tell you about Aretha Franklin. Aretha had just switched over from Columbia to Atlantic at the time because Columbia had her singing stuff that just wasn't her forte. Jerry Wexler, who was one of the vice presidents of Atlantic, took her under his wing and produced her. They sent me a copy of the first album. I was listening to it and one track in that LP was "Respect." When I heard that I said, "Oh my Lord, this is a smash!" I got on the phone and I called Henry Allen, who at that time was the top black in Atlantic Records. I said, "Henry, you got a smash single in this album and it's called 'Respect'." He said, "You think so?" I said, "Yeah," he said, "OK, tell you what we'll do. We're going to have some singles made up on the strength of what you said." And that record jumped off and Aretha has never looked back. But that was a relationship with jockeys and record companies.

Of course the payola things did finally get into it but I never got caught up into it but I had a lot of guys who appreciated what I did for them and they would invite me and my wife to New York and they'd provide us with hotels, food, shows, stuff like that. That was just good business. I built up quite a reputation with the record companies in that I had an unusual ear. I could really hear a hit and if Al Jefferson called you, you better get on that record because that was a smash.

Did you break Otis Redding?

We broke Redding. Of course, his "Dock of the Bay" was his monster. I was the guy that broke the Dells' "Oh What a Night." I was in Washington at the time and we'd been doing the "Teen-o-rama" show and in the course of the show we would bring in about two or three records that we thought would be hits and we would get the kids to judge them. They would listen to the record and they would tell me on the air why they liked the record and whatnot. So one of the three records that I brought in one night was "Oh What a Night" by the Dells. The kids heard the record and said they liked that record and went on to tell me why. So if the kids picked the record then I would play it for a week every day. At the end of the week the Dells were a smash. They came to Washington for the first time, as a group, and appeared on the Howard Theatre Stage and they were just five frightened, little kids that didn't even know how to conduct themselves on the stage. They only had that one record, "Oh What a Night," and they came out and sang that and got off.

Where were they from?

They were from Chicago. When they came back the next time, they had really polished up their act. They had the steps, they had the choreography, they had everything.

Did you promote them? Did you bring them in for that show?

In a way I promoted them because I was always tied into the fact that the record broke on "Teen-o-rama." The kids just loved them and, man, when they came back the second time they had it together, man. They were so polished. So now these guys consider me like their adopted father. So they were in town last week because, you know, they just did this movie with Robert Townsend.

Was that movie called "Five Heart Beats"?

Yeah. They had the background, the story should really be about them. They called it "The Five Heart Beats" but they are doing all of the music. All my kids know them, and so my oldest daughter, she got through to Marvin, the lead singer, who was on a talk show. Marvin said, "This sounds like somebody that should be a disc jockey." She said, "It's funny you should say that. My father is Al Jefferson." And he said, "Whaaat? How you doing?" And so they talked on and he said, "Tell your father that we're going to call him today. We've got to do some record promotion but we're going to call him." So they were going around station to station like you have to do. At about 1 o'clock in the afternoon Marvin called me, so we talked. I've got a project that I want them to do because God has been good to these guys. I've become a Christian in the last four or five years and I just feel that they should give something back, not only to the people, but to God because everything belongs to him and their talent belongs to him. I have an idea for a religious album that I want them to do. The Dells have signed a contract with them so Gamble and Huff are going to be recording them. So I left a call with Kenny Gamble to call me because that is what I want to talk to Kenny about. In the meantime, Gamble's right-hand man, Harry Coombs, called me last week and I went on to explain what I thought would be a fantastic album for the Dells to do. He said "OK, would you be interested in selecting the hymns?" I said, "Sure, I would." So it looks like I might be a step closer to getting the Dells to do that now that they are with Gamble and Huff.

Now, in terms of black radio, is it better or worse today than it was in 1955?

Well, when I first got on the air, black guys on the air were a novelty in that they brought something completely and entirely different to the business of broadcasting. They brought their blackness which was not prohibited at the time and they brought their personalities, which is different from a white man's personality. The selection of music was relevant because they played things that blacks could relate to. They were playing B.B. King, the Clovers, the Flamingos and the Dells and blacks could relate to that. So they were very unique personalities and you had to be pretty bad not to get over as a black announcer or a black jockey or black personality because at that time you had Georgie Woods (WDAS of Philadelphia), the guy with the goods. You had Al Benson in Chicago, who was a monster; you had TV Whitfield, he called himself the only TV on radio . . . he was in Baltimore and worked with us for a while. You had Rocking Robin, who was a big, fat 250-pound dude who upset Baltimore for a while. He used to sign off with the phrase, "Hold on, hold on to what you got until you get what you want," and boy people just loved it. Black personalities were unique and were different and some of them even built up a following with white kids. Fat Daddy, boy, he was tremendous in Baltimore. He built up a big following with white kids. I had a white kid write me a letter some years ago telling me how much he enjoyed listening to me and how I influenced him in his music choice and stuff like that and then he got into playing black music. So you know the black personality crossed over. . . .

In your opinion, was the crossover movement good or bad?

I don't think it was bad because in a way we were ambassadors of good will and we were trying to alleviate a lot of the racism. Now, the older white people in their conservatism and whatnot, they never did cotton to what a black man did on the radio but it influenced the younger white kids. I don't know if it was good or bad and right now it's not important because black stations are not influential, at least in this market, like they used to be. I'll tell you what it did do, it opened up the pocketbooks for the black personalities that came along after this. We got a guy on WKYS in Washington now that is making more money than we ever dreamed we could make. I think he's got a contract that gives him a million five a year. His name is Donnie Simpson.

Was that more than Melvin Lindsay made?

Oh sure. But Melvin made a lot of money. Melvin went to work for the same company that Donnie Simpson was working for and they gave him a nice chunk of change, but he wasn't making that kind of money. And it's amazing that these guys make this kind of money because they are not the equivalent to what we were because we were personalities, we were combo men, we worked hard. When you do four, five, or six hours of what we used to do, you were drained when your time was up because you had to stay on top of your commercials. A lot of the commercials weren't on cartridges like they are now where you just slap them in the machine and hit a button. A lot of the commercials were on big discs and some of those discs had any number of cuts on them and certain things had to be played at a certain time. Certain cuts had to be played on a certain day.

Did you have an engineer with you?

No, we were combo men. We were our own engineers. We sat there between two turntables and the microphone and we did what engineers of a lot of stations do now. A lot of guys just go in and sit there and talk and the engineer plays the records and everything. We did it all. It wasn't easy but we were pioneers and we opened up the way for a lot of these kids today that don't even know what being a combo man is. I would get off the air on Friday night, do a record hop in Baltimore, and have to drive home. The record hop didn't shut down until 2 o'clock in the morning; then I would go back down to the station and get my record list ready for the new week. Then I would finish that up and then drive home. I'd get home maybe about 3 or 4 in the morning, get some sleep and get up and get back in my car and drive back to work for the next day. I was making about $125 a week which was a big deal.

Why do you think black radio is not as influential today as it was in the past?

Because it has lost its identity. You can't tell a black station from a white station.

Do you feel that is a result of crossover music?

That would have something to do with it because you got your singers today who not only record black material but they are aiming at the white market. Whitney Houston records black but her music and the record companies carry it to the pop side. So the music, I'm sure, has a lot to do with it because the black stations are playing what the white stations play and the white stations are playing what the black stations play.

What about the personalities themselves?

I don't know too much about the personalities.

No, I mean, you said with the black, the identity thing is a problem in terms of strength. Do you see black announcers basically sounding the same as all other announcers?

I know what you're saying. Well I'll tell you, the invention of formats hurt the black announcer because you can no longer be yourself. It destroyed the black personality. If you've only got two or three seconds to do this or to do that, or if the format calls for it you give a time check and you know you want to do something else but you've got to give a time check because the format says time check, there is no room for your personality. I fault the black stations for not holding on to their individuality. The white stations started formatting so the black stations followed and they should have never done that because their strength was in their freedom.

Is deejaying something like a performance?

It's a performance. It's show biz and if you begin to feel what you're doing, your audience is feeling what you're doing. And your next record, if the next record that you select hits you a certain way, that record hits that audience a certain way. I have an expression I used to use when I'd play a record that was kind of gospel-oriented. I would say "yeaa" like the people do in church, like break in over the record and do that. A girl wrote me a letter one time, I don't know what I was playing and I used that expression, and she said, "I had to pull my car over to the side and cry." That sort of thing, but you don't have that anymore because of the formats, and by black stations following the formats, by the black stations being basically in white hands, they just changed the color of what black stations were doing.

If you had a free hand and you could change things to the way that you wanted them for black radio, what would you do?

In the first place you have to have a general manager in your corner because there is a chain of authority. The president of the station is over the general manager, the station general manager is over the program director, and so forth and so on. So a program director has to have a general manager who will give him a free rein to do whatever he thinks is right. A program director has to have a general manager who is willing to take a beating for six months while a format is changed or an approach to broadcasting is changed. You've got to have that sort of thing because everybody is number-oriented now and you know a station changes its format if it doesn't show huge numbers when the first book comes out. The general manager gets shook up. Guys start losing their jobs and all that sort of thing.

But if I went back on the air as, say a program director, I would go back to the old free-flow, freelance format. I would find me some strong personalities and put them on the air and say, "Hey, go fellows, we'll see how it goes." But my general manager would have to go along with that and you ain't going to find no general manager today that is going to do that. It's because of what radio has become, very competitive. You've got twenty-two stations in this one market alone and everybody is trying to be #1. Everybody can't be #1. I guess there are some people that listen to radio religiously but television has taken over and radio is not what it used to be. Radio used to be a complete entertainment entity. You could be entertained, you could be educated, you could be informed. I have a radio in my home but I haven't listened to a black station since I quit promoting records. I don't listen to them anymore because there is nothing to listen to. They're all playing the same. WOOK, they had changed their call letters a number of times. They are called WJZM or something like that now, they are playing jazz. They have tried everything, they have tried all kinds of formats and nothing has worked. They are still buried in the book. So I don't know what they are going to do next.

I told the operation manager who is a good friend of mine, "You guys have tried everything else, you might as well try Jesus." I feel that he could operate a very successful religious station because he is a born-again Christian. WKYS ends up being four, five, or six and if they end up three, four, or five, that is considered a good book for them.

Is WHUR leading in the market?

No. WHUR has taken a terrible beating. They have changed personalities; Bledsoe has gone; Bobby Bennett, the program director, is gone; they have had wholesale changes there. They are trying to struggle back. Joe Gorem, the all-night man, is gone. I don't know what they are looking for but it's just typical of what happens to black stations.

If you had to identify one act that really says who Al Jefferson is, in terms of your work in black radio, what would that be for you?

Integrity. One word, you know, I never made promises that I couldn't keep. I tried to manage a station, not from a standpoint of being a hard-nose but I invited input from everybody in the station. You've got talented people working under you, why not delegate authority and stuff like that? You know you can tell when it's getting out of line, you can tell when you got a runaway horse, you know when to rein him in or fire him if you have to. I never fired too many people in the whole time that I was in a management position in radio but there were times when I had to kick a guy out. Integrity, I think. You know, not getting caught up in who you are but trying to realize what you are and trying to make a contribution so that you not only help yourself, your station, but you help your community. We used to have toy drives and food drives and stuff like that. I guess they do it today but . . . the humanity is not in them. They just do it as something to do to build up their ratings but we did it to help out our community. It helped make WWIN the monster station that it was because it represented something, not only to the young but to the old people. We would be invited out to give commencement speeches and stuff like that. They wouldn't ask an educator or somebody else to make the speech, they would ask the disc jockeys to come by and speak to them at commencement time. I've done several of those things.

When was the last time that you heard of a disc jockey being asked to come out to school to give a commencement speech in Washington, D.C.?

It's been a long time since I heard of a disc jockey coming out to do anything, even on a program where he appears as a personality to maybe give out free records or stuff like that. Disc jockeys are happy to be cut off like that from the community. They get in their little cubicle and that's their world and that's all they want to do. There is no commitment to the community outside, so as a result of that the community has no commitment to them.

◆ 11 ◆

Tom Joyner

Tom Joyner's career in radio began when he was a student at Tuske-gee Institute in Alabama, where he was an announcer for the universi-ty's radio station. After graduation, Joyner worked for WMRA in Montgomery, Alabama. From there, he landed an announcing job at WLOK in Memphis, Tennessee and later, Joyner worked briefly in St. Louis, Missouri before finding work at Dallas' KKDA. Later, he worked for WJPC, which was owned by John H. Johnson, publisher of Ebony and Jet magazines.

Joyner credits Johnson with promoting his career and helping him achieve greatness. For instance, Joyner has said that Johnson boosted his career by putting his photograph in Jet magazine and getting him in a commercial with Muhammad Ali.

Joyner left WJPC to take an announcing job at Chicago's WGCI-FM. At the same time, he was also working for Dallas station KKDA-FM. For six years, he commuted 1,600 miles three days a week between Chi-cago and Dallas.

Joyner is known for his quick wit and strong on-air presence. He had helped local communities by highlighting discriminatory practices in his broadcasts. In Dallas, for example, he alerted listeners to speed traps that targeted African-American drivers.

OCTOBER 5, 1991

Would you tell me how you got started in radio?

I got started in radio by accident. I was a sociology major in school; I went to Tuskegee, which is south of my home. I was involved with the student government while in school and my responsibilities included booking shows for the campus, like homecoming and things like that. I was down at the local radio station, which was Montgomery, because we didn't have one in Tuskegee. Montgomery is like forty miles away.

So I was down at the radio station on occasion to advertise my different shows and I met and befriended some of the guys down there. After I graduated from school I didn't have a job for about six months. One day a guy named Tracy Watkin who was programming WRMA in Montgomery asked if I wanted to do news at the station because I had voiced the commercials.

Had you had any formal training in terms of your voice?

No. I did the announcing at the football and basketball games. Most of the guys I went to school with remember me best from the cafeteria because while the meals were being served my job was to play music and make announcements.

This was at Tuskegee?

Yes, it sounds like the cafeteria DJ. It was nothing like what I'm doing now and I always got a lot of complaints. People were complaining about what I was playing or what I was saying. It wasn't morning drive. It wasn't anything very serious so I basically had fun with it. I got a little reputation as being the cafeteria DJ, and then at the different games I didn't exactly straight announce it either.

From time to time I'd get a little loose. One time I got ejected from a basketball game for saying something to the effect that the referee couldn't see. And he ejected me from the game. That went over pretty good because that made me kind of a hero. I was the crowd announcer. And also, Tuskegee is a very unusual town. The town is practically all black but during this time the economic situation was that the whites controlled all the businesses, commerce in the town, even though the town had to be nine or ten black to one white. And this was after the Montgomery bus boycott and all of that. There were two boycotts going on. The Montgomery boycott got all the publicity but there was the Tuskegee boycott as well, where the residents of my town refused to shop in the town and took their business to either Montgomery or Columbus, Georgia, which were both about forty miles away. For some reason, these white businesses survived, including a radio station. And the radio station did not play black music, it played "easy-listening" music, you know, like elevator music. These were the protest years. I mean, we protested every weekend for something, mostly voter registration but that was like the thing to do, "Hey man, what you going to do today? It's Saturday, I'm going to go down here to this protest."

It was exciting, it was a social event. So one day we decided we were going to protest the radio station. We were tired of the radio station not playing any black music and so we protested. If it wasn't voter registration, we always found something to protest for, integrate something; integrate a church one weekend or integrate a school or, you know, and this day it was the radio station. Well, I don't know how many weekends we were out there protesting but they gave in. As a result they said, "OK, you guys can play your music on this daytime radio station from noon to sign-off on Saturdays." I said, "All right, I'll do it, since I'm the cafeteria DJ and most qualified for the job."

Were you paid for doing this?

Did I get paid? No.

Did you have your own records?

Oh yeah, I had to get my own records. I had to get my own records but I got my records from the Record Shop. There were only two record shops in town. I got my records from the Record Shop and I was allowed to plug the shop so that's how I got the music, which was the deal at the cafeteria anyway. I played the music and would say, "You can get this music at the Holland's Record Shop," like there was another place you could get it. The only other way you could get music in my town was if you'd go to Montgomery or Columbus or on occasion, Atlanta. The only other way you could do it was to order it from WLAC. So I got the afternoon show and I did that for, I guess, about a year every Saturday so that along with doing the spots, Tracy knew who I was and we became friends. He said, "Hey, you want to do news?" and I said, "Cool, I'm not working and I'm out of school," so I did news. I was paid $90 a week.

Was this at WMRA in Montgomery?

Yeah, and for $90 dollars a week. I could take care of all my expenses. I got real frustrated because although I was getting the news off the wire service and out of the newspaper, and little Pan-African newspapers and stuff—I was real militant back then—I wasn't getting the kind of attention that I was used to, like in the cafeteria or at the games. The militants knew what I was doing but you knew they were so few. A few militants would say, "Brother, you're doing a beautiful job," but the other folks, they didn't know who the heck I was.

So you moved into entertainment?

Well, not exactly. I started improvising on the newscasts a lot. Even to the point where when it was slow days and I couldn't find anything juicy to talk about, I'd just make up some stuff. My newscasts were not very creditable. I wanted attention and I just wasn't getting enough. So I found ways to juice it up. And also, I wanted to do more than just news because all of the fun was in the studio, you know DJs and stuff. They were the ones getting all the attention that I really wanted so whenever someone was sick or on vacation I worked my way into fill-in positions. I'd do the news and fill in whenever folks were not available. I was doing pretty good at that, plus on Saturdays I was still doing my thing at home. That lasted for about two years and then Tracy got an offer to go to Memphis, Tennessee. He didn't want the job and these people were looking for a whole new staff of DJs. So I put together a tape and sent it to a guy named Chris Turner who was programming WLOK, Memphis. They hired me and I said, "Cool, I'm out of here man, I've got me a full-time DJ job." So I packed, put everything I owned in the trunk . . .

What about your wife?

Put her in the trunk too (laughter). There was just me and her, no kids, so we moved to Memphis. At WLOK, it was a station with just one turmoil after another.

Who owned that station, Sonderling?

No, Sonderling owned the competition. This station at the time was owned by a guy named Dick Oppenheimer. And the station was always turning over their people; no sooner would they get a staff in and they'd be gone, for whatever reason. No one was lasting very long so I was part of a new crop, and I mean from the general manager on down, the station had turned over everybody and so I was doing midday and I was with a really good staff of DJs. The only DJs I had ever worked with were, of course, the ones in Montgomery, and although they were good, they didn't compare to these guys. These guys had a lot more experience than my guys did in Montgomery. My guys in Montgomery were all from Montgomery, never worked outside Montgomery, and these guys had worked at several stations around the country so this was pretty amazing to me. So I learned real fast, you know, tricks on how to make a show sound exciting and stuff and these guys were as close to pros as I'd ever seen. Well, six months later, another turmoil. They was firing everybody, including the general manager. Whole crop, it was weird; they could not keep their people, you know, they would turn over; some stations would have one person replaced, maybe a couple of people; no, here it would be from the general manager on down. There would be nothing left but the receptionist.

Was it a money thing? Was it sales?

I never knew. I was so young and naive and not really into the business of radio at the time. To tell you the honest to goodness truth, I don't know why that station just kept on, all I know was every six or eight months the whole staff would change. What was the deal with this one, I forget now but the whole thing changes, the general manager moved to St. Louis and I was the only one left there. So I was there for about a month and new people came in and the old general manager who had gone to St. Louis called and said he wanted me to come and work there and since I'd had so much fun with this guy, and with all these people turning over, it was kind of scary, so I said, "I'm going to St. Louis." So I went to St. Louis.

Wasn't that a much larger market?

Yeah, and the guys had told me, you know you want to move to a larger market and I worked at WKWK. And they were more screwed up than WLOK. I didn't know it until I got up there. You knew something was wrong because they paid you every week in cash. You'd sign a little receipt. This station was in big trouble financially, obviously. But it was a lot of fun. These guys were the most fun to work with that I've been with in any station. I thought I'd had a lot of fun with the guys in Montgomery, but these guys in St. Louis were truly wild. They didn't have nothing to care about. They got paid in cash and they got paid once a week, every Friday. And sometimes what would happen is they would get paid on a day which was my air shift, so everybody would show up to get their paycheck and leave and I'd be the only one at the station for hours and hours because everybody would leave and go party until somebody would finally come back and relieve me. A lot of times I was doing not only middays, but afternoons and evenings before anybody would show. But when they would show up I couldn't get mad because they'd show up right, you know, they'd bring me a little something.

Was it like a family kind of thing?

Yeah, it was. I didn't stay there long before I got another call from the station here in Dallas, from a guy named Chuck Smith. He's got kind of like a whispering voice and it was kind of eerie listening to him on the phone. Kind of like a Marlon Brando Godfather. "Hello . . . I was in St. Louis (mimicking Brando), would you like to come and work in Dallas?" I said "sure," because this station is about to go under any minute. He said, "Come on down, let's talk." So I went to Dallas and we talked. He wanted me to do a thing on morning drive at the AM station. They didn't have an FM at the time. KKBA. It was a day-timer and it was an amazing-sounding ratio station, it was clean, it was sharp, it was tight. It mostly resembled what I thought was the best-sounding radio station I'd ever heard at the time, which was WLS in Chicago. It most resembled that, but it was black, but it was just as tight, crisp and everything like WLS. So I said, "You want me to work at this station?" and he said, "Ya, I want you to do morning." So I got up the next morning and I listened to the morning guy who at the time was Bobby Elliott. Bobby was smooth! And that was really not me. I knew by listening to him that I was not nearly as good as he was and I said, "Why in the world would anybody want me when you've got this guy here?" The station had only been on the air a couple of years, kicking butt in the market because it was new and it was fresh and it sounded good and it had these clean-sounding DJs on there. But Chuck is a very different kind of guy, he's got visions that seem weird to most people. Bringing me in to replace Bobby Elliott, I'm going to tell you right now, made no sense at all. Not even to me, it didn't make no sense. That's what he wanted to do. It's not like Bobby had bad numbers, he had good numbers, but Chuck thought the numbers could be better.

The people liked him too?

Yeah. So they fired Bobby and put me on the air. Well, during that time you had two books a year and it wasn't Arbitron, it was Pulse. And so Pulse came out and my numbers were low and it looked like they was going to get rid of me; in fact, I knew they was going to get rid of me because I had heard from the guy who was going to replace me. They were going to replace me just like they replaced Bobby. But Chuck worked with me every day. I was obviously an experiment that he wanted to work. He was out to prove something to the man who owned the station that it could work. So he was in with me every morning, he was like my producer because these were the days when no one had a producer but he would coach me every step, every morning and we'd try different things, and lo and behold the Pulse came out and I was doing well and I stayed. This was in '72 and I did real well. I did some things that worked, some unusual things that got a lot of attention and as a result the attention turned into numbers.

Was it a contest or was it a personality-type thing?

No, we didn't have no big contest back then. Had no budget for that. It was personality stuff. One of the things that I did involved the police using radar and roadblock, especially in black neighborhoods. I don't know when police first started using radar guns, in Dallas it was in the early '70s, and they just went wild with the damn radar guns. They wrote tickets right and left and they got real creative with them, they had camouflage, they would be perched in trees and hiding in bushes and putting semi-tractor rigs on the side of the road, all kinds of stuff. And they was writing tickets until they had cramps in their fingers. And then they wrote so many damn tickets that about every couple of months they'd set up roadblocks and check your name off against a list of people who hadn't paid their tickets and they would only do this in the black community. They would set up these road blocks during morning drive, and they would set up a lot of radar during morning driving as well. It just got so ridiculous that we said, "All right, here's what we're going to do. Whenever you see a radar, you call me," we called it "Drop a dime on the man." At the time a phone call cost 10 cents. You call me, you tell me where the radar is and whatever I'm doing, I'm stopping. If I'm playing music, if I'm in a commercial, if we're doing news, just like the President got shot, I'm stopping. And I'm going to announce where the radar is. That got a lot of attention.

Didn't you get any flack from the law enforcement people?

Sure, but they couldn't do anything about it. They wanted to.

There was nothing illegal about it?

No. They tried, they tried to say I was interfering with police business and they couldn't make that stick. They tried to get the City Council to pass an ordinance and stuff like that and we got around it different ways because the station is not licensed for Dallas, it's licensed for Grand Prairie, which is outside of Dallas. It got a lot of attention, it got newspaper, TV and I played it to the hilt. When I did TV interviews, I had them show me in silhouette.

Is this how you were able to develop rapport with your audiences, how people came to love you?

It was things like that that worked for me, plus the coaching I got from Chuck. Chuck completely changed my style.

How was that?

Well, before I got there I was a loud, screaming, rhyming, chiming DJ. I wasn't the communicator that I am today. I didn't talk to people, I just talked. Chuck coached me and I changed all that. I was now a guy who talked to his audience on a one-on-one basis and that's basically my style. I basically do the same thing now as I did then or as I'm doing right now, talking to you.

Like when I hear you on "Count Down," it seems just like you are talking to me personally.

That's very intentional and that's all a result of Chuck's coaching, he taught me that. I changed, I made a 180 degrees, I completely changed.

◆ 12 ◆

Eddie O'Jay

Edward O. Jackson was born in Tennessee on November 30, 1930. His career as a radio announcer began in 1952 in Milwaukee, Wisconsin. He used a contraction of his middle initial and last name to create O'Jay as his on-air name. After a short stint in Milwaukee, O'Jay found work at radio station WABQ in Cleveland, Ohio, where he became the most popular disc jockey in the city. His popularity was so great that a local singing goup decided to name themselves after him. They called themselves "The O'Jays."

While at WABQ, O'Jay had a disagreement with a manager over attending a party given by Stroh Brewing Company. The manager said O'Jay could not attend the affair. He decided to go and was fired. It was not long, however, before he was hired by WUFO radio station in Buffalo, New York. Once again, O'Jay took the city by storm and became a broadcasting legend. He became a force on the air and had a big influence on other disc jockeys in the area, such as Gary Byrd and Frankie Crocker.

O'Jay left WUFO to work for WLIB in New York City, where he was a popular morning personality for many years. Today, he is living in New Jersey and writing his memoirs.

O'Jay has received numerous awards for his work in broadcasting. In 1967 he received the Disc Jockey of the Year Award from Mt. Vernon High School. The Society of Afro-American Transit Employees gave him a Leadership Award. In addition, in 1971, O'Jay received the National Media Award. The National Association of Negro Business and Professional Women's Club recognized O'Jay for his work in broadcasting in 1972.

When I tried to arrange the interview with Eddie O'Jay, I was unable to reach him. First, I called his job and left my name and telephone number. Then, I tried his home. I left a message on his answering machine there, too. Despite my best efforts, it seemed as if I would not be

*able to contact Eddie. Then one Saturday morning my telephone rang. I
hurried to answer and when I picked up the telephone, a deep, baritone
voice said, "Gilbert Williams, Eddie O'Jay." Eddie has the kind of voice
that immediately communicates friendliness. You feel like you've
known him years, even though you just met. From there, I explained my
reasons for calling and we launched right into the interview.*

MAY 11, 1991

Could you tell me how and when you got started in radio?

Around 1950–51 in my hometown, Milwaukee, Wisconsin, I had been
watching the progress of a young fellow from Chicago, Shorty Moore,
who was on a radio station. Shorty was very popular. I think he patterned his show in Milwaukee after the great Al Benson in Chicago. He
was on on weekends, Saturday or Sunday. Shortly after he took ill,
several citizens began to apply for the position to fill in while he was
hospitalized, including myself. They tried me out for two or three
weekends on Saturdays or Sundays. But somehow I didn't fill the bill.
I didn't sound like Shorty, so they called me in to their downtown office and relieved me of my duties. I was very distraught and disappointed because I had told everybody in the community that I was on
the air. Feeling rejected and down-hearted, I noticed there was another station office in the same building and decided to stop there. I
asked to speak with the program director. The secretary, after informing him that "Eddie O'Jay" was here to see him, informed me that he
was busy. I decided to wait. Finally, he did come and crack the door
and stuck his head out and said, "I'm a little busy right now, what can
I do for you?" He wanted to carry on this conversation while he was
standing there, so I just eased my foot in the door and said, "I must
come back to your office, I want to speak privately with you." Obviously, he recognized the fact that I meant business, so in his office we
went and I told him my experience and how determined I was to do a
better job than I had done before. He gave me the name of a Bill Killebrew and told me to contact him and what the possibilities were. Bill
Killebrew had applied for a job at the radio station earlier. We got together and we were supposed to go on from midnight 'til six in the
morning. We decided that our names would be shortened to Bill K.
and Eddie O'Jay. At the start, he took the first three hours from midnight to 3 and I went on until 6 a.m. We were supposed to switch after
a month, reverse our hours. Well, the month didn't go by before he
was released and I never knew really why. I'd just gotten back out of
the army and was working as a bartender during the day and trying to
hustle up spots because we were sustained with commission. If I'd
known then what I know now, we'd probably be fairly rich.

Did you have to buy the time yourself?

We didn't buy it, but we had to sell it which was why we'd have been rich had I known anything about selling. When you sell, you get a percentage of what you sell. The station would sustain you, in other words, there was no salary, only commission. You could sell the spots and I think I got two spots, a barbecue stand and Champale beer. There weren't enough spots to underwrite the full cost of time, and I remember my first paycheck out of the commissions was something like $14.00. But it wasn't all about money then because I was still tending bar, it was just the pleasure of being behind that mike and spinning them records.

Had you had any training or was this something you were just gifted with?

No training whatsoever. I recall listening to Chicago radio and got hung up on WAIT in Chicago who had "Daddio Dailey" on. This guy was burning and I admired him and I decided, if I do anything at all on the air, I'd try to be as swift, but not exactly like him because I couldn't rhyme like him, he was a rhymer. Talk about a rapper, he could do it to death. But I patterned myself after him, not in the way that he enunciated his words but in the air-time space. Our studio had all 78 RPM and 45 records that were big band nature, Les Helgard, Les Browne, and all these big guys. Some Count Basie, some Duke Ellington. That's what I played. Shorty's Record Shop gave some hard 45s to play on the show and I learned that people liked them. I didn't know a darn thing about them. I just knew this was what Shorty had, so his wife let me have a couple of those to play on the air. They suggested that I play more of that soul music. At that time it was called "race music" and that's how it all began. After Shorty passed, the record shop changed hands to a Maney Moreland, Jr. He's the guy who took my place. He came to town when they fired me from that station. I'd go down to Chicago to the George and Ernie Leaner brothers. They had the only black distribution, "United." And they stacked me up with all the soul records to play in Milwaukee and that's one of the ways my popularity began to rise.

How did you endear yourself to the audience?

I played everything that came along and I learned at an early, early stage in my career about playing records. When I'd do a record hop and play what *I* liked kids would be sitting around, I'd wonder, "What's this?," but when I played the stuff that I thought was horrible but the kids had requested, everybody was on the floor. That really spiked my attention to playing the music that the people wanted. I really learned a lesson. In Cleveland, Ohio, I had a rough time because I'd come out of Milwaukee in 1952 very green. I'd listen to all the radio stations, trying to see where I'd best fit in and I used to watch Bill Hawkins do remote broadcasts from his record store. I thought this was so hip. Every afternoon from about 3 o'clock until 6 o'clock it was "Walkin, Talkin Bill Hawkins." People could walk by and wave or blow their horn at him and he'd wave back at them, call their names out on the air and I thought "this is fantastic." This is the way the market should be and I'd stand at the window like all the other people and watch him for hours at a time and see how he'd spin the records and how he would talk his jive. Finally we got a chance to talk, WSRS that's what it was, that's where it was coming from. Bill Hawkins told me that I sounded too white to make it in the market. It was quite a blow but I stuck around in Cleveland because I didn't know where to go and was accustomed to being turned down at stations like KYW. They'd give you some excuse about no openings or that they were satisfied with the staff that they had, stories of that nature. While I was volunteering at Karamu House and selling insurance for a black company, I heard about Teddy Blackman, who started a show in a restaurant, midnight until 6 in the morning. Teddy Blackman was producing that show on WSRS, a remote broadcast out of that restaurant. I went by there to see him a couple of times. He interviewed me and what got me in with Teddy was the fact that he loved to play cards and they all gambled next door and he asked me to fill in while he played cards and he would seldom come back. So I finally became a personality on the air with Sweet Juanita Hayes. She called herself "Sugarlumps," a pretty, healthy woman, too. We were up in a window overlooking Cedar Avenue and people would come into the restaurant and chit chat. We'd announce their names and say a word or two to them. It was similar to New York, at the Palm's Cafe, you know, a little different setting. This went on for months. We made ourselves a name, Juanita and myself and Teddy Blackman. Teddy would open up the show and spend maybe an hour there and he was gone. Finally, I got my big opportunity to open up at WABQ right from the start.

You mean when they signed on the air you were one of the first announcers there?

When WABQ went on the air I was one of the first. I was assigned the morning-man position sign on. Reverend I. H. Gordon, from Texas, was the gospel jock on in the morning following me.

By this time you were into formats?

Oh yeah. Formats and copying off of some of the network stations, I suppose you would call them that. The early openers were called power hitters and I was put in that category. The gospel show was Reverend's, because this was the system. A little later, Ms. Valena Minor Williams talked house chit-chat for the ladies. During that period most radio stations tried appealing to the women because they were the ones who would buy everything because they were the only ones home listening to radio. Harrison Dillard did the sports news because he was an Olympic sports figure. During that period is when I would revert back to playing some of those records I played when I was in Milwaukee (big band music). I thought the folks in Cleveland wanted it. Every morning when I get off the air I'd make my rounds, coffee shops, restaurants, and everybody's telling me, "Man you were cooking this morning." I learned later that your friends would tell you what you want to hear. People who don't know you will tell you the truth. True, these were my friends. Even though they didn't like some of the things I was playing, they'd say, "Ya, you was doing it this morning." And I'd take it for granted that this was good. I began to play blues numbers even though I wasn't too fond of blues at the time because I thought blues were rather sadistic and "how in the world can somebody have these many problems?" The owner spoke to me, encouraging me to play the blues more because that is what people in Cleveland would prefer, especially in the black community. How would he know? He lives in Shaker Heights. I began to do it because it was either that or I would not have no job. I would put on a batch of blues like B.B. King, Bobby Blue Bland, Little Junior Parker, Muddy Waters and I sort of got hung up on the sounds of B.B. King, not knowing who he was or anything else. I began to play more of his music, Little Junior Parker and Bobby Bland, and by golly, I will never forget what happened one day. My wife and I were on our way to the theater one Sunday after church.

You were married by this time?

Yes! To a lovely woman named Audrey, who after thirty-eight years at this interview is still by my side. On our way to the theater we passed a place called Gleason's Musical Bar. Now here it is early afternoon and there is this crowd around Slaughter's Drug Store corner. I'll never forget, Slaughter's was a black drug store I thought looked like it was going to be as big as Walgreens. After the movie, on our way home, it appeared as though that very same line was still extended around the corner. I became curious and made a real quick U-turn and pulled up to the marquee and read the banner "appearing here nightly, B. B. Blues Boy King." I said to Audrey, "That's the guy whose record I played." I double-parked the car and by that time, the owner's son saw and recognized me. I'd never been to his place before. He told me, "Listen, come over here, come here a minute." As I approached, he grabbed me by the arm to take me inside and I said, "Well wait a minute, my wife is in the car." He suggested I park the car and come with him. So I did and Audrey and I went into the bar. He literally dragged us through the crowd, and mind you, I am noticing this, we are pulled past everybody else standing and waiting in line, and it dawned on me that there was something special going on inside. Upon entering, someone said something to B.B. King and he stopped the music and announced, "Ladies and Gentlemen, I have been informed that the disc jockey on WABQ radio who busted my record 'Sweet Sixteen' is in the house and I'd like to meet him." I had a fit, the house went up in the air, people started picking me up. Picked me up off the floor and carried me up to the stage. To myself, I said, "This is it"; that woke me up. So it's been the blues in my life ever since. I learned, on radio you cannot play music for yourself, you have to play it for people. They are the ones who want to hear it. They thought I was a hero.

Now, tell me the story about how the singing group, the O'Jays, happens to have your last name.

You know we always made more money in those days doing sock-hops or dances and the artists and the record companies would actually help us promote them, at a lesser charge than an agency would, especially if they were promoting them. I would have these weekly dances at a nice big ballroom and I would have live music and also records. The place was the Call and Post Ballroom, owned by the local black weekly newspaper in Cleveland.

This was in Cleveland?

Yeah, and there were always groups of singers that wanted to perform. During one of these periods there came five guys, from two little towns called Massillon and Canton, Ohio. They wanted to sing. I never had space on the program for them until finally there was an artist that didn't show and that gave me an opportunity to fill in with these guys. They showed up religiously every week. They literally tore the house up. That's how good they were, so I had them over and over again. My audience grew larger. We got into a lengthy conversation until about 5 a.m. talking about me managing them. I told them that I didn't care for the name "The Mascots." After going through about two dozen names, Walter Williams spoke up and said, "Why don't we call ourselves 'The O'Jays'?" I asked why and he responded, " Because you are so popular and people would really listen to us." So I agreed with them!

As a member of the National Association of Television and Radio Artists, did you actually help save Motown or help launch it?

Not me alone, no, but the organization as a whole. I think we may have had something to do with that but I wasn't an officer then. I didn't become an officer until the later years. There were certain things that went on in the record industry that caused Motown to get crunched by the big ones. We put our foot down and said, "We're not going to have it." We played a big part, we were called Busters because of our defiance of large ofay (white) record companies. We never did get the clout that we really wanted because we had some Judases in the group. When I say Judases, I mean we had some people that were working in direct conflict with what we were all about. They were working for the huge ofay companies and would go back from our meetings and tell their bosses all they wanted to know. Every time we had a NATRA meeting, wherever we went there was some disturbance to create pandemonium casting an unfavorable light on NATRA so that people would say we were no good. We held conventions in towns where we cannot go back again with the name NATRA, because we had someone that gave us a bad name although we had some very smart people like Dell Shields and Tommy Smalls; also Bill Summers of WLOU in Louisville, and E. Rodney Jones of Chicago, Illinois. These were the power hitters.

Was Jack Gibson also there?

Oh yes, Jockey Jack along with all the power hitters who could call the shots, but we still had these Judases and we couldn't figure out who they were. And when we did find out who one or two of them were there was no way of eradicating them. But everything we said in the meetings, the tactics we wanted to utilize were usurped by the big record companies.

So you left Cleveland and you went to Buffalo?

No, I got fired in Cleveland.

Why were you fired?

Let me see if I can put it in a way that sounds intelligent. First off, I was considered the hottest-selling disc jockey in that area of about three states, Ohio, Pennsylvania and Michigan. This is when I really learned that people were listening. A contest was presented to several radio stations by Italian Swiss Colony Wines. They were introducing to the market Ariba wines and the national jingle was sung by Nat King Cole (now you can't beat that!). This contest was for radio stations in Pittsburgh, Cleveland, and I do believe Cincinnati and also

Detroit, and the jock who sold the most would be crowned "King of the Air." That personality would win a Corvette Stingray. The station would get $1,000 cash. I wasn't aware of the enormity because I didn't know what a Stingray was. But with my affiliation with Karamu House Theater and being involved in a couple of plays over there and also being on the air, I decided that I was going to sell some of the stuff. I would tell people on the air, "If you see me and yell 'Ariba,' I will stop my car and give you a taste." Italian Swiss gave you all the samples you wanted or needed. Ariba Italian Swiss Colony wine was all over Cleveland. I'd give Ariba parties. I'd mix half grapefruit juice and half Ariba in a punch bowl and you talk about a hell of a party. This is the kind of activity that really promoted it. In the meantime, things were really going downhill for me. I had bills piled up, you know, I wasn't spending my money the right way, I was getting all kinds of demands for payment. I had opened a ticket office that was failing, creditors felt that you weren't going to respond to a letter or a phone call so they would send wires knowing that you'd open up a Western Union telegram. One morning I was about to leave the station and the secretary said, "Eddie, don't leave yet, you've got a telegram here, let me give it to you." I said, "I'll tell you what to do sweetheart, why don't you read it for me because I don't want to hear no bad news." She opened it up and read it. It said, "Congratulations, you are the 'On-Air King Personality.'" I held that wire for a long time until it got raggedy. I was the owner of a Corvette Stingray. I waited three months before that car came through. Every day I was walking around with that telegram. Finally they called and told me to pick up the car at the Chevrolet dealer. My wife and I went out there and I still have pictures of she and I receiving the keys to the car. I was told, "You're not going to have to pay taxes on it, it is tax free." I had recently bought a new Dodge, so here we are, a two-car family and a new baby. I got a letter from a brewery in Detroit who was advertising on my show, congratulating me for selling their product, also inviting me, along with other jocks on other radio stations, to be their guest at a country club outside of Detroit, in Windsor. Harrison Dillard, who was the program director, told me that the boss didn't think it was a good idea that I go. I said, "You've got to be crazy." I wasn't going to miss an opportunity to go and hob-nob with people and learn some things. But the wind up was "If you're going to go you're going to be fired." See, I didn't know what was going on in the background, all I knew was I wasn't doing anything wrong, making money for the station when you look at the log and the top of the log is full and the rest was practically empty. That means that people are buying Eddie O'Jay. So, I got reckless and carefree. As long as I knew I was making money for the company then I should have no fear. But somebody was telling me something and I wasn't listening. Why, I don't know.

Were you a pretty headstrong person?

Fairly, if I thought I was right. You know, I was the kind of guy that was arrogant to a degree, where I KNOW something is right and I think that you're wrong. I never asked why. How could I be wrong, when I'm looking at the log and it is empty of commercial spots in the afternoon but full in the morning up until noon? So, why shouldn't I go? No one would give me an answer, even Harrison Dillard couldn't give me an answer as to why. So I said, "This is a threat so I'm going." I drove the new Corvette to Michigan and had a ball, but on my return, I didn't have a job. That's how it worked out. I wasn't a member of AFTRA so I'm out of a job. When you don't have protection, or even when you have it, sometimes you don't know how to pursue it if you don't go to meetings to understand what your protection encompasses. However, since AFTRA informed me, I know they had me by the back end. There's nobody to fight. I could have followed up through the FOL (Future Outlook League) in Cleveland and they would have backed me up from a community aspect. But somehow, at the time, I just didn't feel that this was the right way to go. The Future Outlook League, which was big in Cleveland, had more clout than the Urban League or the NAACP, that's how strong the FOL was. They were real activists, advocates of the citizens' interest, black interest.

Did you have plenty of community support?

Of course, but I didn't realize it. I could have gone to the community but I didn't know how to go about doing it to arouse the community to the kind of treatments that I was getting. Eugene P. Weil, a fellow out of Alabama, was general manager for the station owned by a father and son and were considered as liberal Jews. Eugene P. Weil ran the station with an iron fist. He told Harrison Dillard, "Eddie O'Jay can't go there and mingle with those folks from that brewery"—one of our sponsors; now what he had against this brewery, I've never learned.

Was there some sort of conflict of interest maybe?

I asked if it was a conflict of interest because they were on the air, and it could have been. I figured if the white jocks can go, why can't I go? No one else from my station had been invited to go, so maybe that was it. When I got back on Monday, *there was no job*. After being fired in Cleveland, I acquired a job with WUFO in Buffalo, a brand-new station just opening. That was about 1960, and lasted 'til '62. I received several offers to go west. I communicated with management of the possibility of my being advanced to more than program director. Joe Basset, the general manager, said, "Frankly, no, because management feels employees should be beyond reproach and we've gotten a word of your financial downside. They want to repossess your car."

Matter of fact, one of my debtors came and took my wife's car away but our lawyer made them return it because they took it off private property, and I'll be damned if they didn't bring it back. Management told me that they didn't see me going any higher because of these obligations. I said, "Well, I'll be damned." As far as they were concerned that was to keep you down, you're not going anywhere, so I decided to leave. I knew that I had huge popularity in Buffalo, I felt as though they were sitting on gold. At the ninth hour, they said, "Don't go." It was too late then, I had committed myself and had made up my mind. The Plaidlock Society Club gave me a going-away party that was so full I could not even get the band in the house. They had to come up the fire escape. That's the truth. At this time I didn't really want to go but it was too late. I had already committed myself.

Did you like Buffalo?

Oh yeah, Buffalo was something else. Everything I touched turned to money in Buffalo. I was hired by Utica Club beer once a week and made more for just being there, being a personality. They would pick out different bars and clubs for Utica Club night. Word got around town that Eddie O'Jay was going to be there. Even when I'd stop my car at a traffic light, the kids would be all over my car, so many the police would move the traffic. That is how good things were in Buffalo. Frankie Crocker remembers and speaks of those days on the air today. Things were very good in Buffalo. It was a bad move, going to Phoenix, Arizona. My wife, Audrey, never liked Buffalo. So that was my ultimate move; you don't want me, my wife don't want Buffalo, so to heck with you guys. And Jim Titus, the general manager of KCAR in Phoenix, was going to appoint me as assistant general manager. That really drew me out there. This black man was willing for me to have an opportunity to upgrade myself. As bad as I wanted to stay in Buffalo I knew that my wife didn't care at all for it and would not move there so we packed, got Red Ball movers and went to Phoenix. I wasn't on the air two months before Titus fired me. By the way, the general manager was a black man but the station was owned by whites.

Why did they fire you?

The same thing as everywhere else, but out there we was just too big for our britches. Phoenix was not a record market, but we were beginning to create a market. Let me give you a simple example. First off, we made the mistake of staying in their [Jim Titus'] home until we could locate a house. There were a great deal of comparisons Jim Titus would make. He would come home and admonish his wife for not being as active as my Audrey was. We had a new small baby and was doing well, we are living well in Tempe, Arizona. Jim began looking for us a house around 24th and Broadway. We said, "No, thank you." I don't know what his thinking was. This was not it. Many places had outdoor plumbing, this is where Jim wanted us to move, "to be close to the station, you can spend more time at the station." I thanked him and told him that I would look for a place. I became acquainted with some nice people in my everyday tour of the city that told me about the FHA repossess list of houses. Now Jim had a real estate license but he never told us about the FHA repossess list, you follow me?

Was it that he just didn't want you guys to be bigger than him?

I wouldn't say that, draw your own conclusions. We took this list and started hunting for houses. You give the FHA $1.00 for a lockbox key which allows entry into any of these houses belonging to the government. We went searching in Glendale, Arizona, outside of Phoenix. Audrey and I found our dream house. We negotiated and got the house. We invited Jim and his wife out to see it. That did not work well at all. That, along with other things was the end of my career at KCAR. I did nothing to create this tension other than to be myself. I mean, why try and hide? What I was doing was showing that this is what we'd like—it was a nice house, attached garage, three bedrooms, and refrigerated air conditioning. The house came with a redwood fence and it was just fantastic. Audrey went back to Cleveland to pack up everything and have it shipped out by Red Ball, and by the time she got back I was damned near out of a job. It wasn't long before he just completely terminated me. Of course, you know about those contracts whereby you were not supposed to work within a fifty-mile radius of any other radio station.

What was the reason for this contract?

Protective agreement for the station, to keep your audiences from switching. So you couldn't get another job across the street. Those were your terms that you signed. You figure that you are going to be here for quite some time so what need is there to worry about it? Well, they held me to the agreement when KRIZ called me to work some odd shift while their guy was on vacation. I had to get permission from Jim, yes siree. So that gives you an idea of how things were in Phoenix, Arizona. Jim Titus, his wife, and most of the people who worked around us knew that was wrong but what can you do?

Couldn't you sue them?

I didn't have the slightest thought about suing them. When you talk about lawyers, you have to have money and I had none. You don't go to everybody crying. Maybe I could have gone to a person who was the biggest thing since mashed potatoes in Phoenix. Maybe I could have appealed to him. We got along very well. He's a black republican and the biggest man, next to Goldwater, and still is today they tell me.

He was a black man?

Yeah, I was told that. He was Goldwater's right arm. He owns a couple of funeral homes and lots of property there. I think he would have resolved the whole thing for me, but then again I had no idea at all at how close he was to Jim. Let me get back to my stay in Buffalo. You would not even believe this. Some of my co-workers were trying to get me run out of town. My competitors on the air with me warned me the first day there, while we were having dinner at the hotel with the new station owners. One or two drinks and this guy goes hog-wild. He told me, in the presence of everybody, "Now that you are going to be with us I want you to know that you can't do anything in this town without coming through me. I run this town." It was extremely embarrassing. That man was Jimmy Lyons.

Was he the owner of the station?

No, he was one of the jocks who had been hired to go on the air, who said he runs the town. Being outspoken in front of everybody because he knew of the dances I was doing in Cleveland and that were still going on. My Audrey was there taking care of those in my absence. He continued, saying, "I know what you were doing out there in Cleveland, they told me all about it." I later learned that this guy had been doing the gospel show for years, every Sunday on several local stations. He felt that everybody knew the name Jimmy Lyons. Now they have hired him as the gospel jock. OK? I was the morning jock. He then ran down the list of other people who were going to be on the air. We were still having dinner. Although embarrassed, I made up my mind that no one is going to tell me this but I wasn't going to speak of it in the open in order to solidify the statement made by Jimmy Lyons. There was this popular bar in Buffalo where just about everybody went. Sheila, a very voluptous waitress, said to me one evening, "I have someone here who wants to meet you. His name is Trunnis Goggins." Well, Trunnis Goggins was a big, financially successful black man, biggest you ever want to see in Buffalo. I was told that Trunnis was a slum lord. He had about twenty, twenty-five old, big houses in Buffalo. Anyway, Trunnis stood there at the bar holding a glass of beer in his hand. You know, a glass with your index fingers curled in the glass held with your thumb and little pinkie finger? That, I will never forget. I laugh about it because today we are still very close friends. Trunnis also owned the local skating rink and three or four Coca-Cola franchised trucks. You couldn't stop the man. Jimmy Lyons was doing a record hop in Skateland one day a week. Lyons was supposedly Trunnis's right arm. Trunnis knew that Lyons could draw kids. When Sheila introduced him to me, I reached out to shake his hand and he continued leaning on the bar. He wouldn't even shake hands with me but he says, "My man Jimmy told me you were here. I want you to know that you can't do anything in this town without me." I said to myself, "These are the exact words that Jimmy used. So that means they have been rehearsing for me." If I want to give dances, and I've got to have dances at his place, I need to go to them. So I said, again to myself, "We won't do it this way." I backed off and later I began to look around for my own hole because I wanted to do some dances and shows. I knew that the entertainment thing there would be lucrative. I soon found an old catering hall called Washington Hall and the owner had a farm just outside of Buffalo. I was about to negotiate. It would be mine in a couple weeks, now I'm on the air, enjoying life, everything looking good.

What were your ratings like?

I never learned what the ratings were other than they were high. This was during that period when, wherever I went, I drew large crowds. While I was negotiating for this hall we were missing a disc jockey so I had to do the morning and afternoon show. In between I would go get some rest. Trunnis called on the phone and said, "Listen, I met you at the Pine Grill and I'd like to talk with you." And I said, "Well alright" . . . so on my way home I stopped by his house, rang the bell, and his wife opened the door. He's at the top of the step with his hands in his pocket and I said, "Hey, there, how you doing?" He said, "Yeh, come on in. I want to talk to you." So into the dining room we went and sat at the table. He said, "You remember me, don't you?" I said, "Yeah." He continued, "I want to apologize for what I said to you. I didn't mean it that way." (Now that to me is a man or a sign of a man.) He went on, "I'm a business man and I have twenty-five houses where I collect the rent from my tenants myself, in person. I want you to know that at each one of those houses where I go to collect my rent, I hear you." I said, "Say what?" He said "That's all I hear, I hear you and that tells me that you are popular. Now being a business man I'm going to make you an offer. I got New Skateland, the skating rink up there on Main Street, and I want you to pick a time to do a show there every week because you can draw people. I am a business man and I know where it's at." And that's the way the decision was made.

So I chose a day other than the day Jimmy had. I didn't want to conflict with him so I chose Thursdays, usually a quiet night, I thought. I mentioned on the air where I'd be appearing and you could not get in the place. They would skate and then stop and dance for the rest of the evening until time to go home. Trunnis and Lyons had it out in the office and Trunnis let Lyons know that he had had it. He was finished. Lyons walked out and said to me, "I'm not through with you." That was the last word he said to me. He tried everything he could to get me run out of Buffalo. Jimmy Lyons, because of his spiritual show, had good rapport with the Ministerial Alliance. He had the preachers stand up in the pulpit and say, "This young whippersnapper out of Cleveland is a disgrace to the public, he's got women pregnant in Cleveland and he should not be here."

Now get this. In between radio shows I'm at home taking a nap and the doorbell rings and here is this lady saying, "I have to speak with you, it's important, about Cleveland." Well, that perks my interest, you know. So I go down and let the lady in, I have my robe on, we come back, go in the living room, sit down and she says, "I have to go to Cleveland because my family is there and I've got three children and I thought maybe that you could help me." So I said, "You mean help you like give you bus fare, something like that?" She says, "Yes." I says, "Lady, I can't help you. All the money I get is from Utica Club beer and that is once a week, my radio pay goes to my wife in Cleveland." She got up and she says, "Well, I can appreciate that," but on the way out she says, "I've got to tell you something. I didn't come here for that. I was sent here. I'm supposed to get you arrested. You're supposed to grab my clothes." She's to rip them off and have me arrested for attempted rape. I said, "Who?" and she said, "Well, I'll tell you who told me to do it and they paid me $50.00. But you are not the kind of person that they said you were." Now this happened in Buffalo. And one of the fellows is right now in Albuquerque, New Mexico, and the other was Jimmy Lyons, so he is dead now. They paid her to do it. Yes siree. That's what they did to me, friend. So anyway, so many little things happened.

If you could change anything about black radio today, what would it be?

It would be all personality. Every bit of the way. And I'd have control that way. I think the problem is that the station owners feel like they don't have control over personality and that is what is going to sell radio.

Did you ever think about ownership yourself?

No, I never did because I never had the business acumen. I've never had the kind of wherewithal for bottom lines and debits. I was always a little fearful of having people around I couldn't trust. People who always knew more about it than you. The basics of radio I know from my heart, but to have the figures right and to multiply and divide and make sure that we had the right figures to come up right, I never was that astute. So I never even attempted to think about ownership of radio stations.

Did the civil rights movement have any impact upon your career or your workings in radio?

No, none, other than the fact that I had a strong belief in it. I was with Martin when he came to New York. I was with Malcolm X and I believed some of the things that he would talk about. I knew he was a little radical. I was a little fearful at times but we were very close friends, especially when he was in Buffalo and, you know, he more or less owned Buffalo.

Malcom X owned Buffalo?

Oh, of course. Malcolm spent a lot of time in Buffalo. That was our first acquaintance. When he came to New York it was like old home week. We knew each other already. Of course, Farakhan took over after him. He's in Chicago now. All of these people I knew very well personally because I made it my business, not only to follow them but to be involved.

If you could pick out one thing that you would say symbolizes your career or your work in radio, what would it be?

Gee that is a tough one. I think a number of things would be appreciated about what Eddie O'Jay is all about. My idea is to create some endearment of the audience that you are about to speak to. In order to create a desire for folk to really listen to you, you must be an advocate. An advocate of human, not only black, rights. I think that is really where I want to stand. An example is my friend who is not just an acquaintance, who is the major black leader of the city of New York, watching him grow from one level to another in his public career, from a lawyer to a mayor. Watching the media building the garbage against the kind of a person he really is. I don't believe that this man would be elected to be mayor of the city of New York and play patsy to somebody. I know he's got some dues he's got to pay. That's life. And I believe that if you let him continue, he is going to overcome all of this. And there are those of us who are black who believe that he was sold out by the daily media. I'm enjoying great pleasure in being an advocate of the right human causes.

To me you seem like a person who is community-involved; you seem like a people person. I remember listening to you twenty years ago and I've talked to many, many disc jockeys and that is a common kind of bond, a common characteristic. Even though

each one is different, there is this camaraderie that you radio personalities are able to establish with the public.

Well, I think it came about as a result of trying to use the public as a barometer and in doing that I've enjoyed it. People would call on you if they felt that you can handle a problem for them, or if you could resolve a problem, it's gratifying, you feel great.

Did payola have any impact on your career?

Scared me to death. I can't say that I didn't take any money. No checks, anyway. It wasn't called payola before 1958. We were considered consultants. Most got paid a little stipend for making hits. For example, "Tossing and Turning" was a big hit and I had to beg the people to release the record. The artist was Bobby Lewis and I helped make it a hit. The record was owned by a white dude living in a big house out on Long Island right now. He told me to my face, "Eddie, you gave me this house." But I didn't get a quarter. Bobby Lewis didn't get his just due. See how unfair it is. When this payola thing came up over in Newark, New Jersey, the feds started serving subpoenas, and I was told that every dude that went over there before the Federal Communications Commission hearing stated, "You ought to talk to Eddie O'Jay, he knows more about it than I do. Why am I here?" The feds would say, "Oh yes, we heard that name before, tell me about him." But they didn't have a thing on me because I was innocent. They knew who to pick because many jocks could tell them where it's at.

Norman W. Spaulding

When I was working on my doctorate degree at the University of Illinois, a fellow graduate student came up to me and said, "Have you met Norm? You've got to meet Norm Spaulding. He's the old guy who has come back to school to work on his doctorate. Norm's got loads of experience in radio, public relations and everything. And besides, he's the hippest old dude you'd ever want to meet. He even wears his hair pulled back into a ponytail." I had not met Norm at the time but it wasn't long before our paths crossed, mainly because he sought out all of the young brothers to give them advice on making it in this world.

When I met Norm, I was surprised that so much energy and optimism could be packed into his 5'4" frame. Before long, Norm, two or three fellow graduate students, and I were meeting at the local watering hole every Friday afternoon. We'd discuss everything from our sometimes-goofy professors and interpersonal relationships to money and racial politics. Mostly, however, we talked about Norm's love—black radio. He regaled us with stories about what it had been like to work with or know people like Al Benson, "the ol'swing master." Norm said Benson was the most powerful disc jockey he had known. At times, Norm talked about the outrageous antics and personalities of Richard Stams, Jack Gibson, Yvonne Daniels, Studs Terkel and others whose voices were familiar to radio listeners in his beloved Chicago.

Norman Spaulding attended Howard University. Later he graduated from the University of Illinois (Urbana-Champaign) where he received both a master's and doctoral degree in communication. In his early career as a radio disc jockey, Spaulding offered jazz music to his listeners. He worked for WFJL, WNIB, WGN and WIND during the years 1950–1956. In addition, he worked as a record buyer and manager of a music store during those years.

Spaulding had a soft style, in which he infused black idiomatic phrases to establish communication with African-American listeners.

His radio program consisted of white and black jazz artists but black artists dominated. Spaulding became a cultural hero because of the music he played, programs he produced—Dr. Martin Luther King, Jr.'s sermons, for example—and his pioneering research in black radio and music.

Could you tell me how you got started in radio?

I started playing jazz on WFJL, WNIB, WGN and WIND. I first began my broadcasting career in 1950. I worked at all those stations between 1950 and 1956. At the same time as I was spinning records at the radio station, I also was a record buyer and music store manager. You see I was a hustler—not in the negative sense—but I had to work more than one job to support my family.

How would you describe your announcing style?

I used a soft style and at first made no attempt to cater to a black audience. My program was sponsored by white establishments in the "Loop." But I did use black idioms to let my black listeners know that I was black.

You mentioned that you left WIND in 1956. What happened next?

I joined WGES in 1956. While there I tried to blend in the new sounds of rhythm and blues music with popular jazz artists on my afternoon show. In the evening, I played jazz almost exclusively. I also offered my listeners a different style of commentary and discussion.

How long did you stay at WGES?

I left WGES in 1962, so I was there for about six years. In that same year, I created a rhythm and blues and jazz format on WAAF. I also began producing my own shows. I produced and directed Dr. Martin Luther King's nationally syndicated radio program. You see, at the same time that I was a jazz DJ I founded my own company—Feature Broadcasting Company. We produced a series of programs on sports, household hints, and black history. Ethel Waters was the moderator of a program I produced called "Advice to the Housewife."

How well did this company do?

Well, Feature syndicated its programming nationwide. Unfortunately, we had only limited success because most small black-oriented stations could not afford the subscription fee.

Tell me about a little about your programs with Dr. Martin Luther King, Jr.

I produced and directed Dr. King's nationally syndicated radio programs. These programs consisted mainly of sermons. I also produced many radio programs for the Catholic Church and the Chicago Association of Commerce and Industry. I was also the first black person to win the American Academy of Radio Sciences and Crafts Award (1959) for radio announcing.

Did you play mostly white or black artists?

I played some white jazz artists, probably more than other jockeys. But black performers dominated my radio programs. They were artists that whites accepted. Eventually, the format on WAAF lost its appeal among blacks.

Would you say your style appealed to working-class African Americans?

The music I played and language I used appealed to black middle-class aspirations and perspectives. I tried to straddle the fence. I played R&B in the afternoon and jazz at night.

Did you ever promote shows at the Savoy or Regal theatres?

Oh yes! On Friday, Saturday and Sunday nights I promoted dances at the Savoy and Trianon. Those were huge ballrooms, man. They could hold 3,000 to 6,000 people. Our shows featured blues, rhythm and blues and rock 'n'roll acts. I also promoted some jazz acts at the smaller clubs at the Pershing Hotel at Sixty-Fourth and Cottage Grove.

You were a contemporary of Al Benson and other blues and R&B jockeys. How did your popularity compare to theirs?

Benson owned Chicago. Us jazz jockeys were more or less elitists in terms of our musical tastes. Me, Sid McCoy and Daddio Dailey were the most well known. But none of us approached some of the blues jockeys in terms of money earned or even popularity. I tried to create a musical style that the younger generation would follow and keep. I was totally into the music—jazz, especially. I guess that was a sort of elitist approach to musical selections but I wanted to lift up the black community's tastes. I saw my role as a guardian of the jazz art form.

Is that how you became a cultural hero?

Well, the language and idioms I used were creative and improvisational. The music helped endear me to a group of Chicagoans who loved jazz and the rhythm and blues I played. I imitated and helped create some new styles also. I think my listeners also came to appreciate me as member of the entertainment world. My sales style and hustling approach also endeared me to the people of Chicago.

How did black DJs start the practice of "riding gain" and "talking through" records?

"Riding gain" has to do with the fact that many of the small stations did not have engineers, which meant the jockey controlled his own panel board. They would often boost the power, then drop it to accentuate the sound of the music. "Talking through" the music simply meant that the jockey would leave the music under him and then open up the mike and talk while the music was still playing. It is a very common practice now, but back then (late 1940s) it was very unique.

You are a native Chicagoan. Tell me a little about the radio announcers you listened to.

Jack Cooper's style was not black-sounding, as he deplored the use of slang and Negroid language styles. Jack more than many of the later DJs at least established a very dignified style of broadcasting using very good English. The impact of Benson was that this street-talking black appeared on the scene and appealed to the new immigrants from the south. I listened to Jack while I was in high school and when I would come back to Chicago in 1946.

Benson is indirectly responsible for me going into radio. When I heard him with (what I thought) his crude language style and usage, I felt that I could get into radio. While Cooper continued to broadcast up into the '50s, we must remember that he predated the smooth-talking jocks that emerged after World War II. Jack was an old man then and just not "hip" or hip enough for the growing young black population. Benson was entirely different with his black language styles, a shouter and superb pitch man. None of the street-talking jocks copied any white announcer's style. They worked at establishing their own style and gimmicks. They were proud of the fact that they didn't sound white. Proudest, because they considered themselves the best on-the-air salesmen in Chicago. Often they laughed at white announcers'style in Chicago.

Some of the black jazz jockeys did emulate the late Dave Garroway. Not so much his voice, but Garroway's laid-back style, which is still popular on NPR's jazz shows. By the 1950s, the fast-talking, smooth-talking boys were coming in. They were better educated and some, more articulate. They were the forerunners of the black disc jockeys we hear today . . . and also the young white jockeys. I think the fast-talking style evolved out of the urban oral culture. Put down your rap fast, man. And then, too, the successful one . . . the pitchmen often had to talk fast. While it was against the NAB's Code of Ethics, there were times that I had 25 minutes of spots (one minute each) that I had to pitch in one hour and still play the music which I had been paid to play. On my jazz shows, I never took any money, feeling that the music I played was sacred to me and my audience.

While we are on the subject of announcing styles, I can't explain it, but if you listen to a black station in any major market you will find that there is a black sound or flow in the announcer's delivery. This same black announcer could be put on a white station and would sound like a white announcer. My first five years on radio were at white stations. I sounded white and no one in the audience knew the difference. I was at WGN (50,000 watts) doing the classical music show and feeling quite proud of myself until I heard about the money that Benson and some other black jocks were making. I went to WGES, the big black station, with my "proper" delivery and discovered that I had to get a black accent to be accepted by the audience.

After working as a radio disc jockey, you completed a doctorate in communications. Which writers have had the most impact on your thinking and philosophy of life?

In looking back on going to school, I still feel that C. Wright Mills made more sense than anyone I read. I'm speaking of contemporary writers . . . Max Weber. I think Cayton and Drake did the most monumental work on blacks. And of course, Ralph Ellison.

I've been doing a hell of lot of reading lately. Everything from Michael Harrington's *The New American Poverty* (an interesting book), some Marx and Lenin, the Bible, and others. Of course, I been reading a lot about topical matters, too. I mentioned the Bible, not so much that I am looking for salvation, but rather I realized that it has influenced western world thought and behavior, or at least established a reality for perceiving the way we live out our lives, realizing all the time that this reality is a distorted perception of what reality is.

While I have always been dedicated to at least documenting black history and speaking out in favor of all exploited groups, I'm beginning to feel that I am peeing in the wind. I have a clipping from a *New York Times* article about a recent report of blacks in New York. It states that one out of three blacks in New York City live in poverty. Glorious Manhattan and Harlem's blacks have a medium income of only $10,778. One out of every four black males will die before age 28 from homicide, suicide or an OD. That is genocide! I see the Indians in this part of the country (New Mexico) ekeing out a living on $6,000 a year. From my house, I can see the Mexican and Hispanic "pickers" working in the large industrial farms that now own one third of the farms in America, working for $2.50 an hour.

What impact does music have on society? What do you think about jazz? Blues? Spirituals?

I feel music is not only a symbolic form of people expressing their feelings, living out lifestyles . . . but also a way for them to create their own myths. It is more than an appendage to life, but goodness knows, I won't try and be pedantic and explain why. I only look at it as being more than historians and sociologists have acknowledged. Except for print media, music lies subliminally and importantly at the core and the telling of a story or living out the ritual of life. I still feel that DuBois was the only great sociologist who realized music's significance in interpreting certain social phenomena.

The role of language and its own particular sound plays a very important function in musical creativity. Elvis sounded black but had a white face. Listen to the Beatles, they became popular, but listen to the sound of their singing. It is not British, but black. Blues, jazz and perhaps some new musical styles that once had a radio audience and popular support are destined to die. Gospel music is the only remaining black art form that can and will be allowed to develop. And that is because it still reaches an audience on Sunday's broadcasts. It continues because black churches pay their way to broadcast their programs.

What are the ramifications of these trends? Frankly, I don't know. I can only envisage more commercial pablum being turned out by the commercially controlled big business. We as middle-class blacks point proudly to Ella, Count, Roy Eldridge, Peterson and Miles in the jazz field. I feel a certain amount of remorse when I see them appear. All are over fifty years of age. A dying era. The genius and talent of a Michael Jackson is that of a performer and entertainer. His contribution as an innovator of musical styles is nil. I just don't hear any young Muddy Waters, Charlie Parkers or Louis Armstrongs anymore. But still, as DuBois wrote, there is something in the soul of black folk that has and will continue to create new beautiful forms of music.

NOTE

This interview was developed from personal letters from Norman Spaulding to the author.

◆ 14 ◆

Richard Stams

Richard Stams was born in Memphis, Tennessee, where he also attended Lemoyne College. Stams first worked in promotion as a sound truck operator, using it to advertise local and national businesses. He gained broadcasting experience when he worked as a commentator with Jack L. Cooper, the main announcer, on the American Giants baseball games.

Stams became very popular in Chicago radio. He worked for WGES, "The Voice of the West Town," in 1955 where he became known as the "Crown Prince of Disc Jockeys." Stams' radio career has also included disc jockeying stints at WHFC, WOPA and WEAW, all Chicagoland stations.

His announcing style included southern phrases and references to soul food and favorite holidays or celebrations. Stams used his "down-home" background and introduced new phrases from the urban street culture to appeal to listeners. His language and style was southern but not as rural-sounding as Benson's. Nevertheless, Stams was more flamboyant than any other African-American disc jockey, aside from Benson, in Chicago.

I met Richard Stams in 1991. He was in his late 80s and still going strong. I truly enjoyed my conversation with Richard. He is down-to-earth and cares deeply about the welfare of his family, community and people.

AUGUST 30, 1991

Would you tell me how you got started in radio?

Well, I really have to use two dates because when I first got into radio it was with Jack L. Cooper when we were broadcasting the American Giants games. We used a sound truck for a combination P.A. system and hooked it into the radio. That was my first experience in radio.

That year was about 1929?

That was in the '30s. You see, Jack L. Cooper went on radio in 1928 but I went on in 1937. It was 1936 when I acquired my sound truck. In the '50s I was still using the sound trucks as a commercial venture. Sound trucks became sort of popular because we were developing black music at that time and using the sound truck as a commercial venture because we were making money. You see, we'd charge a guy an average price of about $5.00 an hour and we'd drive this truck, advertise a clothing store, 35-chain of stores or Walgreen chain of stores or something similar. An average run would be about three, four, or five hours. The people at WGES saw me working in the sound truck and they asked me to come over for an interview for the radio station. WGES was a 5,000 watt station in the heart of Chicago, and at that time it was the largest black radio station in the United States and it also had black disc jockeys. The first one was Al Benson. It played rhythm and blues.

I'm going into the rhythm and blues era now. Previously, the Jack L. Cooper era was black gospel and jazz. Blues was the big thing in 1948. Al Benson went on the air in 1947 and started playing blues. Al started out with 15 minutes of blues, that was his show, but in a week Al had an hour. And in three months, Al had 14 hours on the air a day. So after Al got going, they asked me would I want to work on radio and I told them "no." I was making a lot of money with the sound truck and I didn't want to go on radio. A week later they called me again, asked me would I come to breakfast and have a conference. I want to say this, in context of the situation, because these were millionaire white people; there were no black radio station owners at that time. Jack L. Cooper owned part of two stations but nobody, no black, actually *controlled* a radio station at that time. I mean absolute control where he could do what he wanted to do. I met for a second conference and breakfast with the people that owned the station, Dr. Dyer, and he was a character within himself. Dr. Dyer was retired from the Santa Fe Railroad Hospitals of which he was in charge of three or four hospitals. He was a medical doctor and a lung specialist. He retired from the railroad to operate radio station WGES because his brother had purchased it and his brother couldn't handle it. His brother ran out. Doc was a millionaire at the time so he moved in to help him out. Doc and his assistant, who ran the radio station, had me to breakfast. So the final question came down to me. "How much money can I make?" and when they quoted it I said, "OK, I'll take the job. When you want me to go to work?" They said, "Monday morning," and I said, "OK, I'll be there Monday morning." Well, they asked me to come in on Thursday, which I did. I worked Thursday and Friday with Rick Ricardo in order to become familiar with the operation of radio station WGES. I took my place on the air Monday morning, one hour from 12 to 1. Rick came on after me for about 2-1/2 to 3 years. This station had a 24-hour license but they only ran fourteen hours a day. Sid McCoy had the night shift right ahead of Rick. There was another black dude by the name of Sam Evans who called himself "Jam with Sam." I used to work with Sam now and then.

How did you open your show?

I opened my show with the record "Open the Door Richard." It's by five different artists and I'd use different ones but I had sound effects that were permanent. I had this creaking, opening door and whichever record I used, I finally settled down to the version sung by the Mac Bays because Mac Bays' ["Open the Door Richard"] was the most comical.

Can you tell me about your community activities?

I worked with the police department in Chicago reorganizing a group of young people. We kept between 800 and 900 young people in an organization that we sponsored. They eliminated that sometime in the latter part of 1990, but we kept that for eighteen years. During those years we raised thousands of dollars to take care of these kids. We'd take kids to the ball games, football, baseball, basketball. Sometimes we'd go as far as blackmailing the owners to get free tickets for the kids. I also worked in various political campaigns. I was very successful in electing some black officials in the city of Chicago, although some of them didn't really appreciate it after they got in office. We would have liked to have them compensate our organizations that helped the community and help the kids, but that never happened.

Did you see yourself as a role model? How did people perceive you as Richard, "Open the Door Richard"? How did people react to you?

I'd like for you to see my scrapbook. I have in there a minimum of twenty-nine pictures of public appearances at malls alone. I gave shows and things which I ignore, that is strictly commercial, like I had B.B. King in Chicago for the first time he ever came to Chicago. I brought him in on a show. I brought Ray Charles in, the first time Ray Charles had ever been on a show in Chicago. That was strictly commercial because we were making money for our pockets for being a role model; sometimes it was turned into commercial situations like there was a small city west of Chicago called DeKalb, Illinois, that is strictly ultra-conservative and ultra-white. There are no black people living there. They had my name on a contest that they held out there every year, as the most popular disc jockey. I was the only black boy on the air there and I won the contest. I went out there to speak and I said, "I'm going to shock these people," so I took a bunch of records with me, popular records with both black and white. They asked me to come up on the platform to get my little plaque, they are going to publicize me, interview me and all that stuff. And I pulled up this box of records and they said, "What you going to do, give the records away?" You know these are all city, county, and state officials. I said, "No, we're not going to give them away. What is this whole thing about?" They said to raise money for Cerebral Palsy. I said, "Good, I thought that that was what it was. And I just wanted to add on a little money for Cerebral Palsy." I said, "I'm going to auction off these records." I auctioned off over a hundred 45s, which at that time were selling for 75–85 cents, took in around $1,500, and gave that money to Cerebral Palsy. It upset those people, those ultra-conservative people, because I was black and successful in raising this money.

I worked for 7-Up for years, very successful. When I went to work for 7-Up, 7-Up was only used as a mixer with alcohol. I turned 7-Up into an ordinary drink in the whole northern area of Illinois. Mr. Joyce who owned the 7-Up franchise said, "Richard, you can't go to Old Orchard," Northern Illinois' largest shopping center. He said, "That's a white neighborhood." I said, "Mr. Joyce, one time let me do what I want to do. I want two trailers of 7-Up." Now I had a crew that followed me. We took the 7-Up to Old Orchard. So I had all these people and two forty-foot trailers of 7-Up brought to Old Orchard. I had a hoist put me on the top of the pile of this 7-Up, which was stacked as high as two stories. I had my microphone up there and I had my crew down on the ground and they were playing records and serving 7-Up, giving away 7-Up, selling 7-Up, doing everything with 7-Up to the kids, mostly white kids. They were hollering, "Richard, come on down. Richard, come on down." And I said, "Can't come down, can't come down, got to get rid of all this 7-Up." When I came down we still had a crowd of maybe 3 or 4,000 of these white kids around and I was on the ground and we had disposed of all this big mound of 7-Up. That is one incidence. It was a commercial project and it changed the thinking of commercial writers that write commercials for television today. They have gone into both black and white on television now as part of it.

One other thing that I used as a role model in Chicago was the Blues Fest. I emceed the Blues Fest one night each year. That's a 15- to 20-minute job and in each instance there is a minimum of half a million, that's 500,000 white people, and an average of 100,000 black people at this Blues Fest each year. And each year, which does me so proud, I got a standing ovation from anywhere from 600,000 to 800,000 mixed groups—and I just loved it! But that is my criteria of being a role model and the feeling and working with the public—it's beautiful.

Can you tell me about the time when Emmitt Till was murdered and how you reacted to that being a personality on the air and how that affected you?

I only wish that this would be shown on live TV so that this story could be told. I was a very viable part in that situation. After Emmitt was killed, his body was brought to Chicago because his family all lived in Chicago. They would not open the casket. Raynor and Sons Funeral Home had the body. They were located then at 41st and Cottage Grove in Chicago. There were thousands and thousands of people standing in line to view the body and thousands of people around with bushel baskets taking money from these people that were standing in line to give to the family, although all the money didn't get to the family. Here was the part I played in it. There's a guy named Dootsy that manufactured records in California and he did a record on Emmitt Till called "The Death of Emmitt Till" and he got that thing on overnight. He had a group that sang the record. I think I have the only copy of that record in the United States today because there was a systematic thing that went on by authorities that destroyed that record. It was the whole story of Emmitt Till and I played it on the air for about half an hour and my boss and station owner, Dr. Dyer, came downstairs. This is the first time he'd ever done anything like this in all the time that I worked for him on the air; he took that record off the turntable and broke it in two. He said, "If you play this record one more time, Richard, I love you and I hate to see you go, but you've got to find another job." He said, "You guys are going to start a race riot," and that was a fact—it would have started a race riot. We didn't think about that then. All we was going to do was play the record. Anyway, I got a copy of the record but I didn't play it anymore, but I saved that copy.

Did you play a role in promoting civil rights for blacks?

We were upset about it [segregation] but we never got a focus on the real situation because we were threatened by the authorities. They did not want us to take a role in it. We were too prominent. We dominated black thinking in Chicago at that time. We owned that particular radio station.

Tell me about your assessment of this whole payola scandal. What was the driving force, in your view?

Greed. Everybody wanted money. We wanted money too as disc jockeys, but for the record companies to come in and give us money to play a record, in my estimation, was the worst thing in the world. And that is what happened. Now if you will excuse me, let's talk about something else. You go to your next question because I will not go any further with that subject.

During the riots in the '60s, did you guys do anything to try to maintain peace and quiet?

Oh my goodness, yes. We did the very best we could. It wasn't very impressive. It wasn't very successful. It was mostly young people that burned up Chicago at that time. They had made up their minds. They completely destroyed Roosevelt Road from like Sacramento, west all the way to Cicero, a highly commercial area with stores on both sides of the streets all the way. They destroyed large residential buildings in that area. They burned them to the ground and we were steadily asking them not to do this, but it was not very effective. The young people were out of hand, they were angry. It did not subside until the state brought in the militia and they were roaming the streets in tanks and other armored vehicles with guns. They claimed they didn't have them loaded, but who knows? It quieted down after that.

When formats were introduced into black radio, did that have an impact on the popularity of black disc jockeys?

It had an impact on the popularity of the listening audience. The disc jockeys were commercially inclined. They had to earn their living and they just had to take it. Radio changed completely at that time. Jockeys couldn't comment. You see we used to be like neighborhood commentators; we talked about anything we wanted to talk. When formatting moved in, DJs were told to play three records, give the commercials, and disc jockeys became robots, which they are today. They cannot express themselves. Only on certain radio stations does a disc jockey have that right to express his own opinion—otherwise, that's gone. We lived through it until they sold the station. It was sold twice within a period of about 3–4 years but I left that station and went to another one. So it didn't bother me, and I stopped even thinking of being a disc jockey. I went into sales and promotion.

Why is that? Why did you give up on that whole concept?

Because of what I just said. You could not be yourself anymore. You became a robot and I don't want to be a robot. I have my opinions, I like to work in my community, I like to do something for my people and if there is any uplifting that I can do, or could do, as a radio disc jockey, that is what I wanted to do. I used to announce for all the neighborhood. People would call me up and ask me to do that, you see, you couldn't do that anymore. And any events that were happening around the schools that would be progressive, you could join in that and you could aid them, you could help them. They don't allow you to do that any more. It changed the whole picture. A disc jockey is nothing but a controlled robot today. All across the whole country, white ones and the black ones. Now and then there is a few exceptions where they are really entertainers and basically a disc jockey is an entertainer, as he is supposed to be. He's not supposed to be a robot. Basically, there is so much greed in this country and the control is so strict. Even the disc jockey who would want to promote himself by aiding the community cannot do it. And I think that is tragic.

If you had to identify one or two events that would symbolize the work of Richard Stams and black radio, that you would have people remember you for, what would they be?

One would be the youth group that we established. When we maintained 800 or 900 kids under complete control the year round.

By communicating love and being a part of the community, is that how you were able to establish rapport with your listening audience?

I still do, and I just love it. I still do a lot of shows and meetings. I make all kinds of meetings; churches, community meetings and etc. . . . I just try my best to shy just a little bit away from politics. I do my duties in politics, I vote and I try to get my whole family and my whole area to vote. I do that, but that is as far as I go. I don't try to influence the politicians anymore because that is probably out. But the neighborhood and the kids, yes, I still build basketball teams and basketball nets, I do the whole thing—baseball teams. We have a baseball team in my neighborhood now and I work with that and I work with the kids however I can to help them, to guide them in the right direction and in the direction where they will eventually appreciate where you came from and be able to make a contribution to their own when I am gone. That's my life, that's the way I think.

You are referred to as the "Crown Prince of Black Radio."

There was a reason for that. There was a reason for the Crown Prince business. Al Benson was the beginning of all rhythm and blues radio in the United States and he called himself the King of Radio. In order to eliminate any hard feelings in the competition between us, I was the Crown Prince. Let him be the king. I was bigger than Benson and I just loved him. He taught me a lot. Benson took me to New York the first time from Chicago just to work on our own accounts; as I said, we brokered. We sold our own shows and naturally in order to do that we had to go to the source which were the advertising agencies. I had never been to an advertising agency. I had worked with local advertisers and local stores and business establishments but I had never been to New York to sell and Benson took me there and taught me how to sell. Benson was tall and he wore funny clothes, he had a lot of money but he wore funny clothes—funny-colored clothes. He wore a purple suit, green shoes, brown hat, a red tie. He wanted to attract attention and he did. And he'd go in these offices and these little girls sitting out front, these secretaries, would say, "Oh, no, you don't have an appointment." I saw Benson actually put his foot on the door of the advertising department of Chesterfield Cigarettes and kick that door in and the agent sitting behind the desk said, "Oh, my God, Mr. Benson, I'm so glad to see you." And Benson had kicked the man's door in.

If you had a free hand today and you could change things in terms of black radio, what would you do?

I'd move it right back to the level that we had it in the '50s and '60s. Let the disc jockey work in the community as long as it was clean and good and contributed to the community and to individual groups, especially charity groups. Any number of organizations that need this kind of help today don't get it. They need it and I would allow them to do that. I'd give them a free hand. It not only would enhance the listening audience of your radio station, it would help the community and we possibly wouldn't have all these bad situations that are in existence today.

Would you like to make a concluding statement?

I have no concluding statement except I appreciate you asking me to do this, but I appreciate more radio itself and what radio allowed me to do in my community. It made it possible for me to be in demand, to make all these visits around the country. It made it possible and gave me the popularity that I needed to do these lectures and so on. throughout the country and be able to help all kinds of children; white, black, Indian, Japanese, all of them. My past gives me the opportunity to do this continually as long as I'm physically and mentally able.

I am a Christian, I like to talk about that. Kids need to be more familiar with what goes on in the right churches. I love that. I'm a member of my church—one of the largest black churches in the United States. My pastor is a role model in the church. He's a role model on television and in radio and I just love my contributions to my church, to my pastor. We have two regular television broadcasts. We have one called "Sunday Morning Sunday School" and then we have our regular broadcast at night. Purvis Spann just bought a new radio station down in Jacksonville, Florida, and we broadcast our New Year's service over it from Chicago. From 10 o'clock at night until 2 in the morning. And we had calls coming in from Jacksonville, Florida, up until 6 o'clock in the morning on New Year's Day from our broadcast. We make a big contribution, we all work hard in the church to make these broadcasts successful and it's beautiful. My only hope in life is that I will be able to continue with that contribution which I deeply appreciate and I believe contributes something to young people and to some older people. Did you know that I'm the oldest living disc jockey in the United States? I'll be 86 on the first day of April.

◆ 15 ◆

Roy Wood, Sr.

I met Roy Wood in 1991 when I was in Birmingham, Alabama, on sabbatical leave. At that time, Roy was a news anchor for WENN-FM in Birmingham. I called him and he invited me to the news studio, where I conducted the interview. I truly enjoyed my conversation with Roy. He was open, honests and forthright. During a brief interruption, he showed me how he announced the news. He used impeccable English and didn't miss a cue. He was the consummate professional, whose intelligence and insight are revealed in this interview.

Wood graduated from Columbia University (New York) and also studied journalism at Columbia College in Chicago. He began his career in broadcasting in 1932. His first job was with Jack L. Cooper in Chicago. He has been a news reporter and announcer for WEDC (Chicago) and WGRY (Gary, Indiana).

Wood's style is best described as articulate, with a middle-American accent. Because of his impeccable English, Woods easily found work at white radio stations and national radio networks, where he introduced radio programs to national audiences.

Wood became program director for KATZ in St. Louis, Missouri, which served black listeners in that area. Later, he produced his own programs and became news director at WYNR and WVON. Wood's nationally syndicated radio program, "One Black Man's Opinion," became a widely used feature on black radio stations. Wood became president of the National Black Network, a distribution service that provided news and features to black-oriented radio stations.

MARCH, 3, 1991

Could you tell me how you started in radio?

It was no accident, it was by design in a sense of speaking. I guess becoming crippled for life by an automobile accident I developed a terrible inferiority complex, became somewhat withdrawn. I was blessed with a mother who had an education, one who decided that maybe psychiatry would help me. After a psychiatric examination the psychiatrist said, "No way do I see anything wrong with the young man except that he has a low self-esteem and ego problem and I think more education would take care of that. And if he goes back to school I think he will overcome it." I had already a Bachelor of Science degree, so when he suggested going back to school I said, "Well, I'm not doing anything else, I guess I may as well. What would you suggest I study?" He said, "Well you have a good voice, why don't you become a radio announcer." And I said, "They don't have any need for negro radio announcers." The psychiatrist's quick retort was, "I didn't say be a Negro announcer, I said be a radio announcer." That put the ball in my court because many people hemmed themselves in with descriptive adjectives that don't amount to a thing. And the word "negro" before announcer didn't have anything at all really to do with being an announcer. So I accepted the challenge and went on to J School at Columbia University.

By the time I had finished my master's degree, Al Benson in Chicago had become a big-time, black disc jockey and rhythm and blues music was blossoming and blooming and being big business. Oscar Brown, Jr., and a fellow named Art McCoo used to do a news block on Al Benson's night-time news. They did such a masterful job of reporting black news, I knew right away that news would be the way to go. Now I hadn't had the kind of expertise when it came to news reporting that I thought was necessary, so I went to the Chicago College of Fine Arts, which is now called Columbia College of Broadcasting, and I took some special courses in broadcast news writing, broadcast news reporting, and I also took some courses in microphone technique because there is a proper, as well as improper, way to use a microphone. I also took commercial advertising and commercial advertising writing so that I could write broadcast commercials and would know how to read them. And hopefully here in the Birmingham area you have heard some of the radio commercials I do for Citizens Insurance Company, Smith and Gaston Funeral Home, and others. I have had several newscasts that have been sponsored by Blue Cross/Blue Shield, for example, national advertisers, Hamms Beer, so many of them. In any event, when I finished that particular course, Mr. Jack L. Cooper, who was a friend of my mother, and who owned even the time that Al Benson was using on the radio because back in those days black people in broadcasting had to buy the time from the radio station to get on the air, hired me to work for him.

Was it different for whites?

Well yeah, white people, they just hired them as announcers and as program originators and presenters. Blacks had to buy the time for their programs like churches buy time on radio today. The black man, Jack L. Cooper in Chicago, bought blocks of time from WHFC, WGES, WEDC and then resold that time. He bought it wholesale and sold it retail to the advertisers who would buy spots in his show. And it just so happened that he had 15 minutes of vacant time on WEDC, Emil Denemark Cadillac Company in Chicago, and it was a news block. And he said, "I don't have a line to WEDC from my house." Cooper did his broadcasting from his home, he had lines to the different radio stations and he did his broadcasting from home, but in the meantime he didn't have a line to WEDC and he said, "Roy, if you want to go out there to do that 15 minute news block, you can go and do it and I can't pay you any money but you can do the news and you will get some air time experience." I thanked him, and I accepted the challenge to do the 15-minute news block, without pay, just for the opportunity to get some experience.

At the time I was an insurance agent for the Chicago Metropolitan Mutual Insurance Company, which at that time was the Metropolitan Funeral System. Lloyd Stanom, white engineer at WEDC, was the engineer on duty when I would do the news, and he said, "Roy, you are good. I have a friend that is an engineer on WCFL who is building a radio station in Gary, Indiana, and I'm going to tell George Whitney about you and suggest that you go and see him so that you get a full-time job." I went to see Mr. Whitney and when WGRY was completed in Gary, Indiana, on November 23, 1947, I was airborne on WGRY as a full-fledged member of the staff of that radio station. I was making the huge sum of $25.00 a week, and it cost me that much to ride the train from Chicago to Gary to get to the damn job.

There was a white fellow in school with me, Howard Fischer, a Jewish boy who got a job in South Bend, Indiana, where Notre Dame is located. In the spring of 1949, Howard called me and he said, "Roy, I have a friend who has a radio station and he needs an announcer and I told him about you and I explained to him that you were black but you didn't sound 'Negro.' " He told Howard that he didn't care what my complexion was, if I was as good as Howard said I was, he would give me a job. So I went to South Bend, took an audition, the radio station was located in the suburb of South Bend called Mishawaka, Indiana. He gave me the job with WJVA, which is now WNDU. I went to work there in the end of the summer and the next spring, 1950, the Indianapolis Speedway Races were scheduled to go. A Mr. Bill Dean of the Mutual Broadcasting Systems, a central division radio network, came to Mishawaka or South Bend to make arrangements for WJVA to carry the Indianapolis Speedway Races that were to run on Memorial Day. He and the man that owned the radio station that I was working for were out late that night and Mr. Dean said he couldn't go to sleep, it was about 4– 4:15 in the morning, so he just flipped on the radio. Whoever was in the hotel room before him had WJVA tuned in and I am on doing the news. I did a wake-up program, "Sunrise Serenade," named after Glenn Miller's tune "Sunrise Serenade," in which I did farm reports, the news, weather, played some music, more farm reports, hog futures, cattle futures and so forth. So Dean is listening to the show and excitedly he called me up at about 4:30 in the morning. He said, "You know you sound just like Gordon Graham, a member of our news team in Indianapolis, Indiana. How long you been here?" And I told him and he said, "How much do you make?" and I said, "$50.00 a week." He said, "How would you like a job paying you a little more money than that?" He said, "My name is Bill Dean and I am with the Mutual Broadcasting System. What time do you get off?" And I said, "9 o'clock in the morning." He says, "Alright, I tell you what. I'm at the Mishawaka Hotel, room 410, you come here to see me. Let's have breakfast together and talk about it." I said, "All right, sir." I hung up the phone thinking it was Ronnie Householder, the owner of the radio station I work for, playing a trick on me. Now Ronnie Householder gets to the radio station every morning about 8:30 or 8:40, so whenever he got to the station he would come in and say, "Good morning Roy, how you doing, so-and-so, you did a good job but—" He'd point out errors if I'd made any. So he came in that morning and I said "Did you have a good time with me on the phone this morning?" He said, "What do you mean?" and I said, "Well you called me about 4:30 a.m. telling me something about a better job and all of that nonsense and saying something about a Bill Dean and the Mutual Broadcasting System." He said, "Did Bill call you? He is in town." I said, "Well, someone who said that they were Bill Dean called me and said I should see him at the Mishawaka Hotel." He said, "Well, he is here and that is the way he is. If he said see him, you go see him." So I did and when I opened the door and came in, Mr. Dean changed colors about five times. He said, "I had no idea that you were a Negro." I smiled and said, "Negro or not, Mr. Dean, you and I had a breakfast engagement and I'm hungry." And he said, "So we did." He said, "Shall we go down the stairs or do you want to eat up here?" I said, "Well, I don't want you to be embarrassed, maybe we could go down the stairs in Indianapolis but in Mishawaka I couldn't get a hamburger inside the White Castle hamburger joint." He says, "You are kidding." I said, "I kid you not." He said, "Well, the state legislature passed a law on nonsegregation in 1949." I said, "Well, they ain't got the news here yet." So anyway, we had breakfast upstairs and after the breakfast, he said, "I am going to be honest with you, Roy, I had no idea that you were Negro. I don't know whether the climate is right yet or not but if I couldn't tell that you were a Negro, and I've been in broadcasting twenty-five years, I doubt that anyone else would know." He says, "You send me your audition tape, personally, and I promise you will hear from me." That was May 10, 1950. By the end of June I'd given up hearing from Mr. Dean but on July 2, 1950 I got the telegram. "Roy the job is yours — you can give your two-week notice and you can come to WIBC, Indianapolis, 30 West Washington Boulevard, Indianapolis, Indiana TODAY, Bill Dean."

How did you feel about being offered the position?

Oh, I felt great! You know I was ecstatic! I showed the telegram to my boss and Mr. Householder said, "Well Roy, I am happy for you. You are a good announcer but I don't think you are ready for that big market and national exposure just yet. You need a little experience." He said, "I'll tell you what I'll do, you go ahead and I'll hold your job for you for thirty days." I haven't been back to Mishawaka, Indiana, yet. And that was forty-three years ago just about. I never went back to Mishawaka but I was in Indianapolis for about four years with WIBC, the flagship station from the Mutual Broadcasting System. I did the intro and the outro for shows like *The Shadow* , *Young Doctor Malone*, *Guiding Light*, *Queen for a Day*, *True Detective Stories*, Mike Hammer's *The Hammer Guy*, and Frank Edwards'*News Casts*. I was his commercial announcer for the Chrysler motor car company and the men and women of the American Federation of Labor. THIS IS WIBC, INDIANAPOLIS, THE FRIENDLY VOICE OF INDIANA. IT IS 7 O'CLOCK, TIME NOW FOR MR. FRANK EDWARDS AND THE NEWS, PRESENTED BY THE MEN AND WOMEN OF THE AMERICAN FEDERATION OF LABOR. And then would come a tone, Mr. Edwards in a moment, and then I would do a commercial—NOW HERE HE IS, FRANK EDWARDS AND THE NEWS. MR. EDWARDS.

How many people would know that?

Very few people. And from 'Nap town, 1954, March something, there was a news story in the *Chicago Tribune*, the *Herald American* and the *Indianapolis News* that in Chicago, Illinois, a black disc jockey by the name of Al Benson had made over $300,000 in 1953 and had been earning upwards of $100,000 since 1950 when rhythm and blues and black radio became big—first black radio station owned and operated by blacks. J.B. Blayton, an accountant and a teacher of accounting at AU, bought WERD in Atlanta and that was the first black-owned radio station. The next black-owned radio station was owned by Dr. Haley Bell and his family in Detroit, Michigan, WCHB. And he was encouraged to do that by, would you believe, Jack Gibson. Gibson said, "Buy and go into the radio business." Another fellow by the name of Larry Dean was on the staff of the radio station but he and Dr. Bell's son-in-law couldn't get along. Dean left. WCHB is still a powerful station. They have AM and FM. Unfortunately, there are more than 9,000 commercial radio stations, AM and FM, in the country. Black people only own and operate 171 at the moment. And actually only 137 of that 171 are licensed to operate. The others are in construction or transition or something. College radio stations are doing a good service in terms of enlightening and educating the African-American community. But they lean heavy on entertainment. They can't do anything commercial. Howard University, where I taught as an Associate Professor under Dean Tony Brown, had the only so-called college radio station that is commercial but Howard University as a land-grant college is owned and operated by the federal government. I was so surprised I didn't know what to do when I accepted a job as Associate Professor and my first paycheck comes from the U.S. Treasury Department instead of Howard University. So it shows that when it comes to the matter of communication, the white man has total control.

In the United States, even today?

In the United States even today. This broadcast facility from which I'm talking to you is not in the condition or position in the economic sense to do the things that we know we should, and that needs to be done in terms of informing and educating the African-American community. The advertising dollar is the life-support system of the media—electronic and print. Who controls advertising? Madison Avenue, advertising agencies who get their money from the people who provide the consumerable merchandise that is advertised on television and radio. But they have a hands-off policy. They will give your advertising agents X numbers of millions of dollars to go ahead and promote the product. You do what you want to do about it. So now if I am doing something that seems to countermand the position of the white hierarchy in a rulership level, then you are going to withdraw your support.

Why should they give money to somebody to undermine their position?

Right. And the general public did not understand that. And this is a nation of their leaderships. First we are fed the illusion of citizens having command of the government, they lie in reality. It looks good on paper but it doesn't work. I base that statement on the reality that political power emanates from a base of economic power. I call this country the United Estates of America. In this country, every time you cross a state line a different set of rules, regulations and laws go into effect. So it is United Estates. If the federal law meant anything, the 13th, the 14th and the 15th Amendments would be all African-American citizens need; see, black people are the only people in this country who were created by law. In 1787 when they drafted and wrote the first constitution of this country, African people who were then slaves were counted only as three-fifths of a human being for the purpose of taxation and representation. Now, next after 1865 they passed a law to make you a citizen. In 1859, the Dred Scott case, Judge Taney went down in infamy for his statement that as far as he was concerned black people didn't have any rights the white would be forced to obey. In 1865 they passed the 13th Amendment which freed the slaves. In 1867, the 14th Amendment allegedly made you a citizen and in '69 the 15th Amendment to the Constitution allegedly made it right for you to vote.They passed the Civil Rights Bill in 1871 that became operative in 1875 and lasted until 1883 when the Supreme Court declared that that bill was unconstitutional. But between '75 and '83, you had all the rights and we had 14 congressmen to pass through Congress and I think two U.S. senators. Today you don't have one U.S. Senator who is black and only twenty-three black Congresspersons and yet we are supposed to be 12 percent of the population. That being true we should have fifty-some representatives in the House of Representatives. Plus the fact that if the 13th, the 14th, and the 15th Amendments were in fact a true part of national law, why do we need a Civil Rights Bill and a Voting Rights Act? Being born in this country, according to the constitution, makes you a citizen. Why is it that a black child is born but is not clothed in every garment that citizenship affords? And then, the Voting Rights Act, now in effect, dies in the year 2009.

The Voting Rights Act expires in 2009?

2009. It was renewed in 1984 for 25 years. You were created by law. So if I create you by law my basic postulation is, if I create you by law, I can uncreate you by law. Black people don't write laws for this country—white people do. Before 1865, in slavery time, you were nothing but chattel—like a cow, calf, or a chicken. I can tell you I can do whatever I want to do with you and it is literally the same way today.

How about radio, how can an announcer . . . ?

Radio, the communications arena, could do much more than it does. I think that, in short, if those persons, who are raping the black people, radio stations, especially those which serve the African-American community and the poor white community, ours is—they call it urban contemporary should do more for the community. The white one is called rock and country, or country rock. Those are poor white folks who are in the same condition and position as we are but they don't know that because they are blinded by the light of the White House that makes them think that they are all-powerful because of their skin color. They don't have sense enough to recognize and realize that they are in no better shape than we are economically, nor intellectually. As a matter of fact, intellectually we are better off than they are because we know more than they know. The difference between them and us is that when they know better, they do better. As long as we keep poor, white folk ignorant, they ain't going to do nothing but if they ever get smart and some of them do, then they move. That is the reason Martin King was assassinated. He was about to do the impossible—form a viable coalition between the masses against the classes. His poor people's campaign on Washington, D.C. in 1968 caused his assassination. When the power structure saw the masses of these underclasses coming together, poor white folks from Appalachia, Georgia, Iowa, Florida, and Indians from Florida and poor folks all the way from the west coast, thousands and thousands strong coming and King talking the right talk, he was letting them know that masses keep the classes on their asses and if the masses withdraw their support, the classes become asses also. And they weren't about to let that happen. That's what the garbage workers' strike in Memphis, Tennessee was all about. And we as a people do not fully understand and comprehend the reality that money is power supreme in a capitalist nation. Now we have some supreme power because our annual spendable income is between, in this point in time, 250 to 260 billion dollars. That makes us, in terms of economic return base line, eighth of the nine largest nations in the world. But ours is expendable, we get 250–60 billion a year and we retain less than three billion dollars of that money. Most of the billions that we save go to the black church, not the black bank and the black insurance company.

Where does the black church invest its money?

The black church invests it money in what I call spook estate. I call it spook estate as opposed to real estate because don't nobody live in the churches, big black preacher thumping his big black chest and talking about "I got myself a million-dollar church." No babies are born there, no manufacturing goes on there and the church affords four jobs if it affords that many. It has got to be a big church to have six jobs. The preacher's job, the assistant pastor, the choir director and the musician and the janitor—that's five, I may have missed one. The National Baptist Convention USA represents about seven million. Most black people in this country are Baptist; they got no business being a Christian in the first place because that's the slavemaster's religion. Now if it was his religion, why am I going to be fool enough to understand that, unlike all the other people in this country who came here, I am the only group who did not come of my own free will. My passage to this country was in the hold of a ship. The man told a lie to the pope he was on to Africa to Christianize the natives as if we didn't have a religion and a God before that white man ever set his foot there, Hispanic, in this particular case, because it was Spain that went there the first time. The point is that since I did have a religion in my native state of Africa and the man claims he is coming there to Christianize me, why is it that I got to be a better Christian than he is? That is a question that we never ask ourselves.

We are better Christians than they are?

We are better Christians, we are. In terms of the ethos of what Christianity is, except we don't practice Christianity with each other. We practice being Christian to the oppressor because we treat him better than we treat ourselves.

Why is that?

It is because of the false images and the false religious education. They freed our body but the man kept our mind enslaved by way of his books, his newspapers, his television set and his radio stations. It all comes back to communication and that is what you and I have been talking about.

So basically, psychology has taught me that you are the sum total of environment, heredity, what you eat, what you read and your over-all environment. All of those in this country are white-dominated, white-promoted, and white-supported. That is why we try so hard to be like white, if not white. Look how black women are dying their hair all those white folks'colors of hair, blond, red, all of that. That is a sign of self-hate but it is told to them that it is stylish. Aesop was black, and Aesop was not Greek, he was a slave.

Aesop was an Ethiopian.

Right, but in any event in one of his favorites, he tells the story of the fox who lost his tail. Now they had been warned about the traps set for foxes. He said, "You be sure now to watch out for those traps. They are so fast that if your tail hits it, it will clip it off, you'll get caught by the tail." To make a long story short, one old sly fox thought he was hip, you know, he's going out and he is so righteous and everything and damn, the trap, you know—to make a long story short, his tail got caught by the trap and somehow he wriggled loose and he come back with a short tail. So when he got back with his short tail they said, "Oh brother fox, you got trapped." He said, "Oh no I didn't get caught, this is the new style. All foxes are going to be wearing short tails next year." So they say, "Where did you get it cut?" And he told them and a lot of the young bucks like him started to rush off to get their tails cut off too and so an old fox said, "Wait a minute child, hold on, don't go so fast. Now if the fox's short tail is the style, tell that smart brother there to bring you his barber." Don't you go to the barber, tell him he's got his tail cut off, bring you his barber.

Now the point is that when it comes to the hair styles and things that women put on their heads and all that, this stuff is decided in some laboratory and they don't know who designs the hair styles, who decides on these colors. It is designed to sell the product. That's what it is all about. And black women are now going to the white beauty shops to get their hair done where the white people are employing black beauticians to do the work and give them the money. You notice how black beauty shops are disappearing. You know that's another sign of self-hate. The white man's sugar is sweeter, his ice is colder, and all of that which is an ideology promulgated in the grammar school books, the high school books and all of that. And then you go to a white institution of higher education as you and I have done and you come out with that perspective. I wouldn't take nothing in the world for my basic foundation, undergrad at Morehouse. You can see the duplicity and the chicanery of the white institutions. But I hate to see young black children finishing high school rushing to UAB or Auburn and to Alabama. I'd like to see them go to Miles, for example.

I have been in the broadcasting business now for forty-three years and the only big change that I have noted in this industry is that blacks in broadcasting are still the lowest-paid and most underutilized people in the business. Except when they work at white outfits. There is a reason for it. This radio station, unlike WZZK which gets a hundred and some dollars a minute for time, they scream and holler like a pig stuck at the stockyards if we charge $75 for a minute and we reach more people with spendable income than WZZK is ever going to reach and black people don't keep no money. They spend all they can get in their hands. The only markets where broadcast people make money are in those markets that are unionized, American Federation of Television and Radio Artists (AFTRA). They have one AFTRA station in Birmingham, out of some twenty-three broadcast facilities. I think that is Channel 6. All the engineers get paid because to be an engineer of a radio station you have to belong to the engineer's union. And no matter what radio station you work at you are going to make the same pay because they have contracts. They have a pay scale.

What about all these changes we have seen in terms of formats and how they have gone to rhythm and blues and how they have come back to urban contemporary?

I'm glad you asked that. I warned E. Rodney Jones who was the program director at WVON in 1972, when they were coming in with what they called "crossover" music, like Madonna. Music you can hear on black and on white radio; that is called "crossover." Now the time was when white radio stations wouldn't play any black artists except Nat King Cole, OK? Now then, the music manufacturers control the ebb and flow of music and they also, essentially, control the radio stations'musical fare because they decide what they want to promote and you get the records for free. If I had anything to do with it, I would buy my records and leave the record manufacturers out in the cold because they control what you hear in terms of music on the radio. But I told Rodney that crossover music meant trying to cross blacks out, and today with automation and with the CD where you can load a CD machine with twelve or fifteen CD records and you can program a radio station for twenty-four hours and don't have nobody there working. You don't have to have spots, a manufacturer produces on a cassette and all you do is put them on a cart and time the machine to play. Crossover music was an effort to cross blacks out of radio.

Why would someone conspire to do that?

They would conspire to do that because a broadcast personality is something else that they have eliminated. Radio stations don't want personality DJs because a personality has too much power—if he decides to leave, you are going to lose half of your audience. So they do everything they possibly can to suppress personality for that particular reason. And yet when black radio started personality was everything. Jack Cooper cannot be given enough credit as he was responsible for Al Benson's start. Commercial broadcasting was born in 1921 and Jack L. Cooper started in 1923. Al Benson got the time on WGES because Mr. Cooper was abandoning an hour and he convinced them to let Al have that time. Al Benson had a personality that sold records and the record companies catered to Al, he was at the hey-day of payola. If you didn't bring a few hundred dollars with your record, Benson wouldn't do it. And fact is that if Benson played the record, the record sold, no matter what it was. It could be bad as all get-out, Howling Wolf, for example, for Leonard Chess sounded like a bear growling in a cave. Benson played the kind of glitzy blues and jazz music that black people had been accustomed to in their native south. He was the first big money maker in so-called black or rhythm and blues radio. Much to his credit, when he got his act together and solidified, he then sublet time to other disc jockeys with personalities like Rick Ricardo, Richard Stams, Norm Spaulding, and Sam Evans. Benson I loved because when I switched to black radio and came home to Chicago in 1957. I worked with him after quitting in Indianapolis in 1954, I went to St. Louis, Missouri, and opened KATZ there.

When you say "opened," what exactly do you mean?

It means that it was a new black radio facility and I was the program director. It was my first job as a program director for a black radio station and Mr. Silverman, a Jewish fellow from Chicago, gave me the job because of my reputation as an announcer and he wanted something good for St. Louis. Spider Burke was the big man in St. Louis at the time. I said KATZ invites you to enjoy our blues in your living room, wherever you are, and if you like you can come down to 800 Center Street, downtown St. Louis, Missouri, and hear the blues in our studio. Spider was dead anyway in a sense of speaking because he belonged to George August Busch's daughter (of the Busch Beer family) and August told the station to fire him. They offered him $25,000 to leave St. Louis, and she bought him a pink Cadillac. Yes, Spider was bad. I left St. Louis and came home to Chicago in 1957. Mr. Cooper again intervened in my behalf. He talked to Congressman Richard W. Hoffman, 10th Congressional District, who owned a foreign language radio station, WHFC, voice of the west town, Cicero, Illinois. They used very little English, if any, but they needed an announcer and because Cooper owned 25 percent of the radio station, Congressman Hoffman hired me. It was a union station and I went to work at this foreign language station where you'd have to introduce a Lithuanian hour, a Ukrainian hour, and so on, all in their native language. I did all of that. This was Cicerio, Illinois, where they don't want no black people to live, there I was, black like I am, a staff announcer at their only radio station.

What kind of a man was Jack Cooper?

Mr. Cooper was somewhat enigmatic, yet he had somewhat of a magnetic personality and he had good business sense. Proof of that reality is the fact that in a time when blacks didn't own radio stations at all and were doing nothing but time brokering, he was smart enough to buy up all the time that was available in Chicago and then sell it himself. He encouraged another man who was a sky-cap, Eddie Honesty, Jr., to buy stock in a station in Indiana, WJOB of Gary, Indiana. Mr. Honesty became a disc jockey there, had time on the station and he owned 25 percent of that station. Jack L. Cooper gave all of these people an opportunity. The man was unselfish. He was known for helping many, including his brothers-in-law, Al Benson, Roy Wood and others.

What about his wife, Gertrude?

Oh yes, but that was his second wife. Very, very nice person, considerably younger than Jack. A lot of entertainers, through Jack's amateur hour, got their exposure on black radio in Chicago through

Jack L. Cooper. A few of them were Mahalia Jackson, Roberta Martin, and James Cleveland. Ethel Waters talked on his station when she came to town. Ethel Waters did a motion picture called "Mamba's Daughters" and she opened a place of business in Chicago, 6324 South Cottage Grove, called "Cabin in the Sky."

So you came back home and you came back to WVON?

No, I came to WHFC, the foreign language station. Now then in 1959 I got the opportunity to get a job at WGES. Congressman Hoffman said, "Roy, please stay here. Everybody likes you." I said, "But I want to be in black radio." He said, "Well, you know, what has color got to do with it, ain't I paying you enough, you want more money? I'll give you $100 per week more money." I said, "No sir, it's not about the money, Congressman, I want to be in black radio." The opportunity for a job at WGES as a staff announcer was open. Now the more the power of the union hierarchy in the station, the more money you make. So I was making $156 a week at WHFC. That was big money then. At WGES the base pay was $196 a week plus time and a half for overtime plus double time for holidays. Aside from that, black radio was growing.

Working at WGES in Chicago, I didn't have to do nothing but sit there and make station breaks and put records on the turntable for the disc jockeys. THE TIME IS FOUR O'CLOCK, TIME NOW FOR THE SWING MASTER, AL BENSON. Let his theme fly and he would give me his signal, I would turn the music down and he would go ahead and rap over the music and when he gave me another signal I'd take my left hand off the record that was cued up, the first record on the show and let it fly. This went on for about six or seven months until Benson and I had a few words over my turning a wrong record loose. I never will forget it. I let that record go and Benson jumped up from the table and called me a stupid, black son of a bitch. I stood up to him and called him a few unmentionable names and said, "If you call me a son of a bitch again I will try my best to kick your ass with my crippled leg." With that he walked out of the studio and went up the stairs and told Dr. Dyer that if Roy Wood is here tomorrow I'm gone! Now Benson was bringing three million dollars a year to the station at that time. How much was Roy Wood bringing? I wasn't bringing nothing, I was taking $196 a week home plus whatever else, you know, overtime. Dr. Dyer called me upstairs and told me I was fired. Now my baby boy Arthur was then four years old. You know, I needed a job. So when Dr. Dyer said that I was fired because Mr. Benson didn't want me to work and the other time slots were taken by staff announcers and said I would have to get work somewhere else Miss Hinzeman said to Dr. Dyer, "Doc, that half-hour that Eddie Plique used to have, 9:30 to 10:00 o'clock, before Sam Evans opens, what if I give Roy that time to go ahead and sell?," because there were time brokers you know. Due to this I got a half-hour show with North-Side TV Repair which stayed on until that station was sold. Do you know how much money I made? With commission, they give you 30 percent of what you sell, right? The man's bill was $1,567 a week, I got 30 percent of that, near $500 a week. The North-Side TV Repair got more business than he could handle. I said when you make that call, let them know that Roy Wood told you. Oh man, I made the money. Then after that Hamms Brewing Company bought me, and after Hamms Beer, Old Style Town Beer which was the number one beer in Chicago. I can sell because I give an air of truthfulness and common sense. I show them a plan that will work to sell.

Didn't Eddie Plique also work at WGES?

Yeah, Eddie Plique did a half hour every night.

What about your parents?

My father died when I was three. My father was a physician, a doctor. My mother was one of the first female black CPAs in the state of Georgia. Her picture hangs in the hall of Morris Brown University as one of the greatest contributors.

What happened after you started selling for Hamms and Old Style?

I was making big money, big money but I had gotten married. I got married in 1947, Roy Jr. was born in 1949 and I had another son born in 1954, and a daughter born in 1957. My ex-wife now is here in Birmingham as we speak. Roy Jr.'s father-in-law died, Mr. Leroy Goree passed away, and so she came to her son's father-in-law's funeral. We are still very good friends. We were married for about twenty-one years, but with me meandering, going here and there and all that, she said, "All of the magnificence that you provided were not what I married you for, you were an insurance man when we got married and I wanted somebody who was coming home every day and having dinner, sit down, listen to the radio, look at the television, and go to bed and get up and do the same thing over the next day." But that wasn't me and she said, "I waited for twenty years for you to come home—you ain't never coming home." That's what broadcasting sort of does to you. It's the hardest field I think for men, in particular, and sometimes women, to maintain a good solid family relationship. There are so many discordant forces that pull against the cleavage of a family. The record promoters and producers pulling on you with all kinds of bribes, inducements and so forth.

And then there's the social side of it. We had many conventions, such as the one to start a black disc jockey organization called the National Association of Black Radio Announcers. Lucky Cordell was an officer in that. Rodney Jones was president, I was the executive secretary at this particular time. We had another convention in Philadelphia with Hy Gold of Gold Disc records in New York. When I got to the hotel and barely got in the door and removed my jacket, I heard a knock on the door. I opened the door and there is a beautiful, voluptuous white woman. She says, "My name is Sandi. I'm from New York and I come to you with compliments of Mr. Hy Gold. I will be your companion while you are in the city of brotherly love." And I looked at her and said, "What?" She said, "Hy Gold says I am to be your guest and your companion while you are here so I am going to be here. Let me call downstairs and tell them to bring my luggage up." I said, "Hold it, pour yourself a cocktail and let me go and put my jacket back on." Because I had the room, you know, flowers and all that stuff.

Gold was a record producer?

Gold was a record manufacturer-producer, yes, Gold Disc Records. I never will forget it. So she sipped a little cocktail, I said, "Now I'll tell you what you do, Capitol Records is having a reception this evening at 6:30 and I'm sure Hy Gold will be here for that. You tell him that Mr. Wood received the package but he didn't unwrap it." So when I saw Gold at the reception I said, "Hy, maybe you have the wrong idea about me, I'm not a personality that can be bought with liquor and women. The woman that you sent up there is beautiful and I don't know how much she is costing you but I have a wife and a baby son and a growing son and something else on the way in Chicago. I need the money more than I need the woman and whiskey. So now whatever you were going to pay that broad, you give me that money." He gave me $500. So I am on record as saying that I got some payola.

But that was when payola was legal, wasn't it?

Well, it's still legal in a sense of speaking but see everything is created by a law—who writes the law? Who says that payola is illegal? Certainly not the people who were giving away the payola. The government, because they wanted a piece of it. They want you to pay income tax on it. But that's just one of the experiences that is proof positive that all these games are played by the purveyors of the music. They want to control you and want you to do what they tell you to do with, by, and for the product that they send. Do you note that on black radio stations you very seldom hear music by Duke Ellington, Count Basie, and you seldom hear music by the new trumpet star from New Orleans, Wynton Marsalis? In other words, jazz, which is our heritage, you seldom hear on black radio stations, especially in the Birmingham area. If you want to hear jazz, you have got to tune in to WUAT, University of Alabama, Tuscaloosa's radio station, or else Sanford University's radio station, except on Sunday when Sahara Glaude is on radio. That should be a part of the total concept of music in black radio. They set aside one hour on Saturday morning here for blues. That is the basic black music, the reason being that they don't sell as many blues records as they do the hip-hop stuff that is coming up. That is for the purpose of selling records. They control the music that is on the radio, the record companies.

If you were to give someone some advice in terms of going into broadcasting today, a young black male or female, what words of wisdom could you tell them?

First of all, LEARN the language of the controllers, meaning advertisers. Learning the language means learn to speak American well. Forget about that line about learning to speak English because we don't speak English in this country, we speak American which is a patois of all the languages of human kind, including African. Next, I would say for you to be a broadcaster, I would advise you to be willing to start at the lowest end of the totem pole and work your way up. The lowest end of the totem pole is some small radio station where you can learn to utilize, not only your talents, but learn how to utilize the equipment that you must work with. You don't get that kind of exposure in the institutions of higher education where they teach communication. You do get a smattering of it but I have learned more on the job than I learned in the classroom.

What about the things in terms of the head, or philosophy?

In terms of philosophy or being able to deal with . . . my philosophy is in a poem taught to me by my almost unlettered grandpa. "Be proud to meet the man who is proud of being black but who also is intelligent enough to be oblivious of that fact. Be proud to meet the person who is proud of being white because every human being has some skin color, any skin color is alright. Be prouder still to meet every person who clearly understands that character and intellect makes a person. Color never made a man."

Conclusion

When African Americans left farms and plantations in the rural south and migrated to larger cities and towns earlier in this century, they needed to stay close to friends, families and traditions. Black DJs helped them keep in contact with each other and to participate in improvisational culture. Black DJs epitomized improvisational culture, which was a blending of West and Central African cultures that African Americans created and used to survive in America.

As the first electronic voices of African Americans, black DJs became cultural heroes. They were hustlers, salesmen, ministers, newsmen, griots and jesters. African Americans loved to hear the music they played, which included blues, gospel, rhythm and blues and jazz. When black DJs combined all these roles and used popular music to tie all the elements in their programs together they gained the respect and admiration of blacks and whites. As gatekeepers and guardians of improvisational culture, black DJs also tried to protect the culture and keep it "pure." Most refused, for example, to play white or "covered" versions of songs that black artists first recorded.

The call-response structure that is so much a part of blues, R&B, jazz, gospel and black preaching style provided a stable structure that black DJs used to display their improvisational skills. They used the call-response technique to effectively communicate with listeners. Moreover, they used call-response structure to encourage African Americans to participate in the music, stories and jokes, which are all elements of improvisational culture.

Over the years, black DJs mastered black English, played blues and jazz and other forms of black music, told stories and communicated their brand of improvisation to listeners. Some whites emulated them. They also became cultural heroes. Alan Freed, Johnny Otis, Hunter Hancock and Hoss Allen are some of the whites who achieved this status in the black community.

Black DJs and the whites who emulated them passed on African-American improvisational culture to future generations. Therefore, they have kept alive such oral traditions as playing the dozens, boasts and toasts, blues, R&B, soul, jazz and rap music. Additionally, black DJs have created new words or given new meanings to words in the English language, a practice that African Americans started during slavery, when slaves realized they needed a communication system that only they could understand.

Although entertaining their listeners is one of the defining features of black DJs, clearly they have done much more than entertain. Some have promoted stay-in-school rallies, money for civil rights leaders, hotlines for people to voice their anger at police brutality, racism and other issues of importance.

Because of black DJs'efforts and work on behalf of the black community, African Americans reestablished bonds and relationships with family members and friends. The electronic village of black DJs served as the meeting place where familiar foods, ideas and ways of doing things helped black migrants participate in their culture.

When black DJs first began working in radio, many were just happy to have their voices radiated through the airwaves. Eventually, their attitudes hardened, as they became aware of the appalling conditions that they worked in. Moreover, they became less accepting of "jive" on-air names that white managers gave them and decided to use their own given names. Moreover, black DJs became less tolerant of unfair treatment and low wages. To fight for fair wages and employment benefits, black DJs formed their own organization, the National Association of Radio Artists (NARA). Eventually, many black DJs decided to buy radio stations, as part of their continuing efforts to achieve economic parity in broadcasting.

The DJs I interviewed gave voice to our concerns and experiences. New voices are now aware of their legacies and the improvisation culture they used and perpetuated. With the help of the new voices improvisational culture—our unique way of doing things—will continue to grow, expand and help African Americans adapt and survive in American society in the 21st century and beyond.

Bibliography

BOOKS

Abrahams, Roger D. *Deep Down in the Jungle: Negro Narrative Folklore From the Streets of Philadelphia.* Hatboro, PA: Folklore Associates, 1964.

Barnouw, Eric. *A History of Broadcasting in the United States*, 3 vols. New York: Oxford University Press, 1970.

Brooks, Tilford. *America's Black Musical Heritage.* Englewood Cliffs, NJ: Prentice Hall, 1984.

Brown, Ina Corrine. *Understanding Other Cultures.* Englewood Cliffs, NJ: Prentice Hall, 1963.

Cantor, Louis. *Wheelin'on Beale: How WDIA-Memphis Became the Nation's First All-Black Radio Station and Created the Sound That Changed America.* New York: Pharos Books, 1992.

Cheek, J. M. *Assertive Black . . . Puzzled White.* San Luis Obispo, CA: Impact Communications, 1976.

Eberly, Philip K. *Music in the Air: America's Changing Tastes in Popular Music, 1920–1980.* New York: Hastings House, 1982.

Fang, Irving E. *Those Radio Commentators!* Ames: Iowa State University Press, 1977.

Foster, Eugene. *Understanding Broadcasting* (2nd ed.). Reading, MA: Addison-Wesley, 1982.

George, Nelson. *The Death of Rhythm and Blues.* New York: E. P. Dutton, 1988.

Haralambos, Michael. *Right On: From Blues to Soul in Black America.* New York: Drake, 1975.

Hecht, Michael, L. Collier, and S. A. Ribeau. *African American Communication.* Newbury Park, CA: Sage, 1993.

Herskovits, Melville J. *The Myth of the Negro Past.* Boston: Beacon Press, 1958, originally published in 1941.

Hine, Darlene Clark. *Black Women History.* New York: Carlson, 1993.

Holloway, Joseph E. (ed.). *Africanisms in American Culture.* Bloomington and Indianapolis: Indiana University Press, 1990.

Hopkins, Jerry. *The Rock Story.* New York: New American Library, 1970.

Keil, Charles. *Urban Blues.* Chicago: University of Chicago Press, 1966.

Lazarsfeld, Paul. *The People Look at Radio.* Chapel Hill: University of North Carolina Press, 1946.

Levine, Lawrence W. *Black Culture and Black Consciousness.* New York: Oxford University Press, 1977.

MacDonald, J. Fred. *Don't Touch That Dial! Radio Programming in American Life, 1920–1960.* Chicago: Nelson Hall, 1986.

McFarland, David T. *Contemporary Radio Programming Strategies.* Hillsdale, NJ: Lawrence Erlbaum, 1990.

Newman, P. *Entrepreneurs of Profit and Pride.* New York: Praeger, 1988.

Routt, Ed. *The Radio Format Conundrum.* New York: Hastings House, 1978.

Siepmann, Charles A. *Radio, Television and Society.* New York: Oxford University Press, 1950.

Smitherman, Geneva. *Black Talk: Words and Phrases from the Hood to the Amen Corner.* Boston: Houghton Mifflin, 1994.

Sterling, Christopher H. *Stay Tuned: A Concise History of American Broadcasting.* Belmont, CA: Wadsworth Publishing, Co., 1978.

ARTICLES

Asante, Molefe Kete. "African Elements in African-American English," in Joseph E. Holloway (ed.) (1990), *Africanisms in American Culture,* 19–33.

"Black DeeJays, Paid to Flaunt their Personalities," *Ebony Man* (January 1992), 44–46.

"Black Radio Pioneer Al Benson Dies at 70," *Jet,* Vol. 55 (September 28, 1978), 57.

Denisoff, Serge. "The Evolution of Pop Music Broadcasting, 1929–1972," *Journal of Popular Music and Society* (1973), Vol. 2, No. 3, 202–226.

"Disc Jockeys," *Ebony Magazine* (December 1947), 44–49.

Gould, Harry M., Jr., "The Sound and Soul of Black Radio," *Philadelphia Inquirer* (August 13, 1983), 13–33.

Heimenz, Jack. "DeeJay Blues: The Story of Rock Radio," *Sound* (September 1975), 28–30.

Love, Walt. "Legends of Black Radio," *Radio and Records,* No. 998 (June 25, 1993), 32–50.

Maultsby, Portia K. "Africanisms in African-American Music," in Joseph E. Holloway (ed.) (1990), *Africanisms in American Culture,* 185–210.

Nidetz, Steve. "Cool Gent," *Chicago Sun Times* (December 3, 1995), 25–26.

"Thirty Years of Payola: The Inside Story," *Pulse Magazine,* Vol. 3, No. 13 (April 11, 1988), 1, 13–19, 24–29.

Williams, Gilbert. "The Black Disc Jockey as a Cultural Hero," *Journal of Popular Music and Society* (Summer, 1986), 79–90.

UNPUBLISHED SOURCES

Black Radio Exclusive Conference, Houston, Texas, 1981.

Edmerson, Estelle. "A Descriptive Study of the American Negro in United States Professional Radio, 1922–1953." Master's thesis, University of California at Los Angeles, 1954.

Spaulding, Norman W. "History of Black Oriented Radio in Chicago, 1929–1963." Doctoral dissertation, University of Illinois at Urbana-Champaign, 1981.

INTERVIEWS

(Unless otherwise noted, interviews conducted by author)

Allen, William T. "Hoss," disc jockey. April 1991.

Castleberry, Eddie, announcer, disc jockey, news reporter. February 1991.

Compton, "Sir Johnny O.," disc jockey, entrepreneur. June 1991.

Cordell, Moses Lindberg "Lucky," disc jockey, radio station manager. September 1991.

Dee, Merri, TV announcer, personality, disc jockey. June 1991.

Faulkner, Greer, wife of Larry Dean Faulkner. June 1991.

Gibson, Jack, disc jockey, entrepreneur. March 1991.

Howard, "Joltin'Joe," disc jockey, public servant. April 1991.

Hulbert, Jr., Maurice "Hot Rod," disc jockey. June 1991.

Jefferson, Al, disc jockey. June 1991.

Joyner, Tom, disc jockey. October 1991.

Mitchell-Beckwith, Peggy, disc jockey, educator. March 1991.

Montague, Nathaniel "The Magnificent," disc jockey, entrepreneur. September 1984.

O'Jay, Eddie, disc jockey, entrepreneur. May 1991.

Smith, Novella, disc jockey, humanitarian. June 1991.

Spaulding, Norman W., disc jockey, entrepreneur, scholar. Personal correspondence, 1985–86.

Stams, Richard, disc jockey. August 1991.

Steinberg, Martha Jean "The Queen," disc jockey, radio station owner. May 1991.

Steward, Shelly, disc jockey, radio station owner. March 1991.

Wood, Sr., Roy, news reporter, announcer, disc jockey, radio station manager. May 1991.

PRIVATE COLLECTIONS

James Edward Saunders Collection (MSS 422), Ohio Historical Society, Columbus, Ohio.

Smithsonian Institution Black Radio Collection, Archives of African American Music and Culture, Smith Research Center, Suite 180–181, Indiana University, Bloomington, Indiana.

Index

About the Author

GILBERT A. WILLIAMS is Professor in the Telecommunication Department at Michigan State University, where he teaches courses on broadcast and cable programming and the history of telecommunications. His research interests focus on African American communications, the history of communications, and health communication.